DR. GEORGE J. STEVENSON
EMORY AND HENRY COLLEGE
Emory, Virginia

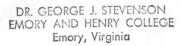

CRIME
WITHOUT
PUNISHMENT

CRIME
WITHOUT
PUNISHMENT

by John L. McClellan

DUELL, SLOAN AND PEARCE
New York

Second printing, October, 1962

Affiliate of
MEREDITH PRESS
Des Moines & New York

Library of Congress Catalogue Card Number: 62-8523

MANUFACTURED IN THE UNITED STATES OF AMERICA FOR MEREDITH PRESS

VAN REES PRESS   •   NEW YORK

For my wife NORMA,
with abiding love and
deep appreciation

This book sets forth some important and recent aspects of the evidence before and the reports of the Senate Select Committee on Improper Activities in the Labor or Management Field and the Senate Permanent Subcommittee on Investigations.

I am deeply indebted to my good friend Theodore Granik, internationally distinguished lawyer and renowned Peabody Award-winning radio and television commentator and producer, for his kind suggestion which sparked my writing of this book. Mr. Granik's public service as former Assistant District Attorney of New York and as counsel to government agencies and Senate Committees, as well as his participation with world-famous leaders during the past twenty-five years in radio and television discussion programs, such as the celebrated "American Forum of the Air," "Youth Wants to Know," and the Reader's Digest presentation "All America Wants to Know," all dedicated to the enlightenment of the people on subjects of national concern, led him to believe that citizens everywhere would be vitally interested in a book chronicling, from the record, the important work of our committees. I shall always be grateful for his intense interest in the committees with which I have been associated in my over-all fight against crime and corruption.

JOHN L. McCLELLAN

Author's Note

THIS book is written because I have a profound faith in America. I am confident that when the American people read from the record of committee hearings and become fully cognizant of the extent of the crime and corruption which fester in our midst, they will demand action.

This record was made during the years that the Senate committees investigating these evils were operating under my chairmanship. However, the extended time during which the record has been developed may have dulled our perceptions of the depth of the danger. Therefore, this book is written to remind some, to inform many, and to alert all.

In my position as Chairman of the Senate Select Committee on Improper Activities in the Labor or Management Field, and as Chairman of the Senate Permanent Subcommittee on Investigations, it has been my responsibility to direct and to preside over some of the most important series of investigations and committee hearings ever conducted in the history of the United States Congress.

No man need apologize for devotion to duty. It is, therefore, somewhat startling to note that attempts are being made to persuade the people, who are the real victims of the soaring incidence of crime and corruption, that Congressional investigating committees do not serve the best interest of the country. Attacks on Senate committees have taken the form of a strong implication and, in some instances, of an open charge that the Chairman and the members of the committees are, because of their attitude and vigilance in exposing crime and corruption in labor-management relations, "anti-labor." (We might then inquire—are the criminals "pro-labor"?)

The revelations made in the committee hearings as reported herein completely refute those unfounded charges and implications. The views expressed in this book make it crystal clear that the Chairman and the other members of these committees are proudly and militantly "anti-crime" and "anti-corruption" and "pro-decent unionism." They have simply been diligent and dedicated in the performance of a most arduous and difficult task.

This work could not have been accomplished without a loyal and competent staff of hard-working men and women. An appreciative tribute is paid to all of them throughout the chapters of this book. It would be impossible to list here all who contributed time and effort to the success of our work, and therefore no attempt will be made to do so. Each of them has the lasting gratitude of the Chairman for his exceptionally fine service.

We were fortunate to have the staff of the Senate Permanent Subcommittee on Investigations as a nucleus for the greatly augmented staff of the Senate Select Committee on Improper Activities in the Labor or Management Field when it was established in January of 1957.

The original staff, under the able and energetic direction of the Chief Counsel, Robert F. Kennedy, included such capable investigators as Assistant Chief Counsel Jerome S. Adlerman, Carmine S. Bellino, Alphonse F. Calabrese, LaVern J. Duffy, Robert E. Dunne, Paul E. Kamerick, Leo C. Nulty, Donald F. O'Donnell, and Paul J. Tierney.

As the Committee's work increased rapidly in the early months of our operations, the staff was expanded to include Mr. Kennedy's able administrative assistant, Kenneth O'Donnell ,and such outstanding investigators as John A. Aporta, John Cye Cheasty, John P. Constandy, Thomas G. Egan, Robert W. Greene, Edward M. Jones, Arthur G. Kaplan, James P. Kelly, George M. Kopecky, Irwin Langenbacher, James J. P. McShane, Joseph F. Maher, Carl F.

Maisch, Joseph M. Mannix, George H. Martin, Walter R. May, Ralph W. Mills, Philip W. Morgan, Francis X. Plant, Harold Ranstad, Downey Rice, Charles M. Ryan, Pierre E. G. Salinger, Walter J. Sheridan, John A. Terry, Martin S. Uhlmann, and Sherman S. Willse.

From time to time, the Select Committee engaged other investigators whose particular talents fitted them for specific investigations and borrowed many from other government agencies. Some of these were Jack S. Balaban, Robert Confini, Ralph DeCarlo, John Flanagan, Gerald Gotsch, James F. Mundie, Thomas E. Nunnally, Levin L. Poole, Carl Schultz, Richard G. Sinclair, and Charles Wolfe.

Many state and local law enforcement agencies were of great help, particularly the District Attorney of New York, Frank Hogan, and his capable chief assistant, Alfred Scotti. We had similar aid and co-operation from the enforcement agencies of most big cities in the United States, such as Los Angeles, St. Louis, and Chicago, to name only a few; former New York Police Commissioner Stephen Kennedy; New York Police Commissioner Michael Murphy; Deputy Commissioner Leonard Reisman, Detectives Joseph Corrigan, Cyril Jordan, Thomas O'Brien, and James Mooney of the New York City Police Department; Detective Natale Laurendi, assigned to District Attorney Hogan's office; and also Captain James Hamilton of the Los Angeles Police Department.

I wish to acknowledge the great assistance we received from various Crime Commissions, including those directed by Virgil Peterson of Chicago; Daniel Sullivan of Miami; Aaron Kohn of New Orleans; Goodman A. Sarachan, Myles Lane, John Ryan, Jr. and Jacob Grumet of the New York State Commission of Investigation; the co-operation received from the Department of Justice and the Director of the Federal Bureau of Investigation, J. Edgar Hoover, and his assistants Courtney Evans and Alfred J. McGrath; and from Joseph Campbell, Comptroller of the General Accounting Office, and his assistant Charles E. Eckert; Commissioner Mortimer Caplin of the Internal Revenue Service, and members of his staff H. Allen Long and Harold R. Wallace; Arnold Sagalyn of the Treasury Department; the Bureau of Narcotics, former Commissioner H. J. Anslinger, Commissioner Henry L. Giordano, Charles Siragusa, and Martin Pera; Immigration and Naturalization Service, former Commissioner J. M. Swing, Commissioner Raymond Farrell, and Assistant Commissioner, Investigations, Austin Murphy; the Department of Defense, Brig. General C. C. Fenn, Army; Lt. Colonel Charles Counts, Army; Lt. Colonel Eric Linhof, Air Force; Lt. Commander LeRoy Hopkins, Navy.

When Mr. Kennedy left the staff, his position was taken by his resourceful Assistant Chief Counsel, Jerome S. Adlerman, to whom I am also personally indebted for his aid and counsel in the preparation of this book. I also thank my personal assistant in the organization and writing of the book, John Brick, and the long-experienced Chief Counsel of the Senate Internal Security Subcommittee, J. C. Sourwine, for his helpful suggestions.

Any acknowledgment of dedicated performance by the staff would be incomplete without full recognition of the splendid work of the committee's Chief Clerk, Mrs. Ruth Young Watt, and her excellent assistants, as well as that of each member of my own highly devoted and greatly appreciated office staff. My special thanks go to each one of them.

JOHN L. McCLELLAN

Washington, D. C.

Contents

Illustrations

PART ONE

CHAPTER 1

The Image of the Underworld

Mounting crime and corruption are insidiously gnawing at the vitality and strength of our republic. These powerful forces pose a tremendous threat to our democratic institutions and to our economic freedom and security. This is a serious challenge to you and to me—to all of us.

The findings of the Senate Select Committee on Improper Activities in the Labor or Management Field, of which I was chairman, and of the Senate Permanent Subcommittee on Investigations, of which I am chairman, are, in my belief, of critical importance to all Americans. This book presents some of the highlights of the evidence these committees have heard and of the reports they have made to the Senate. It sets forth, in part, my views on those revelations and also on some aspects of crime and corruption in the United States.

Its initial emphasis naturally falls upon the widespread criminal activities and the unsavory practices exposed at Congressional hearings since January, 1957. Investigations of crime, improper activities, and corruption on a national scale have occupied a very substantial part of my time for several busy years and particularly so since the Senate Select Committee on Improper Activities in the Labor or Management Field—the so-called Rackets Committee—was established. There probably will be many more such hearings during the next few years.

During nearly three decades in public office, as a prosecuting attorney in Arkansas and as a Congressman and United States Senator in Washington, I have looked into the faces of thousands of witnesses, many of them criminals, and listened to their voices: many of them arrogant, sullen, mendacious, boastful, unrepentant, and unremorseful. Their audacity has often aroused anger difficult to restrain. The descriptions of the sordid actions in which many of them participated, unfolded by millions of words of testimony, produce serious apprehensions regarding the internal security and well-being of our country.

Some of those faces and voices have become and will remain permanent fixtures of memory. There comes to mind instantly the confident, almost supercilious voice of the pompous president of the International Brotherhood of Teamsters, Dave Beck, as he testified eagerly enough at the outset of his first appearance before the Senate Select Committee. He spoke at length, pontifically, as if he were instructing the committee members in an area where they were unfamiliar, about his philosophy on unionism and labor laws. But when the questions sharpened and centered on the $370,000 in Teamster funds that this man had misused, the haughty confidence quickly ebbed from his voice. His eyes lost their spirit and his cheeks paled as he monotonously sought refuge in the Fifth Amendment. Then this astonishing exchange took place:

THE CHAIRMAN: I see a name here we have been trying to locate— a Mr. Dave Beck, Jr. Would you know him?
BECK: I must decline to answer the question.

A few moments later, when order was restored in the great expanse of the imposing Senate Caucus Room, where the public hearings were held, the question was tried again.

THE CHAIRMAN: I will ask the witness these questions and then order him to answer. Do you know Dave Beck, Jr.?
(The witness conferred with his counsel.)
BECK: I decline to answer the question.

THE CHAIRMAN: You are ordered and directed to answer the question.

BECK: I decline to answer this question on the grounds it might
open up avenues of questions that would tend to incriminate
me.

Perhaps it is natural that the easiest sound to recall is the in-
solent rumble of the grating voice that belongs to Beck's successor at the wheel of the gigantic Teamster organization. That
voice never took the Fifth Amendment. However, that voice testified extensively to "loss of memory." Time after time, the chunky
man with the powerful, lumpy face and the thick forearms and
heavy, blunt hands would sit in the witness chair as the voice
grated out the toneless answers: "I don't remember. . . . I can't
recall. . . . I forget. . . ."

At one point, Hoffa was so anxious to stress his poor memory
that he got his words crossed with his meaning: "I am saying that
to the best of my recollection I have no disremembrance of dis-
cussing with Scott any such question."

A cynical grin twisted Hoffa's expressive mouth when Senator
Ives of New York said icily: ". . . I am constrained to point out that
he [Hoffa] has the most convenient forgettery of anybody I have
ever seen." A few minutes later, another grin was forthcoming
when Senator Ives remarked: "I will give you this much credit,
by golly—you have not taken the Fifth, but you are doing a mar-
velous job crawling around it."

The memory of another set of hearings brings to mind the
bleak malevolence in the narrowed eyes of the leaders of the crime
syndicate who read haltingly from slips of paper prepared for
them by their attorneys: "I refuse to answer that question on the
grounds that it may tend to incriminate me." That word "refuse"
usually brought a swift rebuke from the Chair: "You will not say
you refuse to answer. You may decline to answer, but you will
not refuse. Show some respect for your government."

There were those who took the witness chair who professed to be lambs led astray, like the burly strong-arm man for the Teamsters, Barney Baker, who blithely pleaded that he had a big mouth and liked to brag about himself, and that any recitation of his crimes was likely to be greatly exaggerated because of his propensity for talking too freely about himself. Some of his testimony might have been amusing had it not been concerned with such somber matters as a waterfront murder in New York, in which a man named Anthony Hintz, an honest hiring boss of longshoremen, was shot down in the street before his home. The committee's chief counsel, Robert Kennedy, asked Baker about that killing:

MR. KENNEDY: Did you have anything to do with the Varick enterprises?

BAKER: No, I knew the people that did, but I did not have nothing to do with the Varick enterprises.

MR. KENNEDY: Who were the people that did?

BAKER: A Mr. Dunn.

MR. KENNEDY: Cockeyed Dunn?

BAKER: I don't know him as Cockeyed Dunn. I knew him as John Dunn.

MR. KENNEDY: Where is he now?

BAKER: He has met his Maker.

MR. KENNEDY: How did he do that?

BAKER: I believe through electrocution in the city of New York of the State of New York.

The faces and the voices that are shadiest and sometimes difficult to remember are those of the shamed and the frightened who live on the periphery of crime, at the edges of the sordid world that the investigations uncovered. There was a multitude of these over the years. A prostitute was ready to commit perjury at the command of crooked officials in Portland, Oregon, who threatened her with a prison sentence for narcotics addiction if she didn't swear to the false story they wanted from her. A manufacturer of rigged dice and marked cards dropped his voice ashamedly when he admitted that his products probably were used solely to fleece the unwary victims of crooked gamblers. The ex-wife of a labor goon testified with varied emotions—sometimes she was obviously afraid of what might happen to her, and again she exulted that she was repaying her husband for his infidelity and his grossness.

There have been more than two thousand witnesses who have appeared at committee hearings since 1957, testifying or declining to testify about crime in nearly every state of the Union and in many segments of American enterprise and endeavor. The guilty ones have often denied their guilt; many of them have protested that their actions constituted no crime at all, because they were not specifically so defined by statute, and when their voices were loud enough and their resources great enough, many gullible people believed them.

At the outset, then, we have need for definitions in the use of the word "crime." The dictionary * that is closest to hand supplies these meanings for "crime":

An omission of a duty commanded, or the commission of an act forbidden, by a public law. . . . includes all grades of public offenses, which at the common law are often defined as treason, felony or misdemeanor . . .

Gross violation of human law, in distinction from a misdemeanor or a trespass or other slight offense. . . . any aggravated offense against morality.

Criminal activity; conduct violating the law.

Any evil act or sin . . .

Something reprehensible or disgraceful . . .

Each man has his own interpretations of these meanings, assessing their weight and import according to his conscience, his concept of principle—of right and wrong, and the environment in which he dwells. A district attorney attends heavily to those declared by the statutes, as does his adversary in the courtroom—

* *Webster's New International Dictionary of the English Language* (Springfield, Mass.: G. & C. Merriam Co., 1955).

the defense attorney. A clergyman covers much wider areas of transgressions, as do parents and teachers. A policeman ranges less widely because he is restricted by the limits of the legal meanings. The average citizen usually thinks of crime simply as "breaking the law," and too often he carelessly believes that he is exposed to crime and criminals only by way of television whodunits or by the dramatized fiction of paperback novels. The Select Committee's hearings demonstrated time and again that no man, woman, or child in America can completely escape the immoral pressures and the financial tributes that organized crime extorts from the populace because of the criminal's greed for power and the dishonest dollar.

The first of the Webster definitions, the one that identifies crime as "an omission of a duty commanded," was rarely expressly touched upon by the two thousand witnesses. In many respects, however, it is one of the most vital aspects of crime in America today.

What is the crime of omission? What is the neglected duty? Certainly one of them is, fundamentally, our failure to meet the responsibility for crushing the criminal menace. Our duty is to destroy the twining tentacles of the national crime syndicate; to break its grasping hold upon business and upon labor; to put the confirmed and professional criminals in jail where they belong; to wipe out the viciousness of syndicated gambling and prostitution; to end the terrible and heartless traffic in narcotics; to destroy the gangsters, thieves, cheaters, racketeers, hoodlums, and panderers who gain their evil profits by preying upon decent and honest people everywhere in this great land of ours.

This neglect of duty is probably the most common crime in our society. It is evil; it is a sin by any proper ethical standard, and all of us are guilty in varying degree, although we may not be acutely conscious of our guilt. This is surely true for each man, no matter how much he rejoices in freedom, no matter how justly and honestly he rears his children in our ancient traditions of devotion to God and country, no matter how properly he earns his living. Each of us may be charged in his conscience with some crime related to the omission of a duty commanded.

If we are to prevail against the Communist conspiracy, then we must be, and we must remain, better and stronger than the Communists. In terms of armaments and wealth and resources, we are stronger. In terms of ideology and purpose, we stand far above them. We stand firmly in opposition to international gangsters with all the vigor of the greatest republic the world has ever known. We are completely committed to the struggle for peace and freedom wherever they are threatened in the world. We must, however, use the same strength and determination against the frauds, the cheaters, and the gangsters who infest our economy and who operate within our national borders.

The international Communist conspiracy is undoubtedly the most dangerous and most powerful enemy that the free world has ever faced, and we are presumed to be armed and united against this massive threat. Inside our nation, however, we have a foe that can destroy us without help from Soviet missiles or Red Army divisions. The secret web of crime and corruption has spread its malignancy through almost every structure of our society. It has been stealthily generated and sheltered by the terrible apathy of the American citizen.

While gambling and stealing, narcotics and prostitution, extortion and exploitation, are linked through criminal conspiracies from coast to coast, and while one thieving racketeer after another grabs the funds of gigantic labor unions, while outwardly respectable businessmen pay tribute to gangsters or conspire among themselves in corrupt and fraudulent deals, while the police departments of big cities are afflicted with widespread venality, what is the general reaction of the average American citizen today?

He is usually shocked and fascinated, but the scandals tend to be seven-day wonders, soon forgotten. Instead of getting angry and flashing into vigorous action, he figuratively shrugs his shoulders and turns to the next sensation that comes along. He has his own concerns; he must get ahead in the world; he must devote his attention to making a better living. The ability to acquire material possessions, and the opportunity to enjoy them in expanded leisure, seem to have dulled the responses of a large percentage of our people to sharp questions of morality, spiritual values, and good citizenship.

Most Americans have been exposed to Congressional hearings through the past several years, but not enough of them have been sufficiently aroused to enlist in the fight against crime. There are, of course, many variations among the reactions of the populace, but one of the most usual of them, unfortunately, goes something like this: "What does it matter to me if the Senate Investigating Committee points its finger at Jimmy Hoffa and complains about how Teamster dues were spent, or why there were so many racketeers and ex-convicts in the union's employ, or why the Teamsters were tied up with reputedly Communist-infiltrated outfits like the West Coast International Longshoremen's and Warehousemen's Union or like the Mine, Mill and Smelter Workers Union? What does that all mean to me? I'm no teamster. It is not my problem nor my concern."

But in truth these matters are vital to him. They are crucial to his future and that of his family. The burgeoning crime and sneaking corruption and slackening morality touches him and his loved ones in a thousand insidious ways. Irreparable damage can be done to this great country unless we all work to prevent it. We need action by vigorous and indomitable people, to cut away the criminal malignancy before its ravages become intolerable. The national government, in its three branches—executive, legislative and judicial—cannot succeed alone. It must have the help of every American who cherishes the ancient verities and the spiritual values that are the very pillars of our republic and the source of the freedoms and strengths that we enjoy.

Our investigations are not ended, nor should they be as long as the need for them is so strikingly apparent. We should continue, for legislative purposes, to expose gangsters and racketeers in every section of the nation, in every sphere of influence in which they operate. Evil will not vanish, however, merely because the bright light of investigation shines upon it. The men who foster it will only duck into another dark corner or hide for a while until the lights are turned off. We need concentrated study of many areas of our laws against crime of all kinds. Many statutes are obsolescent today in view of the changing image of the underworld; many others have never been strong enough or specific enough to combat crime successfully. Congressional investigations are designed to provide studies and gather information that will aid in drafting legislation necessary to correct the faults in existing statutes and to define additional crimes and fix penalties therefor.

Much of what I know about crime and criminals and the nature of their minds was learned from an outstanding lawyer who frequently represented defendants in cases that I prosecuted in Arkansas. He was my father, Judge Isaac McClellan. If a man was arrested in his county for stealing, assault, moonshining, or some other crime, he was more than likely to have my father defend him. That would be a wise move, too; my father was an excellent lawyer, and moreover, he possessed an almost uncanny knowledge and understanding of human nature. He personally knew the jurors of our rural area, their weaknesses and their strengths, their faults and their virtues, just as well as he knew the occasional impetuousness and overzealousness of his son as a prosecutor.

In one case against me my father won an acquittal. Naturally he was pleased with his somewhat unexpected victory, but when we ate dinner together that night, he said to me: "You lost that case, John, because you had not prepared well enough—you took the defendant's guilt for granted." Two good reasons for losing. A lesson I never forgot.

That just criticism is pertinent to this account of the long series of investigations of improper activities in the fields of labor and management, of organized crime, of the evidence of damage to our country's moral welfare. The tireless and brilliant staffs of the Select Committee and the Permanent Subcommittee never lost sight of those two vital concepts contained in my father's advice. Congressional hearings are not trials, but their success is dependent upon thorough investigation, a tremendous amount of hard work, and constant attention to justice.

Our hearings can be described as at least fairly successful, in view of legislation that has been enacted and the labor and business reforms that have been instigated. The job isn't finished, however, and won't be until the nefarious activities of racketeers are made unprofitable and punishable. This is a continuing fight, and it requires and should receive the aid and support of all decent citizens everywhere in the country. To help with this great purpose, the people should know the nature of the enemy and the type of operations that he has been carrying on in furtive fashion on so great a scale. It is hoped that the chapters of this book will serve usefully in advancing public understanding toward that objective.

CHAPTER 2

The Teamsters Under Fire

THE officials of the International Brotherhood of Teamsters, who have been intermittently investigated by
congressional committees over the past decade, have nobody to
blame but themselves for the creation of the Senate Select Committee that shook the foundations of their tarnished fortress, and
for the lengthy investigations that revealed the venality and corruption with which this mighty union was infected.

Investigation was nothing new to the Teamsters in late December, 1956, when the Senate Permanent Subcommittee on Investigations began to look into the continuing reports that Teamster officials all over the country had misused the union's vast
treasury for their own personal advantages. This was certainly a
proper domain for the subcommittee's staff to investigate under
the direction of the energetic and enterprising chief counsel,
Robert F. Kennedy. The committee directed Mr. Kennedy to go
ahead with the probe. The union was required to file certain reports under existing laws, the filing of which were matters of interest to the parent Government Operations Committee. Since
union funds are tax exempt, we believed their expenditures and
the correctness of union financial reports were subject to scrutiny
by the Permanent Subcommittee on Investigations.

Accompanied by the able chief accountant of the staff, Carmine
Bellino, Counsel Kennedy started almost innocently on a West
Coast trip in December, 1956, intending to look into the admin-

13

istration of Teamster affairs in that area. Data supplied the committee by informants, and subsequently testified to before the committee, revealed that Frank Brewster, head of the Western Conference of Teamsters in Seattle, was misusing Teamster funds. Neither Mr. Kennedy nor Mr. Bellino had an inkling, however, of the gigantic storm that their visit was about to unleash.

Teamster officials refused to co-operate. They apparently thought that if they made the job difficult enough, the Committee's activities would be diverted to other tasks. This had happened before in the course of some government probes of their financial affairs, and they expected it to happen again. The Teamster leaders would not produce records; they repeatedly challenged the jurisdiction of the Permanent Subcommittee to probe the inner workings of the union; they exerted considerable and constant pressure upon members of Congress in both houses to have Teamster activities rest in the traditionally gentle hands of the Senate's Labor Committee.

Mr. Kennedy and the staff proceeded, nonetheless. Quick developments of the West Coast trip were valuable leads from confidential sources which attracted Mr. Kennedy's attention to Dave Beck, the high potentate of the Teamsters Union. There was already an internal struggle for power within the organization. James Riddle Hoffa was thirsting for the presidency. Dave Beck was expendable. The staff investigators were told that Beck's personal financial records would reveal an intricate maze of manipulations of Teamster funds for his own personal gain and profit. A man named Nathan Shefferman, a labor relations counsel in Chicago, was supposed to possess vital records of Beck's operations. Mr. Kennedy and Mr. Bellino turned from Frank Brewster, flying to Chicago to subpoena the Shefferman records.

The results disclosed in the record were astounding. This man, Dave Beck, top officer of the greatest union in the United States, had a salary of $50,000 annually, an unlimited expense account, and a rent-free house in Seattle worth $163,000 of Teamster money. He had built it with Teamster money, then sold it to the

Teamsters, and thereafter lived in it without cost. In addition to this excellent arrangement and freedom from financial worries, Beck virtually converted the Teamster treasury into a personal bank account to gratify his vanity further. He used Teamster funds, through Nathan Shefferman, to pay such items as these: $1,918.15 for gardening and $2,159.77 for landscaping; twelve pairs of binoculars, $354; Sulka ties and shirts, $192.65; two aluminum boats, $196.50; three mattresses and three springs, $222.69.

There were coats, ties, undershirts, a radio, golf balls, golf clubs, sheets and pillowcases, football tickets, twenty-one pairs of nylons, five dozen diapers, typewriters, outboard motors, furniture, a deep-freeze, a vacuum cleaner, a rifle, and hundreds of other items, totaling about $85,000. This money was systematically looted from the Teamster treasury.

There was a bill for $90.92 from Saks Fifth Avenue in New York for the purchase of socks. When Dave Beck sent this bill to Shefferman for payment, he wrote across the face of it: *Tell them their socks I purchased are terrible, full of holes.*

About the time of this discovery we had word that Dave Beck was ready to leave on an unannounced tour of Europe—a trip that presumably would last until the heat died down. Bob Kennedy raced to New York to intercept him, and they met in the Waldorf-Astoria Hotel. Beck was asked for a reasonable explanation of the accounts.

For better than an hour, Beck talked about everything under the sun, lecturing young Mr. Kennedy on his duties, ridiculing Congressional investigations, issuing veiled threats to use the power of the Teamsters on the one hand and, on the other, pontificating about how he personally would clean out any racketeers that could be found in the vast union.

Bob Kennedy kept trying to get to the point. He is a most persistent man, among his many other excellent qualities. He finally reached it, after an hour and a half. What did Beck have to say about these Shefferman records that indicated he had stolen $85,000 of Teamster funds?

Beck had nothing to say. He would have to confer with his personal lawyer, even though there were two Teamster attorneys present in the suite with him at the time.

Mr. Kennedy then handed him a letter, signed by me as chairman of the Permanent Subcommittee on Investigations, which was to be given to Beck when and if Beck couldn't, or wouldn't, give a proper explanation of his financial deals with Shefferman. The letter told Beck that there would be hearings in January, 1957, concerning his misuse of union funds. The letter asked him to appear to hear the charges and to answer them.

The great man raged. "You'll hear about this," he told Mr. Kennedy. He meant what he said. The Teamsters thought they were powerful enough to defy the Senate of the United States.

Beck went to Europe. Mr. Kennedy and Mr. Bellino came back to Washington to plunge into the tremendous job of preparing for the hearings that would examine the fiscal affairs of the International Brotherhood of Teamsters as well as the shady finances of Dave Beck. The staff was pretty certain at this point that Teamster officers' thefts would mount into the hundreds of thousands of dollars.

It was now clearly obvious that the investigation would be concerned with items and amounts far more important than fourteen-dollar neckties and Sulka shirts costing forty-three dollars each.

The pressure of the Teamsters soon was felt. Banks where the union kept its vast treasury refused to produce their records for inspection. Vital documents disappeared from Teamster offices; others were disfigured or so changed as to make them difficult to identify. The union's attorneys, numbering in the hundreds—so many that our investigators referred to them as "The Teamsters Bar Association"—worked long hours preparing challenges to the committee's jurisdiction and roadblocks to its investigations.

Whispering campaigns vibrated through the Washington atmosphere. McClellan was anti-labor, they said; this Teamster investigation was really designed to strike a telling blow at all organized labor. What would happen, the wise voices asked, if

The Select Committee meets in the famed Caucus Room of the Old Senate Office Building. Seated, from left to right, are Senators Pat McNamara (Michigan), Barry Goldwater (Arizona), and the late Irving M. Ives (New York); Chairman McClellan (Arkansas); Chief Counsel Robert F. Kennedy; Senators John F. Kennedy (Massachusetts) and Carl T. Curtis (Nebraska). Standing at right is Mrs. Ruth Young Watt, Chief Clerk of the committee.

Teamster boss James R. Hoffa is sworn as a witness during one of his frequent appearances before Senate committees. The late Senator Ives commented in a hearing on Hoffa's convenient "forgettery." *Wide World*

LEFT TO RIGHT: Mrs. Mollie Baker testifies about her ex-husband's activities and exploits as a Teamster strong-arm man. Barney Baker, three-hundred-pound former boxer, tells the committee his ex-wife's words are those of "a vengeful woman, a woman scorned." Joey Glimco, once boss of Chicago's cab drivers, now heads a union whose members deserted him in droves. *Wide World photographs*

ABOVE: Anthony "Tony Ducks" Corallo (left) listens to his lawyer. The former Teamster, a leader of the New York "paper locals," has been convicted of bribery. LEFT: Chief Counsel Robert Kennedy questions James R. Hoffa during a hearing recess. The attentive listener (center) is Walter Sheridan, staff investigator on Teamster affairs. *Wide World photographs*

Handcuffed jukebox racketeers James Rini (left) and Alex Ross, both of Chicago, take the oath before the Senate Select Committee. They were brought to testify from cells in Illinois State Prison at Joliet. *Wide World*

The chairman asks Mike Miranda (left) and Vito Genovese to identify themselves in the photograph before them. Genovese took the Fifth Amendment. Miranda said his glasses were home; he couldn't see. *Wide World*

LEFT TO RIGHT: Lloyd Klenert (left), power in the United Textile Workers, tells his story to newsmen outside the hearing room, while Alphonse Calabrese, who led the investigation of the union, listens skeptically. James G. Cross, Bakers Union leader, whose short reign almost destroyed one of the nation's oldest unions. *Wide World photographs*

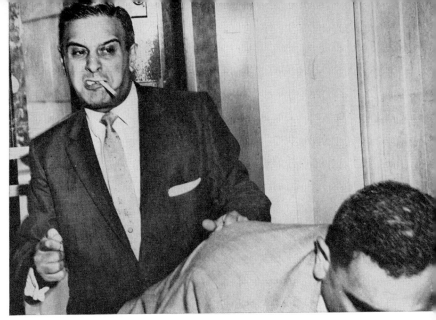

Johnny Dio slugs a photographer outside the hearing room. He is now serving time in Atlanta for extortion.

LEFT TO RIGHT: Thomas Lucchese, also known as "Three-Finger Brown," testifies he is neither a Mafia member nor a leader in New York City crime. Vincent (Jimmy) Squillante, king of the garbage rackets in New York, is missing. He is a fugitive from justice. Don (The Professor) Modica refuses to talk. He tutored Albert Anastasia's son and other racketeers' children. *Wide World photographs*

Chicago crime leader Tony Accardo wears dark glasses to ban bright lights as he takes the Fifth Amendment. *Wide World*

Carlos Marcello, baron of the New Orleans underworld, also wears dark lenses in his appearance before the Senate Select Committee. *Wide World*

A pre-hearing conference includes (left to right): Senator Pat McNamara of Michigan, Chairman McClellan, Chief Counsel Kennedy, and Senator Karl Mundt of South Dakota. Standing is investigator Pierre Salinger, now press secretary to President John F. Kennedy. *Wide World*

Wide World

Max Block (right), of the Butchers Union, confers at the witness table with his attorney, James M. McInerney. Block failed to explain many manipulations of union funds.

Abraham Teitelbaum, erstwhile Capone lawyer, assumes these expressions while pleading the Fifth Amendment and suggesting that he take the First, Sixth, Fourteenth, and Sixteenth Amendments.

Wide World

"That's the man," testifies Michael Bruce, pointing to Frank "Lefty" Rosenthal and identifying him as the gambler who tried to bribe him to fix a football game.

Marked cards are examined by the Permanent Investigating Subcommittee. Left to right are: John Scarne, gambling expert (back to camera); Senators Karl Mundt (South Dakota) and Sam J. Ervin, Jr. (North Carolina); Chairman McClellan, and Jerome S. Adlerman, Chief Counsel of the subcommittee.

the political balance in Congress were switched? The answer was
clear, they said; Senator McCarthy of Wisconsin would take over
the chairmanship of the investigating body once more. The
whispers said that this would be a calamity for labor. The best
thing to do, according to their experts, was to keep labor matters
in the hands of the Labor Committee.

We prepared and presented a resolution asking for more
authority and a special appropriation of $350,000 to enable us to
do the job properly. Already pending, however, before the Senate
Labor Committee was a resolution by Senator Ives of New York,
asking that a special subcommittee of the Labor Committee
undertake this investigating assignment. In this atmosphere of
competition and dual requests for jurisdiction and authority to
proceed, the labor lobbyists worked around the clock to prevent
any investigation at all.

Our subcommittee continued with its preliminary work during
the early days of January, 1957, under its authority from the
parent body, the Government Operations Committee.

The barriers of Teamster defiance appeared in quick succession.
Frank Brewster refused to answer questions at these initial hearings because his lawyers said the subcommittee lacked jurisdiction. In sequence, the same stand was taken by Einar Mohn, who
was Beck's executive secretary, and by Nugent La Poma, secretary-treasurer of Seattle Local 174, and by Harry Reiss, an
officer of one of the soon-to-be-noted "paper locals." These locals
are disclosed in the record as having existed only on paper char-
ters improperly issued by the international union. They were
fictitious. No rank-and-file members thereof could be found. Although Beck was invited to be present, he didn't bother to appear
at the hearings.

A few days before these first hearings began, Einar Mohn sent
a telegram to all Teamster vice-presidents, which was made an
exhibit at the hearings. This telegram advised that Teamsters
should refuse to answer any questions put to them by the committee. He added, in effect, that the union would back them sol-

idly if they took the Fifth Amendment. The entire Senate was quickly informed that the International Brotherhood of Teamsters was challenging the authority of the Federal government.

The response from the Senate was prompt and decisive. An eight-member bipartisan select committee was established, to be called the Senate Select Committee on Improper Activities in the Labor or Management Field. There were four Democratic members—Senators John F. Kennedy (Mass.), Sam J. Ervin, Jr. (N. C.), Pat McNamara (Mich.), and John L. McClellan (Ark.). There were four Republicans—Senators Joseph McCarthy (Wis.), Irving M. Ives (N. Y.), Karl E. Mundt (S. Dak.), and Barry Goldwater (Ariz.). To avoid the fears of many people both in and out of Congress that Senator McCarthy might succeed to the chairmanship, Senator Ives was named vice-chairman of the committee. This Select Committee was launched with a unanimous vote on the afternoon of January 30, 1957.

The Select Committee was empowered to conduct investigations into corruption and improper activities in both labor and management. We were given the appropriation we had requested. We assembled a staff that probably has had no equal for ability and dedication in the long history of Congressional investigating committees.

The Teamsters had chosen to fight all our previous inquiries on the grounds that we had moved beyond our jurisdiction. Now the Committee had a specific charge from the Senate to proceed, and the Teamsters, by their antagonism and refusal to co-operate, had certainly assured their role as primary targets.

The chairman of the committee has been attacked many times since January, 1957, for his alleged "anti-union" philosophy and for spearheading a "union-busting" campaign.

Although this book is about the findings of Senate committees and revelations in the hearings on certain aspects of crime and their evil influences, and not in any sense about me and my life in Arkansas and in Washington, I would like to make clear my views about organized labor. They have not changed since January, 1957.

I have never had any quarrel, nor will I ever have, with honest and well-managed labor unions. They have their proper place and sphere of influence in our national economy in this twentieth century, along with the great corporations with their multitudes of shareholders and the smaller private businesses that have historically formed the bulwark of our free enterprise system.

For several generations, my family in Arkansas has largely been made up of working people. Until recent years they were mostly tenant farmers who were hard-pressed to make a living from poor and unproductive soil. When I was a boy, living near and part of the time in the little county seat town of Sheridan, my father was a part-time schoolteacher and farmer. By studying law at night, he passed the bar examination and became an attorney when I was eleven years of age.

I followed his example, and while working on our farm I studied law under his direction.

There were two incidents in my boyhood that probably had a great deal to do with launching the long series of events that culminated in my handling of the gavel during the life of the Senate Select Committee. The first was when my father, before he was admitted to the bar himself, had to hire a local attorney for twenty-five dollars to make a day's journey by train to and from the county seat in an adjoining county to settle a small timber claim against a sawmill company on behalf of my uncle's estate. At the age of ten, I was astonished to learn that a man could receive so magnificent a sum for one day's work. I immediately resolved that I, too, would become a lawyer. Seven years later, at the age of seventeen, I was admitted to the Arkansas bar.

If the first incident was a factor in my decision to become a lawyer, the second one similarly influenced the direction of the long journey that has taken me from the pine forests of central Arkansas to the Capitol in Washington. When I was eight years old my father took me to a political rally in Sheridan, where

Governor Jeff Davis, seeking an unprecedented third term, addressed a cheering crowd of his partisans. I was so impressed by his rousing oratory that I went home and made my own political speech. I had no platform and no audience. So I used the chopping block at the woodpile to speak from, and I stood sticks of stove wood on end before me for my listeners. I harangued this make-believe audience with all the fervor that Jeff Davis had used the day before on the real crowd in the court square at Sheridan. That day had sparked in me a political ambition. Some few months later, I wrote to the Congressman of my district, John S. Little, for whom I was named, to tell him that I had picked some seventy-five pounds of cotton in one day. My letter also enthusiastically informed him of my recently acquired embryonic political ambition. He replied most graciously, predicting that someday I would go to Congress. From that day on, I was a candidate.

Three decades later, I left Arkansas to take a seat in the House of Representatives in Washington.

One of the most important votes I cast during my early years in Congress was in favor of the Wagner National Labor Relations Act, the Magna Charta of present-day organized labor in America. In 1947, as senior Senator from Arkansas, I voted for the Taft-Hartley Act.

In all these years, as a young attorney in Sheridan and in the small cities of Malvern and Camden, and later in the Congress of the United States, I have advocated decent unionism. Labor unions, honestly directed and properly operated, can be a vital and stabilizing force highly beneficial to our modern economy. But dishonest and corrupt leadership in unions or in management is a harmful and disrupting force that generates economic instability, hardship, and suffering.

My criticism of labor leaders is directed only at those who drive for national power at the expense of the rest of our society; at those who are thieves and scoundrels; at those who cheat and lie to the dues-paying rank-and-file members; at those who consort with gangsters; and at those who run their unions like feudal empires in total disregard of the traditionally fundamental democratic process.

Elements in the leadership of the International Brotherhood of Teamsters, as the record sets forth, had been guilty, individually or collectively, of all of these crimes when the investigations began in the winter of 1956–1957. The current regime evidently still condones many such practices. This group has stepped up its drive for power which will enable it to threaten the nation's economy by devastating strikes. It has in fact not only failed to cleanse itself of known criminals but in some instances has lifted them to positions of prominence and power. Direct testimony in the hearings linked 141 Teamster officers with improper or criminal activities in connection with their duties; 73 Teamster officers took the Fifth Amendment in their appearances before the committee during the first eighteen months of the hearings; testimony named 49 nationally known gangsters and racketeers who were closely connected with the Teamsters.

Finally, the union's current regime has apparently not only failed to nurture the democratic process from top to bottom but has railroaded constitutional changes that plunge the dues-payers even deeper into bondage.

The Teamsters drew our fire first in 1957 not because they were the biggest union in the nation, nor because the committee and its staff were out to destroy unionism by exposing the corruption that infested important unions—in the beginning we were not even aware that most of it existed—but because the Teamster leadership chose to challenge the power and authority of the United States Senate.

While Dave Beck was in Europe, choosing to ignore the subcommittee's requests that he come to Washington to talk about his finances, and while Einar Mohn and Frank Brewster and other Teamster leaders were refusing to testify on the grounds that the subcommittee lacked jurisdiction, the work of the staff went on with unrelenting vigor. As a seemingly endless series of amazing

revelations unfolded, the working hours of the staff were length-
ened long into the night and into weekends as well. The first set
of hearings held by the Select Committee exposed a network of
crime and vice in the city of Portland, Oregon, in which Teamster
officers and civil officials had conspired together to corrupt the
city.

In the meantime, an FBI arrest of Jimmy Hoffa was to have a
tremendous effect upon future hearings and upon the subsequent
history of the Teamsters' union.

Jimmy Hoffa was charged with conspiring to bribe a committee
investigator. The story unfolded in the record follows.

A New York lawyer named John Cye Cheasty came to Robert
F. Kennedy to tell him that Jimmy Hoffa had offered him two
thousand dollars a month if he would get a job as a committee
investigator and then pass on information from the committee's
files about the progress of the investigations into the multiple
scandals of the Teamsters. Mr. Kennedy brought Mr. Cheasty,
who was a former Navy officer and a Secret Service agent, to my
office, where he repeated his story. Within a matter of minutes,
J. Edgar Hoover of the Federal Bureau of Investigation was in
full charge of the case, advising us to hire Mr. Cheasty, who had
already turned in more than seven hundred dollars of Hoffa's first
payment of one thousand dollars—the rest of it Mr. Cheasty had
used for expenses in round trips by plane to Detroit and Washington. Subsequently, Mr. Cheasty was furnished on two occasions
with innocuous material about the Teamster investigation, which
he turned over to Hoffa at the Dupont Plaza Hotel on Dupont
Circle in Washington. The two men were under the constant
surveillance of FBI agents during the meetings. At the end of the
second meeting, Hoffa asked Mr. Cheasty if he wanted his money.
"Nobody ever said no to money," replied Mr. Cheasty. Hoffa
shook hands with him and left in Mr. Cheasty's palm a wad of
money totaling two thousand dollars. That was at approximately
11 P.M. on March 13, 1957.

Hoffa was immediately arrested by FBI agents who took him

to the Federal courthouse. He was subsequently indicted for bribery and conspiracy.

Hoffa was acquitted by the jury. He took the stand and testified that he had hired Mr. Cheasty only as a lawyer, and that there was no intent to bribe.

On July 19, 1957, the jury returned its verdict. It is interesting to note that the defense used several tactics which may have played a decisive part in the trial. A combination of these resulted in eight Negroes among the twelve jurors—Hoffa's attorney used his challenges to exclude a large number of white jurors and managed to indicate by adroit cross-examination that Mr. Cheasty had been employed to thwart the National Association for the Advancement of Colored People in its drive to integrate buses in the city of Tallahassee, Florida. This implication was wholly unsubstantiated, but the seed was planted in the jurors' minds. At the same time, the former heavyweight champion of the world, Joe Louis, appeared in the courtroom "to see what they're doing to my good friend, Jimmy Hoffa." He and Hoffa put on a display of affection for each other that certainly was not missed by the jurors.

Just as important as these tactics, however, was the conduct of the government's case. The government underestimated Hoffa's shrewdness, and obviously did not prepare adequately for it.

Consider the jury, for example: one juror had fourteen convictions on his police record, another had nine. Most of these were for drunkenness and disorderly conduct. Another had a son who was in jail on a narcotics charge, and still another had lost his job with the government because he had declined a lie detector test to determine whether or not he was a homosexual. The government attorneys should have given more serious attention to the backgrounds of the jurors selected and to their probably biased opinions and prejudices as jurors in a criminal case.

The government attorneys seemingly were overconfident. They failed, in our opinion, to prepare adequately for the vigorous examinations that the facts warranted and the circumstances required in a case of this importance. Hoffa, who had not at that time been called to the witness chair before the Select Committee, took the stand in his trial and indicated that he certainly had no reason for great interest in the Select Committee's activities, since the Central Conference of Teamsters, which he then headed, was not likely to attract any attention from the investigators. In those days, Hoffa scoffed at the suggestion that there might be a searching probe of his union activities. The jury accepted Hoffa's testimony, and thus he was acquitted.

Since this court proceeding took place early in the life of the Select Committee, we had not yet gone through the long and grueling months that lay ahead of us, during which time we would become acquainted with and would understand better the cunning tactics of the powerful Teamsters. We had not yet witnessed the intriguing spectacle of Hoffa engaging in verbal gymnastics in the witness chair and testifying to forgetfulness.

Hoffa survived his trial and prevailed in his union. He was ready to launch himself across the prostrate form of Dave Beck on a swift smashing drive to the pinnacle of Teamsterdom.

Once the Hoffa trial was over, the committee became free again to resume its investigations. It thereupon took office space in Detroit. One of Hoffa's first reactions to the invasion of his stronghold by the staff members was typical of Teamster toughness. He snarled at the committee's chief accountant, Carmine Bellino: "I've looked into you, Bellino. You've got seven kids, and you're going to have to earn a living."

The most significant result, however, of these early months of astounding revelations of venality was the scores of thousands of letters and telegrams that inundated the committee from all over the United States, pleading for help against racketeers and pledging aid to the investigators even though some of the correspondents were afraid of violent reprisal. Many of these messages are discussed in detail farther along in this book.

In the meantime, the committee was holding the first of a long series of hearings that gave graphic illustration of corruption in a major American city. The 1,109 pages of testimony on the campaign to establish criminal control of the city of Portland, Oregon, unfolded an astounding tale of a cynical conspiracy to organize and operate a network of vice hidden below the bustling activities of a modern metropolis.

James B. Elkins was a racket chief and long-time gambler. He had his hand well into most of the illicit enterprises in the city of Portland. He had a long police record that included prohibition violations, a twenty- to thirty-year sentence for assault with intent to kill, a one-year sentence for possession of narcotics, and a number of arrests on gambling charges. During the early years of the last decade, he was the pinball king of Portland. He was a powerful and well-known leader of West Coast crime. Then he ran into trouble; he began to deal with the Teamsters. He became disenchanted with the conspiracy to enmesh his home town in a tight web of corruption, and finally he became so fearful for his own future that he used a tape recorder for documenting the entire sordid conspiracy.

As he told it on the witness stand, Elkins had good reason to be worried. He described the story of his meeting in Seattle with Frank Brewster, head of the Western Conference of Teamsters:

ELKINS: As near as I can remember it, I came into his room and I first sat down in his little waiting room. Three men came in and looked me over for a couple of minutes and then went out. Then he came in. . . .

He said, "I am going to tell you to start with I don't like the people you represent." I said, "I don't represent any people, just Jim Elkins."

He said, "Well, I am going to tell you something else. I make mayors and I break mayors, and I make chiefs of police and I break chiefs of police. I have been in jail and I have been out of jail. There is nothing scares me."

He talked a little more and he got red in the face and he

said, "If you bother my two boys, if you embarrass my two boys, you will find yourself wading across Lake Washington with a pair of concrete boots."

Brewster called Elkins' testimony "a fantastic story" and denied it.

The men whom Elkins was dealing with were two Seattle gamblers named McLaughlin and Maloney, whose operations were financed with Teamster funds. The gamblers had in mind the organization of vice and crime in the city upon a profitable, businesslike basis.

They intended first to take over the city's pinball operations, using Teamster pickets to stop deliveries of bread, milk, and beer, as well as other commodities, to those storekeepers who wouldn't co-operate.

Elkins went along with that, all right. He drew the line, however, when the others of the combine proposed to open up the city to organized prostitution. He took measures to protect himself, setting up the tape recorder, with a microphone capable of picking up conversations in Tom Maloney's apartment, where the other conspirators held their meetings.

There were seventy hours of tape recordings that resulted in the explosion of the conspiracy to share in underworld profits. Elkins turned over the tapes to Wallace Turner and William Lambert, reporters for the Portland *Oregonian*, and they subsequently won the Pulitzer Prize for their articles on the criminal combine.

Some of the tapes were played during Elkins' testimony before the Select Committee. Listening to them was an ordeal for every decent man and woman who heard the voices of the conspirators setting forth the details of their infamous plans and attempts to corrupt the wonderful city of Portland, Oregon.

The committee was well aware that Elkins' police record and his criminal career did not make him a witness of sterling character, but almost all of his long and involved story was corroborated by other evidence. In contrast, the Teamster witnesses were artful dodgers in the witness chair, often making incredible explanations of their roles in the Portland affair.

Tom Maloney, Joseph McLaughlin, and other witnesses, including William M. Langley, the then district attorney of Portland, all took refuge behind the Fifth Amendment.

The exposure of the sordidness beneath the façade of righteousness in Portland's urban administration involved testimony from all strata of the city's citizens, from top-ranking officials all the way down to the furtive denizens of the underworld, prostitutes, and narcotics addicts.

The hearings disclosed that Frank Brewster and John J. Sweeney, the ruling officials of the Western Conference of Teamsters, were fully aware of the drive of their underlings to seize control of crime in Portland and aided the attempt by making the Teamster treasury available to pay for the racketeers' expenses. The committee also found, in its report to the Senate on the Portland hearings, that other Teamster officials were guilty of grossly improper activities, chicanery, and callous misuse of union funds in the attempt to grab control of Portland's underworld.

Some of the most bizarre testimony ever heard in a Congressional hearing came during the Portland sessions. Much of it was contributed by the operator of a "night club and restaurant," Nathan Zusman, who received the close attention of the Portland vice squad.

ZUSMAN: My show was censored by nine of the vice squad.
MR. KENNEDY: By what?
ZUSMAN: Nine of the vice squad, which is the censor board.
MR. KENNEDY (*incredulously*): Nine of them?
ZUSMAN: I guess there were nine of them. The whole front row was taken.

Zusman was questioned about some of his associations. He was asked about a person named Bob Van Bable.

ZUSMAN: Yes; I know Bob Van Bable.
MR. KENNEDY: Where is he now?
ZUSMAN: Atlanta, Georgia.
MR. KENNEDY: Is he working down there?
ZUSMAN: Working for the government.
MR. KENNEDY: What is he doing?
ZUSMAN: I guess he is on the road gang.

Nathan Zusman was questioned at length about various aspects of the Portland situation, and a glance at the record these several years later shows that it is still difficult to make head or tail out of much of his testimony. Both Mr. Kennedy and Senator Goldwater questioned him closely about two cars financed for a known racketeer, an Oldsmobile and a Cadillac. The confusion went on and on, because nobody ever was quite sure which car Zusman was talking about—both of them were in accidents. In one accident a man was killed ("He should have been killed twice," said Zusman.) and in the other accident, the car—Cadillac or Oldsmobile?—was loaded with stolen TV sets and a thousand pairs of crooked dice.

MR. KENNEDY: Was this the same incident?
ZUSMAN: No. It was an Oldsmobile in Reno and a Cadillac in Chicago. Can't you get your stories straight?

The problem apparently was that Zusman couldn't get his own tale straight. Shortly afterward, Senator Goldwater took up the tangled trail of the cars:

SENATOR GOLDWATER: You put that Oldsmobile in your name?
ZUSMAN: The first car was a Ford, sir. . . .

At that point, everybody gave up trying to figure out Nathan Zusman's relationship with the American automotive industry. If we'd kept on that road, we might have had Volkswagens buzzing through the corridors of the Senate Office Building.

Zusman was accused by the operator of a call house of referring customers to her. He denied it vigorously, saying that while he visited the place twice, in company with Tom Maloney, a partner in the combination, he was there for this reason: ". . . I delivered some sandwiches to them and I used to make barbecue sandwiches and barbecue spareribs there and I delivered sandwiches to them. I took the stuff in the kitchen, and what they talked about, I don't know."

Zusman demanded a lie detector test, to be taken with the women who accused him. He finally took it alone, answering seven pertinent questions about vice operations in Portland. The chief of the United States Secret Service, U. E. Baughman, gave a laconic report on the results: "Analysis of the test results by the polygraph specialist who conducted the examination reveals specific reactions which are indicative of untruthfulness on the part of Mr. Zusman in his responses to the relevant questions."

The Portland investigation was tremendously valuable to the Select Committee for three reasons: (1) it shocked the nation into attention by focusing the glare of the news media on a single city and the dubious adventures of law enforcement officials, of underworld characters, and of Teamster union officials in the netherland of prostitutes, pinballs, and politicians-without-conscience; (2) it flushed out the first odious mass of corruption that could be directly attributed to the supposedly respectable leaders of a great American union, and therefore it keyed the committee to the astounding revelations that lay ahead; (3) it firmly established the methods and procedures by which the committee would conduct future investigations and hearings that would always strive for justice and fair treatment and in which corroboration of condemnatory material was one of the fundamental characteristics.

The Portland hearings led directly into the probe of the Western Conference of Teamsters, headed by Frank W. Brewster. This was the initial investigation that cracked the shell of Teamster corruption wide open.

In the Western Conference, Brewster was emulating his boss

and close friend and associate, Dave Beck. There were about eight hundred thousand dollars spent in dissipation of the treasury and other funds. Several of the malpractices revealed by hearings were these:

Frank Brewster threw union dues to the winds, particularly to support his large stable of thoroughbred race horses. He purchased a Palm Springs, California, apartment, luxuriously fitted for the use of the union's top officers. He used four thousand dollars of union funds for a down payment on a house for himself in the same town. Four hundred thousand dollars of union money was used in an attempt to salvage the financial affairs of a Canadian trucking company, supposedly for the benefit of its ninety union employees, but without much prospect of any return for the Teamsters. Indeed, the company was destined to end up in the hands of a State of Washington trucker who hadn't invested a penny in it. Brewster and Beck owned a filling station that got most of the Teamster business. Finally, there was a definite conflict of interest in the business dealings between Frank Brewster and a broker for the Western Conference's welfare funds. In all of his operations, Brewster was found by the Senate Select Committee to have mishandled $849,309.98, a figure which includes the $440,000 loan to the Canadian trucking company.

Not all of this money, of course, was for Brewster's personal benefit. He spread the wealth with a generous hand. A great deal of the money went down the drain, however, with little prospect that much of it would ever return to benefit the union and its members.

The basic principles of sound and decent union leadership are set firmly in a foundation of trust and responsibility. A union leader, just like a banker or a stockbroker or an insurance executive, should always have uppermost in his mind the nature of the trust reposed in him by the multitudes of men and women who belong to his union and who furnish the hard-earned dollars that fill the treasury and the welfare funds placed in his care. Frank

Brewster, a high-ranking official of this International Brotherhood, by his own testimony, was a careless, profligate, and unreliable custodian of the loyal membership's money.

He was somewhat of a piker, however, in comparison to his friend and leader and business partner, Dave Beck.

CHAPTER 3

"His Majesty, the Wheel"

THE International Brotherhood of Teamsters demonstrated cynical arrogance in their moves to frustrate and flaunt the preliminary efforts of the Select Committee. Nobody, they said, not even the United States Senate, had the power to poke and peer into the files of the Teamsters. The files were shut up tightly, the doors of the international's office building were closed to the committee's staff, and orders were issued that no union officials had to answer any questions. The top echelon of the Teamsters then relaxed, at least briefly. The suggestion and expectancy was that since other similar investigations had died away, this one would also.

Hoffa, who was a direct man everywhere but in the witness chair, told the noted Washington newspaper correspondent, Clark Mollenhoff, winner of the Pulitzer Prize, whose critical writing about the union had helped to arouse national interest in Teamster leadership, that nothing would come of the probe. "Why don't you give up?" said Hoffa. "We're the Teamsters."

Evidently believing that money and the pressure exerted by large sums of money can solve any problem at all, Hoffa said cynically to Mr. Mollenhoff: "Everyone has his price. What's yours?"

At that time, Mr. Mollenhoff had long been engaged in a thorough study of questionable practices in the labor-management field, particularly those of certain echelons of the Teamsters

Union. His articles on Hoffa and other officers of the international union, published in the Des Moines *Register* and *Tribune* and the Minneapolis *Star* and *Tribune*, were very helpful at the start of our vast investigations. His advice and ideas on improper activities in areas of the committee's jurisdiction proved to be soundly based upon fact, and his achievements in the field were most impressive.

James R. Hoffa wasn't yet the president of the International Brotherhood, however. That dignitary, Dave Beck, was still ducking all efforts to get him seated at the witness table to face the eight senators who wanted specific answers to some specific questions. He probably knew that his appearance was inevitable, but he tried desperately to prolong his absence. First he went to Europe, for his health. Then he went to Puerto Rico, this time for his wife's health. He returned and went into seclusion in his mansion in Seattle, pleading ill health again.

During all the time that Dave Beck was traveling and taking care of his health, the legion of Teamster lawyers was busily trying to discover ways and means of diverting and dissipating the committee's insistent attention as well as the mushrooming publicity that was focused upon the big union.

The Teamsters at first had reason to believe that it would not be difficult to reduce the heat. They were, after all, the power elite of the American labor movement. They had a history of muscle and violence that went back to 1867, when team drivers in Chicago banded together to improve their conditions or to put down their reins. They joined the A.F.L. in 1899 and were ruled by Dan Tobin from 1907 through 1952, a reign of almost unparalleled length in American labor, during which Tobin became a noted political power in the nation and his rough, brawling Teamsters burgeoned in strength to more than a thousand locals grouped in four conferences that cover the nation. It has been estimated that about 90 per cent of the over-the-road truck drivers in the country are Teamster members.

Dave Beck became "His Majesty, the Wheel" (an apt nickname taken from the union's seal) in 1952, and he ruled in lordly and solitary splendor, looting the treasury at his whim, while he evidently paid little or no attention to the furtive infiltration of racketeers and hoodlums into the lower levels below the throne.

In 1957, the Teamsters were the biggest labor union in the United States, with a membership of about one million and a half. They controlled the movement of almost all the raw and finished materials that supplied business and industry across the nation. They possessed the power to whip the American economy into a knotted snarl, literally overnight.

Let us take a look at the awesome strength of this single union as it might apply to one great city: the biggest union in the world versus the biggest city in the world, the Teamsters against the City of New York.

There is a huge administrative authority that controls and directs all commercial traffic that approaches and enters the sprawling metropolis. All the waterways and their piers and docks in Manhattan, Brooklyn, Staten Island, and along the New Jersey waterfront are under the administration of this agency, which is called the Port of New York Authority. It also has jurisdiction over tunnels, bridges, and ferries that pour commercial vehicles into the great city from all directions of the compass. What would happen if the Teamsters decided to pull a strike against the vast Port of New York at dawn tomorrow?

As the sun came up over the bay and the North and East rivers, the swift-wheeling columns of tractor-trailer units that roll through the night from all the states on the eastern seaboard toward Manhattan would begin to jam the parking lots of diners and turnpike restaurants in New York, New Jersey, and Connecticut. Soon there would be no more room in the lots, and the highways and turnpikes would begin to choke with trucks. All the bridges and tunnels that lead into the heart of this metropolis would be empty, their approaches jammed with silent trucks. The rows of piers in Brooklyn, Manhattan, Staten Island, and New Jersey, servicing ships that ply all the trade routes of the world, would stand silent and empty in the early-morning sunlight. They would be empty because the longshoremen would honor Teamster picket lines.

The great produce and meat markets in the Bronx, Brooklyn, and Manhattan couldn't open for their ordinary frantic early-morning activity without Teamster-driven vehicles to supply them.

Incoming ships would stand out in the bay, unable to dock without the tugboats that guide them to the piers; tugboat crews would respect Teamster picket lines. Railroad trains wouldn't come south of the great transfer point of Harmon on the Hudson River nor east of Newark, New Jersey.

The busy garment industry on Manhattan's central West Side would have to close up shop—Seventh Avenue traffic, for the first time in the memory of any living New Yorker, would be free of thousands upon thousands of trucks.

Manhattan Island would be almost a paradise for motorists, without its usual daily snarl of huge trucks from almost every part of the nation, although there probably wouldn't be too many motorists other than taxi drivers to take advantage of the freedom. Incoming drivers would be frustratingly jammed into the tremendous flotillas of motionless trucks in upstate New York, suburban New Jersey, and nearby Connecticut.

Industry would grind to a stop during the day, while retail businesses would try to keep going without bread, milk, meat, fruits, vegetables, newspapers, and literally hundreds of other commodities under daily delivery schedules. It has been estimated that Manhattan uses two million gallons of fuel oil every day to heat its towering forest of buildings. There would be few oil trucks on the streets during a Teamster strike. Buses and subways would stop running; the operators would be out in sympathy, and fuel and power would be limited. Within a matter of hours, the great city of eight million people, and its surrounding urban areas with millions more, would be reduced to complete chaos. If the strike were prolonged for only a few days, tragic disaster conditions would prevail. Some people would be starving; the city's electrical system would begin to fail; troops would have to take over to maintain law and order.

That picture does not come from idle speculation. It could happen, and the Teamsters have the power to do it, although it is difficult to conceive that the most heartless and conscienceless union leader would deliberately speak the words, "Pull 'em out!" that would cause such cruel havoc. James Hoffa knows he can do it. He has been quoted about the prospect of laws that would restrict labor's right to call strikes that might cripple the nation: "The only answer is that if such a law passes, we should have all our contracts end on a given date. They talk about a secondary boycott; we can call a primary strike all across the nation that will straighten out the employers for once and for all." Later, when these words were published nationally, he said he had been misquoted.

Let no one make any mistake about it; the power is there.

The Teamsters, at the beginning of our hearings, were also tremendously strong in the titanic national labor organization, the AFL-CIO. Of every ten members of the labor alliance, one was a Teamster. They had a treasury so bulging that they were the financial peers of the greatest industrial concerns. Their welfare and investment funds were so huge that few of their leaders had even the vaguest notion of the amount of the Brotherhood's gross wealth. The former president, Dan Tobin, had been the intimate of presidents of the United States. Their leader, Dave Beck, who sported Sulka shirts costing forty-three dollars of dues-payers' money, was a former truck driver who had become one of the most powerful men in the country. Beck was the friend of high officials in the national government; he had great influence in Congress, where he was regarded as a tough and effective labor leader; he'd had his picture taken on the steps of the White House, shaking hands with President Eisenhower. Dave Beck's endorsement of Mr. Eisenhower's candidacy was national front-page news. About the only man in unionism who apparently viewed him with any lack of respect before his downfall was James Riddle

Hoffa. There are those who believe that Jimmy helped the great man's fall with an ungentle push.

With their power and prestige, the Teamsters also had public opinion pretty generally on their side as the hearings started, for millions upon millions of people who had witnessed the growth of unionism to maturity and respectability in our time simply refused to believe that "big labor" could be grossly corrupt. In the popular mind, particularly in urban areas, labor leaders were generally regarded as unselfish men who lived simply and who were dedicated to the rights and advancement of the rank and file.

The Teamsters had all these factors going for them as they came into the hearings of the Select Committee.

They had stature, and as has been said, they were sure that they were equally as powerful as the United States Government. The imposing "marble palace" that contains the union's headquarters is a five-million-dollar building that faces the Capitol, just across the plaza from the offices of the eight senators who comprised the Senate Select Committee. Through the bare limbs of the trees in winter, the Senators can look across and see the gleaming windows and shining marble of the Teamsters' building, which was placed to face the working halls of the Government so that, as Dave Beck reportedly said, "we can keep our eye on Congress." Incidentally, the testimony is that Nathan Shefferman managed to net an agent's fee of twelve thousand dollars of Teamster money for his services in getting the land. When Mr. Shefferman discovered that the land was for sale at fifteen dollars per square foot he suggested an intermediary corporation to buy it at fifteen dollars and sell it to the Teamsters at eighteen dollars. However, the representatives of the American Legion, which owned the property, would have no part of such a deal.

In the beginning, therefore, the hierarchy of the Teamsters probably lost little sleep over the impending hearings. After all, who were the two men who had moved to the principal posts on the firing line?

One of them was a handsome young man from a noted family

who had come to national prominence as counsel for the Demo-
crats during the Army-McCarthy hearings. Any Teamster could
tell you that he was "a dumb kid" and completely inexperienced
in the law, compared to the top-notch quality of the Teamsters'
legal staff. He was surely going to founder, they said, in the
crashing waves of deterring action that the countless Teamster
attorneys would launch against him and his relatively small staff.
Bob Kennedy, the wiseacres said, was going to be a sorry young
man for his audacious sniping at the mighty men across the plaza.

The other was the senior Senator from Arkansas, who would be
up for re-election within three years. A stern-faced man, they said,
with a reputation for stubbornness. But the union leaders weren't
much concerned about him, either.

This Senator had manifested many times his deep concern for
the dignity of the United States Senate; there was no doubt that
McClellan would call a halt to the proceedings once the investigation and the subsequent hearings began to degenerate into a
three-ring circus. Right from the beginning, Hoffa brazenly referred to the hearings by the name of a noted television dramatic
show—he talked about "McClellan's Playhouse 90."

Furthermore, the wise men said, if McClellan persisted in his
folly, he would be informed quietly that the power of the International Brotherhood of Teamsters would be thrown against him
back home in Arkansas when he ran for re-election. Perhaps it
was, but it was hard to find; the Teamster candidate never made
an appearance.

So the union made the mistake of ridiculing and under-
estimating determined men, and then compounded its errors.
Teamster leaders dismissed the qualities of honesty and integrity
and loyalty. They predicated all their moves on cynicism, and
they discounted the dedication and public service of the highest
order that was lined against them in a splendid staff of men and
women. One of the remarkable qualities of the committee staff
has never been understood by the parade of crooks, criminals,
and frauds which has passed in review over these years; these

people just couldn't comprehend the motivations of investigators. "What's your angle in all this?" was a question frequently put to staff members. Criminals cannot fathom the concept of an old-fashioned set of moral standards that puts a man into a fight to the finish against venality.

On Tuesday, March 26, 1957, Dave Beck arrived at the Senate Caucus Room, affable and smiling as he chatted with reporters and photographers. With confidence he moved forward at these words:

THE CHAIRMAN: If there is nothing further, the witness, Mr. Beck, will come around. You are present and you will stand and be sworn.

Fresh from his voyages, and looking as if he had recovered the health that had allegedly failed him, Dave Beck sat in the witness chair, prepared to discourse at length with the gentlemen of the Senate on whatever great affairs of state they cared to discuss. The long series of direct questions started to flow, and before the morning session of the hearing was over, Dave Beck's aura of respectability started to seep away from him, and then to flow more swiftly, and finally to flood. There was left exposed the naked image of a man who betrayed a great trust and stole from the honest working people who had lifted him to power.

When he was elected to the presidency of the union in 1952, Beck pledged his honor to the task of safeguarding the funds of the membership and the integrity of the union. Yet during the five years of his term, he ignored the rights of the membership, carried out with greedy shamelessness a campaign to enrich himself from the treasury, and so neglected his duties that when he left office in disgrace, there were thugs and thieves in positions of power in the International Brotherhood.

We recall that his avariciousness became so widespread and so petty that he purchased five dozen diapers with union funds, presumably for a niece who had several children.

It is true that Beck eventually returned $370,000 to the Teamsters, as restitution, but he did so only when the Internal Revenue Service began to follow his labyrinthine financial trail. The record showed that $370,000 had been used for many purposes, but principally for the construction of his home and the homes of four of his associates in Seattle, and for payments to Nathan Shefferman in the amount of $85,000 to pay for his personal bills and those of his son and nephew. The attempt to cover this squalid dealing was apparent in the testimony of Shefferman, who said he acted as "purchasing agent" for Beck but admitted that Beck and his relatives did a great deal of the buying themselves and had the bills sent to Shefferman for payment, whereupon Beck would send Teamster checks to reimburse Shefferman.

Beck received kickbacks from placing Teamster mortgages with a company in which he had a financial interest.

On the land deal for the "marble palace" in Washington, mentioned earlier, Beck got eight thousand dollars of Shefferman's agent's fee of twelve thousand dollars.

The testimony also showed that Beck received a twenty-four-thousand-dollar kickback when Shefferman supervised the interior decorating of the international headquarters, while also setting up a new bookkeeping system for the union. Shefferman's system was a singular one; with exasperating frequency during the long series of hearings on Teamster affairs, the committee's accountants found that records had been shifted for storage to cellars or attics, and then, according to testimony, thrown out as useless junk.

Beck pressured Anheuser-Busch, the St. Louis brewers, to favor a liquor distributing company whose president was none other than Dave Beck, Jr.

The committee heard testimony that a large part of the money that Beck repaid into the Teamster treasury was lent to him by the Fruehauf Trailer Company—a major supplier of the nation's commercial trailers, as should be evident to every motorist in the United States who has driven the nation's highways.

Beck repaid the loan in full (with interest), in part from funds he realized when he sold his home in Seattle to the International Brotherhood of Teamsters for $163,215. The astonishing feature of this sale was that the house had been built in the first place with Teamster money. But that isn't all. After his retirement as president, Beck continued to live in the house.

There were twenty-one findings of the Senate Select Committee detailing the activities of Dave Beck. One of these involved toy trucks. It was reported that Fruehauf Trailer Company and Associated Transport Company were approached by Beck and contributed fourteen thousand dollars, which they testified they understood was to be used for industrial promotion. The Teamsters came through with twenty thousand dollars, and with this pool of money a company was formed to manufacture and distribute toy trucks to Teamster locals throughout the country. The promotional campaign for selling the trucks to Teamsters came to about twenty thousand dollars of the union's money.

Here is how Dave Beck, the national man of distinction, occupied some of his time as the leader of fifteen hundred thousand union members. He sent telegrams to push the sale of the toy trucks. Two examples are sufficient, one to the Joint Council in St. Paul, and the other to the Joint Council in Milwaukee:

We do not have a single purchase letter, wire, or telephone call of any kind or character from the St. Paul local union or the joint council, although we have had Hoffa and others trying to make contact. Please advise why we get no cooperation. If special meeting of council has not been called or special meeting of secretaries has not been called, please do so immediately and advise me by wire or telephone this afternoon what is the matter in St. Paul.

Twenty-three trucks is the total purchased by local unions affiliated with Joint Council 50 [Milwaukee]. Sixteen of them are from your own local union. All over the United States locals are averaging about five trucks per local. Please give me an answer this afternoon, either by wire or telephone, the reason for the situation in the Milwaukee joint council.

Why was the great man so interested in toy trucks bearing the union emblem and costing fifteen to thirty dollars apiece? Why did he want every local in the nation to order at least five?

The answer is brief and simple. The Shelton Company handled the trucks at a profit of eighty-four thousand dollars. This neat return on thirty-four thousand dollars was split between Shelton Shefferman (son of Beck's "purchasing agent"), Dave Beck, Jr., and Norman Gessert (cousin of Mrs. Dave Beck).

The second transaction disclosed to the committee was so gross and shameless that it disgusted every person who heard it unfolded at the Beck hearing. Ray Leheney, a veteran Teamster and very close personal friend of Dave Beck, died and left a widow for whom Dave Beck wished to do something. He organized a voluntary contribution fund called the Leheney Memorial Foundation, with funds given by Teamsters throughout the country. Then Beck and a mortgage banker from Seattle proceeded to use Teamster funds to purchase mortgages for $71,407.03. According to Teamster records, these mortgages had been purchased for the account of the union. The mortgages were bought in May, 1956, and held until December, 1956, by which time payments had substantially reduced their value. Thereupon Beck and his associate transferred the mortgages to the widow, Mrs. Ray Leheney, at the par value of $71,607.32. They paid the union what the mortgages were actually worth, and then put the difference, which was $11,585.04, in their pockets, splitting it as profit on the transaction. The depth of dishonor has ever been described as the practice of "robbing widows and orphans." Beck went that low, and then a step lower, because the widow happened to be the wife of one of his best friends.

Beck and his son were tried and convicted of larceny, and Beck was convicted of filing fraudulent income-tax returns for a Teamster subsidiary.

The revulsion of the national Teamster membership caused Beck to step down as candidate for re-election to the presidency; he was burned in effigy by the members of a West Coast local.

He went to the Florida convention that year to preside as his last official act.

He made a speech to the representatives of Teamsters from all over the nation. He said he was leaving after thirty-one years, and that he had a last request:

"I am going to ask you to judge me as I would judge you. I only ask you to try, if you possibly can, just here and there, somewhere along the line, to see if you can't find something that I have done that is perhaps just a little bit over on the credit side—just a little."

To that plaintive plea, the Senate Select Committee had its own answer: "This committee can only conclude that the labor movement is well rid of Dave Beck, as it would be well rid of others like him. The public and the seventeen million union members in America deserve better."

As Beck made his farewell, the chunky figure of James Riddle Hoffa waited impatiently in the wings. He would now move to center stage.

CHAPTER 4

The "Simple Life" of James R. Hoffa

JUST a few weeks after Hoffa clambered over the fallen might of Dave Beck to mount the throne, there were several dramatic scenes played in a convention hall in Atlantic City, New Jersey, where the AFL-CIO was meeting in convention. One of its main objectives was to decide the case of the corruption-riddled Teamsters. A committee recommended expulsion.

Einar Mohn spoke in defense of the Teamsters. Alex Rose of the Hatters Union said that the truck drivers must go in the name of decency and honest unionism.

Then John English, secretary-treasurer of the Teamsters, who had served many long years under Tobin and Beck, rose to his feet. He spoke passionately:

". . . For fifty years every time you came to us we helped you. . . . When you were on strike and you couldn't get it from anybody else, when you knocked at the Teamsters' door they helped you. . . . Are you going to expel us today while our case is on in Washington? Do we deserve that from you after fifty years?

". . . There are some men sitting on that platform there, and if it hadn't been for Dan Tobin they wouldn't be there. . . . Then you sit up there and you are ready to vote against us. Don't forget, Mr. Meany, you never had a better friend than Dan Tobin, and you never had a better friend than the Teamsters. I have been with you all my life, Gompers, Green, and you. The Teamsters stood by you. What are you going to do for us?

"... We ask for one year. After giving you fifty years, giving you all our time and our money, we ask for one year to clean up our house. Beck is gone, Brewster is gone, and Brennan is gone. There is only one man—Jimmy Hoffa. And Jimmy Hoffa has done more for our international union than anybody connected with it, including myself. How in the hell can we kick him out?

"... Oh, it makes my blood run cold. I am coming near the end of my days. I never thought I would live to see this. . . . We won't forget our friends, Teamsters never forget their friends. As far as our enemies are concerned, they can all go straight to hell."

The house of labor didn't listen to the plea of John English. The vote was taken and the verdict was announced. It was thumbs down. The Teamsters delegation rose and walked silently from the convention hall.

Sadly for the cause of unionism in America and for the citizenry whom it is supposed to serve, John English's promise "to clean up our house" in one year was not fulfilled. Five long years have gone by since the veteran Teamster asked for a little time, "one year," and the conditions for which the Teamsters were expelled have not been corrected. A committee report filed in the summer of 1962 indicates that in some respects they may be worse than ever.

Consider the man who took over the Teamsters at the mammoth organization's low point of decency. Consider his record.

James R. Hoffa was born on February 14, 1913, in Brazil, Indiana. He was the son of a coal prospector who died while Hoffa was a boy. Hoffa had to quit school at an early age and go to work. He became a stock boy in a department store. "Then I got a job at Kroger's. And that's my whole life. Pretty simple life."

It was by no means simple. He organized a union at Kroger's, which was a grocery chain, and took his outfit into the Teamsters in 1932. He became president of Local #299 and was in the middle of Detroit's labor troubles during the 1930's. He was arrested on the picket lines a total of eighteen times in one day. He was asked about his police record, not including picket-line arrests, during his appearances before the committee:

MR. KENNEDY: Since you have been with the Teamsters union, you
   have been arrested a number of times, have you?
HOFFA: That is correct.
MR. KENNEDY: How many times, approximately, do you think?

Note the supreme self-confidence and hail-fellow-well-met attitude of Hoffa early in his testimony as illustrated by his answer to that question:

HOFFA: Well, I don't know, Bob. I haven't counted them up. I
   think maybe about seventeen times I have been picked up, took
   into custody of the police, and out of the seventeen times, three
   of those times—in many instances these were dismissed—but in
   three of those times I received convictions.

It is interesting to note Hoffa's use of the familiar nickname in his answer. Just a few months before, he had taken up the habit of pleasantly addressing Mr. Kennedy as "Bobby." At this point, as he sat in the witness chair for the first time, it was shortened to "Bob." Before many days went by, it became much more formal: "Mr. Kennedy." During his later appearances, he had abandoned the chief counsel entirely as a person to whom he might address his answers. He looked pointedly away and started his responses aggrievedly: "Mr. Chairman . . ."

There probably is little purpose in tabulating all the committee's findings on Hoffa's transgressions one after another in the pages of this book. Several of them will be highlighted to illustrate the qualities of leadership that he provides, but the details of dozens of them already fill huge volumes of the Select Committee's record, where more than 20,000 pages and more than 11,537,-500 words attest to an almost incredible story.

The courts of the United States are the setting in which Hoffa is being called upon to answer for some of his conduct. The process may be slow—he has had the services of a multitude of lawyers employed by the Teamsters, who were at his beck and call. A long, drawn-out legal battle can well be anticipated.

James Hoffa is a shrewd and forceful man, and endlessly through the years since he took over the Teamsters, he has shouted his story to sixteen hundred thousand members of his union, and to all other union members who would listen—the impassioned story of a life dedicated to only one purpose, that of bettering the working conditions of Teamsters all over the country. All criticism directed at him, all the indictments, all the charges of crooked dealing, all the "fantasies" about racketeers, were part of a conspiracy, according to him, against a valiant labor leader who worked ceaselessly for the members of the union. He has been persecuted, he says, by McClellan and Kennedy only because he is the head of the nation's greatest union and for that reason is the biggest target for the "union-busters."

In these pages, therefore, the findings of the committee about his activities are being examined once again. These show that his favorite theme—"they are just picking on Hoffa in order to smash unions"—is manifestly false.

In point of fact, the committee stated its conviction that one of Hoffa's chief interests in life has always been, is now, and always will be his own advancement to power.

There have been many adverse findings, reported by the committee, concerning Hoffa's rule of the Central Conference of Teamsters and the International Brotherhood itself.

The committee declared in its report "that if Hoffa remains unchecked he will successfully destroy the decent labor movement in the United States. . . . If Hoffa is successful in combating the combined weight of the U.S. Government and public opinion, the cause of decent unionism is lost and labor-management relations in this country will return to the jungle era."

A fitting course to take is to let Hoffa speak for himself. His words can then be countered by the testimony of others.

When he accepted the presidency of the Teamsters on October 4, 1957, at Miami Beach, Florida, just a few weeks before the union was thrown out of the AFL-CIO for corruption, Hoffa made a speech to the assembled delegates. He makes many speeches every year all over the country, but this was one of the most important of his career because it stated the conditions of his trust as he saw them, and it contained the promises he made to carry out that trust. He held forth at length, denying the charges against him and against those with whom he surrounds himself. He spoke forthrightly to the delegates, as he never did in all the days he was in the witness chair before the Select Committee. Five years have gone by since he made the speech. What did he say about his role as Teamster leader?

HOFFA: "We have taken action at this convention to comply fully and properly with proper ethical demands of the AFL-CIO."

Almost a year later, Hoffa was again in the witness chair. He was questioned at length about his promise to clean up the Teamsters. For example, on the very day that Hoffa testified, a small-time hoodlum named Frank Kierdorf died in Pontiac, Michigan, as a result of burns incurred as he set fire to a dry-cleaning shop in a shakedown racket. Kierdorf was accused of running a Teamster shakedown in Flint, Michigan. Hoffa was asked what he'd done about it. "I discussed the matter with Frank," said Hoffa, "and he flatly denied it."

Then there was Frank Kierdorf's uncle, Herman Kierdorf, who was shaking down Detroit automobile dealers for the Teamsters. The elder Kierdorf was an ex-convict who had served several prison terms in between stints as a Teamster organizer. Hoffa was asked if he'd done anything about Kierdorf's alleged Detroit shakedown and whether he'd thoroughly investigated the complaint about his man extorting money. Certainly he had. He'd asked Herman Kierdorf if it was true, and Herman had told him it wasn't. "I tried to find out from the only man that could have told me, Senator."

THE CHAIRMAN: Well, if you found that your agents were acting that way, you could do plenty about it, and do it fast.

HOFFA: If they deny it, what could I do, Senator?

Another Teamster ex-convict named Lawrence Welch was accused of using pressure in the auto-washing business in Detroit. Again, here is the testimony less than a year after the righteous speech in Miami Beach.

MR. KENNEDY: Did you ask Welch about it?

HOFFA: Yes, sir, and Welch said he didn't do it.

MR. KENNEDY: Did you make any further investigation?

HOFFA: Where would I investigate?

The prize situation of them all, however, was that of Glenn W. Smith, president of Teamsters Local #515 in Tennessee. Smith had admitted that he had used twenty thousand dollars of Teamsters' money in order to bribe a judge in a case in which he and ten others were defendants. (Smith's lawyers successfully used the argument, when he was tried for income tax evasion, that the twenty thousand dollars wasn't income, since he was only a channel for the money's route from Teamster funds to the judge, and furthermore, if that defense wasn't allowed, then the huge sum wasn't income for another reason—Smith had embezzled it!)

THE CHAIRMAN: Mr. Hoffa, this is almost beyond comprehension, that a man will come in and admit that he took twenty thousand dollars of union money and state it under oath before a legal or properly constituted tribunal, the Senate of a sovereign state, acting as a trial court on an impeachment, and make that statement, under oath, that he took union dues money and used it to fix a criminal case to keep him from being convicted or going to the penitentiary, as likely he would have had he been convicted. Now, do you mean to say that as president of this great international union that doesn't cause you any concern to act, to protect your membership?

HOFFA: Certainly it is disturbing news, but since there are charges filed, and the due process will take care of the question of that.

Next case: another Smith, this one W. A., "Hard-of-Hearing Smitty," who was business agent of Local #327 in Nashville, whose penchant for solving labor problems was to punch somebody into senselessness, as he did a Nashville trucking executive —first having the courtesy to ask the man to take his hands out of his pockets. Of this man Smith, the question was asked:

MR. KENNEDY: He has been arrested fourteen times prior to that, and he had a number of convictions, and he has just been sentenced from two to ten years and he is still business agent of Local 327, and you haven't taken any steps against him?
HOFFA: You are right.

A further note on the Smith boys: Hoffa was asked by a newspaperman, Clark Mollenhoff, why they had been given positions of power. He replied, "We need somebody down there to kick those hillbillies around."
Then of course came the question of the infamous mobster, Anthony "Tony Ducks" Corallo, vice-president of Local 239 of the Teamsters, a vicious hoodlum with a long police record.

MR. KENNEDY: He has been arrested twelve times, ranging from robbery, grand larceny, and narcotics. He was identified before the committee as an important figure in narcotics, and he was a close friend of Johnny Dioguardi. My question is, Have you made any investigation of him? . . . Have you taken any steps against Mr. Tony Ducks Corallo?
HOFFA: As of now, no.

The record of the hearing goes on: Milton Holt, secretary-treasurer of Local #805, indicted for extortion—no steps taken; Abe Gordon, administrator of the welfare fund of Local #805, receiver of kickbacks—no action taken; John McNamara, official of Local #808 and Local #295, in jail for extortion—no action taken; "Shorty" Feldman, Local #990, 18 arrests, 2 convictions, 2 prison terms—no steps taken; nineteen officials of Local #107 with 104 arrests and 40 convictions, a local run by Ray Cohen, a vice-president of the International—no action taken; Al Reger, secretary-treasurer of Local #522, serving 5 to 10 years for extortion—no steps taken to remove him; Joey Glimco in Chicago, 38 arrests—no action.

MR. KENNEDY: What about Mr. Frank Matula, out in California?
HOFFA: What about him?
MR. KENNEDY: He has been convicted of perjury.
HOFFA: Frank Matula is up on appeal. I have taken no action.

Let us move to Detroit, to Hoffa's own home local, #299:

MR. KENNEDY: You have Roland McMasters out in Detroit. Does he work for you?
HOFFA: What did he do so bad?
MR. KENNEDY: Does he work for you?
HOFFA: He does, Local 299, my own local union.
MR. KENNEDY: How long has he been with you?
HOFFA: I believe Mac came with us somewhere around the 1940's.
MR. KENNEDY: . . . Was he under indictment on a charge of felonious assault against Leslie Smith and Brother Hugh Smith, these two brothers being assaulted with baseball bats and knives?
HOFFA: I don't remember if he was or not. I don't remember the indictment.

The long rollcall continued—Jack Thompson, Local #332, attempted killing with an automobile; still working for the union.

MR. KENNEDY: . . . Are you frightened of these people, Mr. Hoffa?
HOFFA: I am not frightened of anybody, Mr. Kennedy, and I don't

intend to have the impression left, as has been stated publicly, that I am controlled by gangsters.

THE CHAIRMAN: . . . This has become a sordid story. Lord Almighty, you are the man at the head of it. You have the responsibility. But apparently instead of taking any action you are undertaking to do everything you can to perpetuate this situation. You can make any comments you like. . . .

There, from Hoffa's own lips, is the story of how he used the year for which John English pleaded to clean up the evil in the Teamsters.

The committee, in its report to the Senate on Hoffa and the Teamsters, compiled a list of 141 Teamster officials who showed up in a derogatory light during the hearings. Of the 141 officials, 55 were no longer with the Teamsters at the time the report was made, but, according to the record, Hoffa himself had not removed a single one of them. Of the 141 people, 73 had taken the Fifth Amendment to a total of 3,044 questions.

Speaking at the Miami convention, Hoffa said: ". . . We are decent trade unionists and useful citizens. . . . I have been beaten, threatened, abused and smeared."

Let's take another look at the record, which quotes a Senate guard who testified that Hoffa said, of a witness who had just testified to corruption: "That S.O.B., I'll break his back." Two days later, Hoffa testified that he couldn't remember saying it.

A former business agent for Local #614 in Pontiac, Michigan, Robert Scott, testified that he wished to quit the Teamsters. He reported that Hoffa said: "I will break both your arms and legs."

Hoffa was quoted by a witness before the committee, talking about the rights of membership: "In the Teamsters Union every man stands up and has his vote counted, and God help him if he votes the wrong way." Hoffa said he couldn't remember making exactly that statement, either.

"This union will be a model of trade unionism," said the chunky little man when he was inaugurated. "I believe in good honest trade unionism. I believe in the welfare of our members."

However, Hoffa was charged with concealing from the union members his participation in the Sun Valley land scheme in Florida, where he had an option under which he stood to make a fortune if things had turned out successfully. The Teamsters, their families and friends bought at extreme markups the poor building lots that were offered. At this writing he stands indicted for fraud in that matter.

The committee found that over $2,400,000 of Teamster funds, principally of the Central Conference of Teamsters, had been misused; funds in the amount of $174,870 were used to aid union officials accused of extortion, dynamiting, kickbacks, and accepting bribes; the Teamsters paid large amounts of money to lawyers to defend Teamster officials accused of such crimes. Typical of loans made out of Teamster funds was one made to a New York accountant who did some work for the Teamsters, and who managed to obtain a loan of $150,000. The Marberry Construction Company, owned by Teamster employees, got $175,000. Northville Downs Race Track in Michigan received $50,000; Teamster leader Bert Brennan's horses were running there.

Teamster welfare funds in the amount of $1,200,000 were invested in a Minneapolis department store run by Benjamin Dranow. This store went into bankruptcy soon thereafter, and Dranow, an associate and friend of Hoffa's, drew out $115,000 of the company's funds immediately before a bankruptcy petition was filed. Dranow is now required to answer for this withdrawal before the Federal courts in Minnesota.

Hoffa gave two union employees $3,750 out of union funds to work on a hunting and fishing club in Michigan owned by Mrs. Hoffa and Mrs. Brennan; the union gave $5,000 to a fellow who was running for the presidency of a Philadelphia local; the union spent $155,000 to buy the home of the old Capone mobster, Paul "The Waiter" Ricca, and said it was to be used to train Teamster employees in their jobs; $5,000 was paid to have a business agent go West to bring back the runaway wife of Hoffa's brother Billy. The record goes on and on and on. And through it all Hoffa keeps insisting that he deals in cash; time after time one associate or another gave him $1,000 in cash as a loan, or $5,000, or $2,500, or $2,000, even though sometimes these lenders had to go borrow the money. Everything is in cash, including Hoffa's annual race track winnings. His late crony, Bert Brennan, would do all the betting, and then they'd split the proceeds at the end of the year. Senator Kennedy asked Hoffa about his winnings during his last appearance before the Senate Select Committee.

SENATOR KENNEDY: I have never been completely convinced, Mr. Hoffa, to be frank with you, that Mr. Brennan did win this money at the race track.
HOFFA: Why don't you ask him?
SENATOR KENNEDY: I did, and he took the Fifth Amendment.
HOFFA: Maybe he has a reason.

Whenever he was asked direct questions about these and a host of other malpractices, his answer was almost always a plea of poor memory, while he often suggested that the committee ask the question of one of his cronies who would then plead the Fifth Amendment. This is the kind of answer from Hoffa that the committee was forced to accept on many occasions, as when he was asked a question about his association with Johnny Dio: "To the best of my recollection, I must recall on my memory, I cannot remember."

Hoffa said in Miami: "I believe in the welfare of our members. This union will practice democracy. . . ."

The Select Committee reported on this matter to the Senate, saying, "On more occasions than we can recount, Hoffa has told the committee (and anyone else who would listen) that no matter what else may be said about him, he is first and foremost interested in the betterment of the working conditions of his union members. . . . Time and time again the committee has found Hoffa to be faithless to the members of his own union." Time and time again Hoffa has denied this charge.

Out in Detroit, one of the business agents of Local #299, Hoffa's home local, had two businesses that didn't do much for the welfare of union members. This man, Zigmont Snyder (another ex-convict, of course) had the Great Lakes Cargo Handling Co., which unloaded grain ships on the Detroit waterfront. Snyder, a union officer, used derelicts and teenagers for the jobs, paying far under union scale. His other business was the Fort Wayne Manor Car Wash. Teamster business agents, according to the testimony, used pressure to drum up customers for Snyder's carwash, where he employed nonunion help at shameful rates of pay. One washer testified as follows:

Mr. KENNEDY: How much do you make a week, approximately?
Mr. WADLINGTON: About six or seven dollars.
Mr. KENNEDY: About six or seven dollars a week?
Mr. WADLINGTON: Yes; seven days.
Mr. KENNEDY: That is a seven-day week?
Mr. WADLINGTON: Yes.
Mr. KENNEDY: Eleven and a half hours?
Mr. WADLINGTON: Yes.

That was a nonunion shop, run by Ziggy Snyder. Now let us look at the record for a "union" shop. The local is 985, Teamsters, and the witness is a man who waxes cars for a living:

Mr. KENNEDY: Did you ever attend a union meeting?
Mr. LEWIS: No.
Mr. KENNEDY: Were you ever notified about a union meeting?
Mr. LEWIS: No.
Mr. KENNEDY: How much do you pay to the union?
Mr. LEWIS: He deducts ten cents each day.
Mr. KENNEDY: How much do you receive a week, approximately?
Mr. LEWIS: The most I have ever drawn, the department I am working in now, is eighteen dollars.

MR. KENNEDY: For sixty hours a week you make eighteen dollars; is that right?

MR. LEWIS: That is right.

MR. KENNEDY: That is about thirty cents an hour.

Consider that hourly wage paid to a Teamster union member under a Teamsters' contract in the home town of the great Teamster leader. Then consider this statement by the same great Teamster leader at Miami Beach: "No one has said we have failed to bring to our membership a program of wage gains and improved security never equaled in the history of organized labor."

Moving to other matters of welfare and union democracy, we find "sweetheart" contracts scattered through the record. A "sweetheart" contract, of course, is one in which collusion between management and labor results in substandard pay and low benefits for the union member.

Hoffa's home local, #299 in Detroit, didn't like Negroes to drive over-the-road trucks. A driver named Ross Hill testified that he had to sell his truck, his car, his house, because he was discriminated against as a Negro. This testimony was corroborated by another witness, George S. Maxwell. Hoffa was quoted as saying that Local #299 "did not like over-the-road drivers of the colored race coming into Detroit; that if this were repeated, it might not be healthy for those drivers."

Part of the testimony on the matter:

MR. KENNEDY: Will you deny you made the statement to Mr. Maxwell on the telephone, telling him that he had better tell the employer to keep those Negro drivers out of the city or they would get into difficulty?

HOFFA: I do not recall any specific conversation concerning what Maxwell said. There was some problem concerning Negro drivers on the highway. I may have discussed that problem with him. I will not recall from memory the exact quotation that he made until I have talked to Maxwell.

MR. KENNEDY: Well, you wouldn't deny it, then, his testimony here before the committee?

HOFFA: I have made my statement for the record.

MR. KENNEDY: So I understand it, I assume that to mean or gather that to mean that you do not deny it.

HOFFA: I have made the statement for the record.

For many years, it has been almost impossible for the rank and file, assuming they have an interest in how the International is operated, or misoperated, to vote at the national conventions. Only delegates can vote, and the way to get to be a delegate was always to get elected to the post, and for a man to get elected, folks had to vote for him. The trouble always was that when it came time to elect delegates, in many of the locals, most of the people who had votes were the officers of the locals, who voted for themselves as delegates and then careened away to sunny Florida on fat expense accounts. Why was it principally the officers and their friends who had the votes? Very simple—the Teamster constitution provided that only members who have paid their dues by the first of the month could be candidates for office. The officers always paid theirs on the first, but the rank and file usually had their dues collected by the company they worked for, in the well-known practice of "checkoff" of dues. These dues were transmitted to the local after the first of the month, and therefore few rank-and-file members were entitled to vote.

That's the way it used to be, but even that has been changed. There was too much chance of the dissidents getting together to make sure their dues were paid on the first of the month.

At the 1961 national convention of the Teamsters, Hoffa urged some changes in the constitution. Now the rank-and-file member is barred from participation in national meetings almost completely, unless he is heart and soul a Hoffa man. Here's how it was done: the constitution as amended now provides that a man who wants to be a delegate must have served at least two years in local office, and he must have attended at least 50 per cent of the meetings held by his local union. The convention was asked to vote for a provision which would make officers of locals delegates to the national convention automatically.

There were a few scattered howls from the floor. Dissenters argued that each local union has a quota of convention delegates, and that the quota is strictly limited by a local's size. How could a rank-and-filer make it, if the officers automatically were designated?

Hoffa had the answer. The whole thing was very democratic, he said, because any rank-and-filer could run for a local union position, and when he was elected, he could attend all the conventions he wanted to. That was fair, wasn't it?

One delegate from Oakland, California, a man named Edward H. Painter, declared that the proceedings would be dominated by the Hoffa machine. Hoffa immediately accepted a motion to strike out Painter's comments. "Hoffa don't have no machine," he is supposed to have growled, according to AP and UPI reports, "Let the record show the vote was unanimous, including Painter. Now we'll have no more of that."

This was democracy in action in the International Brotherhood of Teamsters.

Also railroaded through were provisions that the union would pay the legal expenses of all the union officials who are indicted on charges of kickbacks, extortion, shakedowns, embezzlement, assault, or whatever other crime is decided to be "unfounded or politically motivated." However, since the convention, a decision of the U.S. Court of Appeals, in the District of Columbia, by Judge Charles Fahy, has laid down a principle that should have required no judicial assertion. "The treasury of a union," he declared, "is not at the disposal of its officers to bear the cost of their defense against charges of fraudulently depriving the members of their rights as members."

The convention also raised the dues by one dollar per member per month (possibly to pay for all the trials and costly appeals), and set up a pretty system of mighty comfortable pensions for union officers. Last but not least, the delegates shouted through an increase in the boss's annual salary from fifty thousand to seventy-five thousand dollars per year. Hoffa said he deserved it.

One Cincinnati delegate is reported to have said: "I could have written the new constitution in twenty-five words. What it means is: In the Teamsters Union, Jimmy Hoffa will do what he wants when he wants to, and anybody who doesn't like it will be thrown out."

It was significant that Hoffa kept a tight rein on proceedings. The press reported that he ran an electronic console of push buttons that controlled the microphones on the floor.

A newsman counted three dozen lawyers at the convention.

Somehow in these perilous years for labor, the dissidents who are now scattered throughout the ranks of the mighty Teamsters must demonstrate that democracy in union affairs need not die. Some of them already have; the AFL-CIO stands ready to give them a helping hand if they revolt. The national government, even when urged by the general populace, cannot do the job alone. It needs the help of all decent Teamster members—surely a majority of them now understand that a serious setback to their own rights and privileges occurred at that convention. And the government needs the help of the rest of the house of labor, who must realize that their own organizations are critically damaged every time any union moves toward dictatorship or suppresses the rights of the rank-and-file membership.

Finally, let us consider most somberly the warning given in a report to the Senate by the Select Committee, that "if Hoffa remains unchecked he will successfully destroy the decent labor movement in the United States." Hoffa has given it new and significant meaning. Since that report was made, he has taken the Teamsters far along a new and dangerous road. He seeks even wider power over the nation's labor movement. He has linked himself with other labor leaders whose unions have been outlawed from the AFL-CIO, and some of them are strange companions indeed for James R. Hoffa, who has insisted that the Communist philosophy has no greater enemy than himself.

Before considering his actions, let us consider his words:

MR. KENNEDY (*reading from the union's magazine,* The Teamster): If Communist unions ever gain a position to exercise influence in the transport lanes of the world, the free world will have suffered a staggering blow.

HOFFA: I am not interested in politics and philosophy. I am interested in workers.

MR. KENNEDY: Do you agree?

HOFFA: No, I don't agree.

MR. KENNEDY: Do you know who made that statement?

HOFFA: I don't know. Probably Beck. It sounds like him.

MR. KENNEDY: Mr. James Riddle Hoffa.

The Teamster leader and Harry Bridges, head of the International Longshoremen's & Warehousemen's Union, who has long been regarded as a labor leader whose sympathies are with the left wing of union activity, have, to the detriment of decent unionism, concluded working agreements regarding the movement of freight on this nation's roads and waterways. The gigantic Teamster organization, most of whose members are undoubtedly vigorous opponents of Communist philosophy, has entered into an arrangement with a union that has been reputedly influenced and manipulated by Communists for many years.

This alliance is undoubtedly part and parcel of Hoffa's aggrandizement program by which he seeks to found his own union federation to rival the AFL-CIO. He doesn't always find willing partners for this opposition movement; witness his attempt a few months ago to coax the Bakery and Confectionery Workers into the Teamsters—he was rebuffed by the reform movement in that formerly corrupt union, which was seeking to return to the AFL-CIO. He found a willing confederate in Harry Bridges, though; the lean and hawk-faced longshore leader probably grinned and licked his chops when that pact was signed. The Communists welcome any opportunity to infiltrate any organization. They are always confident that, once inside, they can take over.

Hoffa's plan is to have a series of mutual-assistance pacts by which transportation unions will support each other in collective bargaining proceedings and in the settlement of labor disputes. The consequences of such an alliance among all the transportation unions are frightening to contemplate.

Hoffa and his satellite unions—satellites at least for a time—if they had the power to exercise a paralyzing influence over the entire system of free enterprise in this country, could then, upon their own initiative, or in co-operation with criminals or Communists, compel the nation to submit to whatever arbitrary terms, unfair conditions, and unreasonable demands they might choose to make.

They could halt the traffic in raw materials to our factories across the nation; they could stop in a matter of hours the flow of manufactured products to consumers; they could bring to a halt our foreign trade and our military transport abroad. They could keep the essentials of food, clothing, and heat from the general populace.

This kind of monopoly, if attempted by business concerns, would result in government action very quickly to prohibit the national damage that would result. Hoffa and Bridges and their kind should not be granted or permitted to possess or exercise such devastating powers—powers that transcend those of government itself. This threat to our internal economic security is no myth—it is real; it is no fantasy—it is a fact. It cannot be tolerated with impunity.

It is the duty of Congress to enact legislation to remove this danger of national disaster, lest we remain at the mercy of Hoffa's arrogance and Bridges' politics.

Legislation has been introduced in the Senate that would make transportation unions subject to anti-trust laws and would therefore outlaw such pacts as those Hoffa has concluded with the

Longshoremen and the Mine, Mill and Smelter Workers. Both ILWU and Mine, Mill and Smelter Workers were expelled from the C.I.O. because of their domination by Communist leadership. Such conspiracies are now, and have been for many years, forbidden by law to the corporations and business enterprises of this nation.

The power that Hoffa and Bridges and their satellites have taken through alliance is actually prohibited to the federal government itself. It can regulate commerce between the states, but it cannot prohibit it or stop it. The public should insist that Congress forbid Hoffa and Bridges to do what the government itself cannot do.

Hoffa puts on a different hat whenever he has a different object in view. After his vehemently anti-Communist testimony before the Select Committee, he appeared in the fall of 1961 before the Senate Internal Security Subcommittee to declare that the Teamsters had found it advantageous to form alliances with labor organizations that are reputedly Communist-dominated. He used the specious and dangerous reasoning that he wouldn't accept the charges of Red domination of his allies until the charges are fully proved in courts of law. He prefers figuratively to look into the muzzle of the gun to see if it is loaded.

The Teamster president has also signed a mutual aid pact with the International Union of Mine, Mill and Smelter Workers, which has been labeled as Communist-infiltrated by the Subversive Activities Control Board. That union was thrown out of the C.I.O. in 1950 because the policies of the union were "consistently directed toward the achievement of the program and the purposes of the Communist Party rather than the objectives and policies set forth in the C.I.O. constitution." Nine of its officers were convicted for filing false non-Communist affidavits under the regulations of the Taft-Hartley Act. These convictions were reversed, and seven of the nine are now up for retrial. (Hoffa testified he wouldn't judge them until their appeals from the convictions had been decided.)

It is significant to note that an earlier alliance between the big mine union and the Western Conference of Teamsters, signed in 1955 before Hoffa was its boss, contained a non-Communist clause, abrogating the agreement if the signatories were discovered to have lied about Communist affiliation. The 1961 agreement between the two unions contained no such clause. Hoffa explained that: "I don't have to put something in the pact to dress it up, to make it sound like something other than what it is."

Hoffa was questioned closely at the Internal Security hearing in October, 1961, about the sum of one hundred thousand dollars that the Teamsters had allegedly made available to the Mine, Mill and Smelter Workers Union. Funds of tax-exempt labor organizations cannot under law be used for such purposes as helping Communists to defend themselves in legal actions. Hoffa was interrogated by Jay Sourwine, the capable and long-experienced chief counsel of the Senate Internal Security Subcommittee. Mr. Sourwine asked specific questions about the defense fund for the convicted Mine, Mill leaders:

MR. SOURWINE: Was there a hundred-thousand-dollar loan?

HOFFA: There was an arrangement made at a bank to loan one hundred thousand dollars to the Mine, Mill & Smelter Workers for the benefit of the strikers that were on strike at that time for trade union principles, and the security was guaranteed by the international that it would be paid back.

MR. SOURWINE: Was that money guaranteed by the Teamster Union for the use of the Mine, Mill defense fund?

HOFFA: It was not. It was for the strikers.

The Teamster leader then said that he and the secretary-treasurer of the union had the authority to arrange for the loan and that they did so.

That was Hoffa's sworn testimony in the matter. Now let us read what the February, 1960, issue of the *Mine-Mill Union,* official publication of the Mine, Mill and Smelter Workers, an exhibit in the same record, had to say about this financial aid:

The general executive board of the biggest union in the country, the Teamsters, acted "to extend financial aid and support" to Mine-Mill "on behalf of nine leaders of that union whose recent conviction is now on appeal."

In a letter informing Mine-Mill President John Clark of his union's action, Teamsters General President James R. Hoffa declared: "The outcome of this appeal is of vital importance to the entire trade-union movement . . . we believe it is urgent for us as trade unionists to assist financially in efforts to reverse these convictions through appeal."

Hoffa's testimony under oath said the money was for strikers. The Mine-Mill newspaper quoted him as saying that it was extended for the aid and support of the nine leaders convicted for filing false affidavits. There is a conflict between these two stories.

When he makes alliances with unions considered to be Communist-infiltrated, Hoffa is probably crossing the thinnest ice of his career. He may think he is big enough and strong enough to swing all the necessary weight in such a curious combine. But there is doubt that he is. The Communists are not primarily interested in unionism, or workers' welfare, or collective bargaining, or in any other wholesome aspect of the labor movement in the United States. They are interested only in advancing the Communist international conspiracy. They've had almost half a century of experience in the job. The loaded gun that Hoffa is looking into may go off in his face.

CHAPTER 5

"I Cannot Sign My Name"

THE very same pressures that resulted in the formation of the Senate Select Committee on Improper Activities in Labor and Management also had a great deal to do with the sudden tremendous growth in the volume of work that the relatively small staff of the Permanent Investigating Subcommittee had been handling. There were, of course, several investigations running concurrently with that of the Teamsters, and almost immediately, because of the news stories that featured the new committee and because of the bursting scandals within the Teamsters and other unions, the staff found itself swamped with work. The force of investigators, accountants, and office workers began to grow until there were, at the peak of the committee's investigations, more than one hundred people whose headquarters were in the crowded suite of rooms designated as Room 101 in the Old Senate Office Building. All of the investigators were dedicated to their jobs, putting in seven-day weeks and often twelve- to fifteen-hour days. Each was capable in his own fashion at a particular type of job. The diversity of talents and skills was most rewarding. All of our personnel were carefully selected from an avalanche of applications which came from detectives of municipal, state, and federal agencies, from investigators with experience on government committees, from lawyers, accountants, newspapermen, and from people in many other fields of endeavor.

The staff had an infinite number of trails to follow in the beginning, trails that led directly into the tunnels of corruption below the surface of both unions and management. Investigations of this kind of malpractice and criminality did not, by any means, start with the Senate Select Committee in 1957. There had been other probes over the years, both in the House of Representatives and in the Senate. Some of them had gone so far as to result in an increasingly critical eye being cast by members of Congress upon certain segments of both labor and big business.

For the most part, however, previous investigations had been either abortive or inconclusive. There were several compelling reasons why some of them had passed into the oblivion of dust-covered filing cabinets. Oftentimes, the chairman of a Congressional committee had not pursued with vigor the evidence unearthed by his investigative staff, either because of the pressure of other duties or because of distaste for the rigorous ordeal that required countless interviews, endless study, and seemingly interminable hearings. Sometimes a chairman seemed to have been dissuaded from launching a thorough probe into the tremendously powerful union movement, since such investigations are bound to be unpopular in their initial stages. Labor has long been regarded as a sacrosanct province of public life, and almost all unions were commonly believed to have selfless, dedicated men as their leaders.

There were some investigations that made progress. The late Senator Tobey of New Hampshire was a militant foe of gangsters and racketeers, and he was well embarked upon an investigation of Teamster corruption in the Midwest when he died in July, 1953.

There were, of course, other reasons for the faltering of previous investigations—lack of sufficient funds was one reason, and the lack of competent personnel was another. Paramount among them, however, was the tremendous pressure that labor and its friends could marshal within the Congress and the executive department to stall probes of various unions, particularly of the giants who were grouped within the protective coalition of the AFL-CIO. Labor was lined up fairly solidly against Congressional investigations into unionism at any level.

Union leaders believed that they had reason to be suspicious and fearful; even the honest labor executives were convinced that Congressional investigating committees had as their prime purpose the weakening of the labor movement in the United States.

In the beginning, the Select Committee felt the pressure, intense and manifold. When the initial investigation of Teamster corruption under the leadership of Dave Beck began to reveal the startling rottenness under the gleaming façade of the great brotherhood, the committee was attacked from all directions for "union-busting."

The first single clear manifestation that this new investigation was not going to wither and die like some of its predecessors was the swift and decisive approval by the Senate of the resolution creating the Select Committee and the quick voting of its first appropriation. As has been said earlier, this blunt action by the Senate was largely a direct response to the arrogant and contemptuous conduct by the Teamster officials in refusing to answer any questions put to them by the Senate Investigating Subcommittee and its staff, as well as the telegram sent to Teamster leaders across the country, advising them to follow the same defiant course if they were questioned. That telegram helped to insure the unanimous vote of the Senate that established the committee.

It is certainly true, however, that the quality of the staff, the clear trails that were ready for trained investigators, and the warm and inspiring confidence placed in us by the United States Senate were never in themselves enough to insure the success of the work. There were so many other factors, tangible and intangible, that they are too numerous to detail. One of the most vital, however, was the anguished cry that rose from within the ranks of organized labor.

As soon as the large corps of Washington newsmen began to take notice of the first tentative probings into the practices of unions great and small, and of venal management associated with them, the communications began to trickle in—a few letters a day at first, from cities and towns scattered all across the nation, along with an occasional telegram, as well as phone calls from union members to the committee offices.

The newspaper, magazine, radio, and television stories grew more frequent as the staff's round-the-clock efforts began to furnish plenty of material for hearings. The dispatches that were written about the investigations began to be used daily on the front pages and on the television screens. Articles were featured in national magazines and in the Sunday feature sections of great newspapers; weekly news magazines ran sprightly articles about the new probe and its targets.

At that point, the trickle of communications to the committee began to swell. Daily the reception desk of the Select Committee's offices was piled high with letters. They came in infinite variety: some of them were carefully typewritten, with attention to style and grammar; others were neatly written in pen and ink; many were painfully inscribed in pencil. One arrived with an address scrawled in bright crimson crayon. Its huge block letters directed it to: *Mr. J. McClelland, the Chief Racket Buster, Washington, State of the District of Columbia.* In spite of its garish appearance, it was read, answered, and filed as carefully as all the others.

Congressional investigations draw communications of all kinds. Some of them are invaluable in pointing out new leads or procedures to the investigators. (One unsigned, neatly typed letter received by the committee went into complete detail on the corruption in a union under investigation: names, check numbers, amounts of money, fraudulent book entries, false expense accounts, a dozen other matters—showing an intimate relationship with the scoundrels who headed the union.) Other communications suggest remedial legislation to correct the conditions being exposed—and often these are helpful. Many are simple expressions of praise and appreciation for the work being done. There are always some that are critical in any one of several ways.

Never before in the history of the Congress, however, not even during the highlighted Army-McCarthy hearings, has any investigation drawn the cascades of mail that descended upon the members of the Select Committee and upon the staff. There were hundreds of telegrams, and literally countless numbers of telephone calls arriving night and day. Some Senators on the committee received so much mail every week that their office staffs could not possibly handle it all. Most of it was forwarded to the committee offices, where each letter, if pertinent to the investigations, was answered. The office staffs of committee members, each of which normally devotes the major part of its time to assisting a senator in his work as representative of the people of his state, were kept busy answering endless telephone calls and signing for telegrams relating to the work of the committee.

Estimates made by veteran members of the committee staff place the total number of communications received by the Senate Select Committee somewhere in the neighborhood of two hundred thousand. There were some correspondents, of course, who wrote more than one letter, or sent more than one telegram, or were in frequent contact with investigators by telephone. The figure of two hundred thousand communications of all kinds, however, does not include the routine incoming mail connected with the administration of the committee's offices, nor does it cover the many thousands of messages and telephone calls received by investigators in the field, nor their interviews with informants and possible witnesses all over the United States. This figure of two hundred thousand, which is a conservative estimate, also excludes many anonymous letters and phone calls that were of no real value to the investigations.

Where did the tremendous volume of mail come from? The overwhelming percentage of it was sent from rank-and-file union members in all fifty states, as well as Puerto Rico and some overseas outposts of the American economy. It did not always represent the views of one union member; many letters and telegrams came in with multiple signatures—often ten to fifteen pages of names, which apparently constituted almost the entire rank-and-file of a single union local.

So small a percentage was critical of the Select Committee and its work as to be almost negligible. Most of this type of correspondence was anonymous, and one of its curious features was that the writer very often castigated the committee for ineffectuality, and, in extreme cases, actually for collusion with the very scoundrels it was investigating. These critical letters were likely to tell us that we were licked before we got fairly started. Union corruption was so strong, they said, that the committee was foolish to try to do anything about it.

There is a most significant factor in the amount and type of correspondence received by the committee, and it has a definite bearing on the future of the American labor movement. The important point is this: the Department of Labor recently estimated that there are about 17,500,000 union members in the United States. The receipt by the committee of more than 200,000 communications clearly shows that we received at least one letter, one phone call, or one telegram for every 100 union members in the nation.

That is a factor that deserves reflection by every public official, by every union officer and union member, by every American citizen who is concerned about his country's future. The hard-working employee that we all know is usually content to put in his eight-hour day, his forty hours a week, and then relax with his family in his leisure time, so that he may engage in those community or personal activities that are closest to his heart. It is no exaggeration to say that most citizens would sooner go fishing than sit down to write letters to United States Senators. (One of the high officials of the Teamsters said that the membership was only interested in the "extra nickels in the paycheck.") Yet scores of thousands of citizens wrote the letters, pouring out their grievances, their fears, their indignation, and their heartfelt disgust with the evils that sorely afflicted them as union members or as businessmen who were caught in the squeezing tentacles of corruption, violence, and greed. It is certainly fair to say that there were hundreds of thousands of other union members who wanted to write letters to the committee but were afraid to do so. Printed in their entirety, the letters and telegrams would make a massive volume. Not a single person on the committee staff has been able to read them all; none of the many writers who have published comprehensive stories about the committee's investigations has done more than scan a few hundred of them. Yet each of them was answered whenever it was possible and proper to make reply, and not a single one of those was ever cast aside in cursory fashion.

What did they say? The variety of topics was almost limitless; the objectives, however, were overwhelmingly and startlingly similar. They called for help against racketeering and against totalitarianism. They spoke of brutality and coercion, of kickbacks and shakedowns, of rigged elections and fraudulent vote counts. They asked the committee to put an end forever to bestial tactics of goon squads. They were philosophical and patient; they were outraged and frantic; they were strident and they were quietly courteous; they were remarkably erudite and they were naively simple; they were belligerent and they were timorous. Yet in their multitudes, they cried out the same plea: "Help us!"

Naturally, many of these communications came from people who were in arms against some fancied slight or trespass to their interests by the union leadership, and others came from the perennial writers of letters-to-the-editor. It must be pointed out, however, that a large part of the "crank" letters were not placed in the permanent records of the committee. And the proportion holds true without them—slightly more than one union member in one hundred throughout the country communicated with the committee to plead for help.

The startling observation that is invariably made by the curious examiner of the committee's files is that so many letters followed exactly similar patterns. This was true although they came from members of unions without the slightest connection, and although the writers ranged in education from Ph.D.'s to workingmen with little schooling. One of the latter was a member of the Painters Union who politely concluded: *Sir, I hope you will understand my writeing, I did not go to school to much.*

These were the subjects that cropped up day after day in thousands upon thousands of letters: fear, threats, undemocratic procedures, rigged elections, disappearances of union funds, assessments for political purposes without consultation of the rank and file, discrimination by reason of race, creed, or color, "sweetheart" contracts that callously sold the membership down the river, kickbacks, Communism, domination by known racketeers, locals placed in trusteeship (often unjustly and for the sole purpose of protecting the national leaders' positions of power) for periods of one to twenty years. In one instance an Operating Engineers local was in trusteeship for thirty years! The letters cried out about violence and intimidation, bombings, graft paid to public officials, withholding of union books and membership cards, featherbedding, coercion upon small businessmen to join unions under threat of violence, failure to audit union books for periods ranging from one year to a quarter-century, no meeting notices, no meetings, boycotts, goon tactics, self-perpetuating dictatorships, shakedowns, paper locals, vandalism.

Finally, there were hundreds of communications which charged to union officials the crimes of murder, arson, dynamiting, larceny, embezzlement, fraud, assault, and extortion, as well as almost every other felony contained in the statute books.

Examination of some of these letters will serve to show how, in spite of the wide geographical and social and cultural ranges among the writers, the identical patterns were repeated in a daily flood that was both piteous to read and stimulative toward renewed action upon our part against the racketeers who inspired them.

The desire for anonymity was expressed in countless ways, but always for similar reasons:

Please Keep My Name Secret.

I regret that I do not feel secure enough to sign my name, but my children also play in the streets.

I am not giving my name and address because I fear reprisals in the form of acid in the eyes, being waylaid, or being pushed in front of a truck.

I cannot sign this letter. . . .

I cannot divulge my name because I am afraid what their goons would do to my family. . . .

I can't sign this letter. I have a wife and three small children and these fellows are too rough for me to handle alone. . . .

I won't sign my name because I know their power. . . .

Please do not use my name—please—I'll be a gone goose if you do.

Just call me X.

Sir, I am sorry that I can't not reveal my name because their goons will be right on my head. . . .

Those valedictory messages, which asked that the writers be excused for seeking anonymity, were taken at random from among 906 letters which were withdrawn from the files of the Select Committee in anticipation of the desire of the Senate to hear about the national reaction to the committee's work. The only selective process in picking the letters was that they be readily legible and generally concerned with malpractices in union and management. The letters were fully representative of the kinds of communications the committee received. They came from union members, business executives, and even from a few labor leaders who were sick at heart over the crimes being committed in the name of trade unionism in their international brotherhoods. The 906 messages ranged geographically from Boston to Los Angeles. By actual count, almost exactly half of them, a total of 451, were not signed, or else bore such signatures as "A Hard-Working Driver," or "A Loyal Union Member Until the Crooks Moved In," or "An Honest Union Member."

Most people quite properly follow a policy of ignoring and discarding letters that are unsigned, and this is good practice for almost any individual to follow. These letters were certainly different from most anonymous correspondence, however, since the reason for the anonymity was quite clearly stated—the writers feared for their jobs and for their families' welfare. Indeed, in many instances, they bluntly said that they were afraid of assault and even death. Let no one imagine that violence in labor is a thing of the past. In January, 1962, in the city of Baltimore, a man who refused to participate in a Teamsters' strike was set upon as he came out of his house one morning. Four men with clubs attacked him; one of them slugged him and then shot him through the abdomen. Many similar cases have been brought to the attention of committee investigators. The newspapers of the nation carry daily stories of labor violence.

It is a saddening reflection upon the integrity of too many union leaders that almost exactly half of the men and women who wrote to the committee and whose livelihoods and welfare are in trust to unions are, according to the record, afraid to sign letters addressed to the Senate of the United States.

The concern for democratic processes, for honest elections, and for representation in the affairs of the international brotherhoods was frequently a prime motive evident in the correspondence. Viewing the correspondence in retrospect, one remembers that these matters seemed to be of far greater import in the minds of the writers than the actual material benefits that were being denied them by corrupt or dictatorial leaders. The rank and file who wrote to us went directly to the heart of the matter in assuming that if they could have participation in the affairs of their labor organizations, then they would have no problems with benefits, pensions, insurance, and all other economic and fiscal affairs.

It was also a source of pride and of inspiration to read every morning the outpourings of honest men who likened their union membership to their role as Americans, and who demanded no less from their unions than they received as free citizens of this republic.

Thousands upon thousands of them vehemently stated that they had been union members most of their adult lives, and that they were willing to fight for honest unionism if we could show them the way. They repeated time and again that in these days working conditions were good, and wages in their various industries were the best they had ever received, but they did not attribute these economic benefits to the union in which they were held in bondage. They said that their relations with employers were usually excellent, but that they did not any longer want to be dominated by crooks and goons in their local unions or in the internationals. They wanted honesty and dignity to govern their labor affairs.

As illustrations, a few letters have been drawn from the massive steel filing cases that contain the committee records, housed in a vast room on the first floor of the Old Senate Office Building. Here, in excerpts from these letters, are accusations, pleas, and bursts of outraged indignation. The letters were selected at random, and their proportion to the total is akin to a few angry hornets buzzing around a great nest full of their kind. Language, grammar, and spelling in these excerpts are all those of the correspondents:

Teamsters: . . . they have the men picked before a meeting come up— one of our officers will get up and say he thinks that we should go along with Hoffa 100 per cent. One of his pick men will say I second the Motion. Motion made & Second and there are nothing you can do.

Amalgamated Meat Cutters & Butchers: Could it be possible for the rank and file to vote for someone other than the persons selected by the present officers?

A Businessman Harassed by Labor Racketeers: Give us laws that will make it impossible for anyone to hold any labor office who has ever been convicted of a felony.

Teamsters: Help us get rid of these rats. [Signed] A disgusted driver.

Hod Carriers: Our books have not been audited in twenty years.

Plumbers: Please Senator hear this plea and investigate our union.

Wine Salesmen: In all my years of membership in this union, I have witnessed neither an open election nor an accounting of the finances.

Teamsters: No Benefits
No Death Benefits
No Hospitalization
No Sick Benefits
No Insurance
No Membership Card
No magazine or bulletin
No notice of meetings
No Hope
Please!

United Textile Workers: You have a blessed opportunity to free more slaves than Lincoln did.

There were letters full of dignity and eloquence and pride, like the one from Akron that started: *I have been a union member for 25 years, and until lately, have never been ashamed,* and this one from Philadelphia, *Please come in and restore our union rights and privileges to us. If we can get this exposé going we can kick them all out, with open elections.* Another from Philadelphia: *Is this the America that I went out to fight for, and then come back & be run by a bunch of criminals?* And one from a member of the Millwrights Union: *We don't live under the Constitution of the United States. We are forced to live under the Constitution of the Millwrights Union.*

There were occasional bright spots in the deluge of bitterness. The top letter on my desk on March 12, 1957, was from Hamilton, Ohio, written by a member of the Brotherhood of Railroad Trainmen. The salutation brought a smile; it was a good start for a day's work: *Good morning, Mr. Senator!*

Another correspondent was a truck driver, certainly serious and probably unaware of the wry humor of this language: *I say nothing because I just have 3 more years to go for my Pension if there is any. If they keep on going there wont be none left when I get to it.*

It was of course an arduous task to try to stay even with the tremendous volume of correspondence, and sometimes our efforts didn't bring happy results. Paul Kamerick, the committee's capable assistant counsel and one of its finest investigators, remembers how he and a stenographer managed one mishap. Mr. Kamerick dictated an answer to a long letter from an erudite union member who had appended a handwritten postscript in the form of a quotation from the works of Ralph Waldo Emerson. Mr. Kamerick handed the original letter to the stenographer so that she might take the name and address from it for the reply she was about to type. Later in the day, this letter was one of many read and signed by the chief counsel, Robert F. Kennedy, and it was sent on its way—without anyone noticing that it was addressed to Mr. Ralph Waldo Emerson of Chicago, Illinois.

Above all others, however, the letters that caused the most sickness in our hearts were those that cried of threats, violence, and assault by the goon squads. From Akron, we had word of beatings of outspoken union members, of discrimination against Negroes, of the bombing of homes and the tossing of stink bombs into business establishments. From Youngstown: *He landed in the hospital as the goons beat him then and there. . . .* A textile worker in New York wrote about his business agent: *He says at meetings it is voluntary* [assessments upon members] *but if we don't pay, we lose our jobs. When we complain at meetings, he sends 4, maybe 5 guys to scare us. . . .*

A motion picture operator in Buffalo told us: *You would have to talk to the rank and file of this union to find how they fear talking out of turn or saying anything that isn't liked by the business agent.*

A corner newsboy in the City of Brotherly Love sent us this story of viciousness: *When I walked out of one of our meetings, 3 men approached me and told me this—"Do you remember about 3 years ago an* Inquirer [Philadelphia newspaper] *driver was beaten to death?" I said, "Yes." So one of the men said, "The same thing will happen to you if you don't keep your mouth shut."*

They poured in by the thousands—reports of bestiality that made a man shudder with horror and revulsion as he read them.

While it is true that much of the correspondence dealt with heart-warming emphasis on democracy in unionism and the need to expel dictators and racketeers, there was also a vital concern with the material benefits that in general form the central economic core of the organized labor movement. Some astonishing practices came to light and were investigated by the committee through the communications from the rank and file of many unions. Most labor leaders are well aware of the dangers and are usually willing to correct injustices and criminal practices, but we found that in some unions the crimes began at the top and filtered down through the organization.

A widespread grievance brought to the committee's attention by many union members concerned hospitalization benefits. Many men expressed their regret that they had never read the fine print in their contracts for sick benefits. An insurance policy approved by some union leaders stated that a man who is ill in the hospital is entitled to have his charges paid according to regularly scheduled rates, *if he worked a certain minimum number of days in the current quarter of the year.* Problem: How was he to work the minimum number of days when he was flat on his back in a hospital bed, or unable to work during preceding weeks of the quarter because of a drawn-out illness that finally sent him to the hospital?

Another frequent plaint concerned retirement funds for which men and women had worked twenty or thirty years and more. They retired, and after a few months of patient waiting, began to ask angrily where their monthly checks were. The answer was that they were on the way. It would take just a little while longer. Legal barriers stood in the way, they were told; there were documents to be signed; the company's attorneys were blocking action, but of course the union's attorneys were working night and day to get the matter expedited. There were dozens of other reasons, most of them patently false, given in some unions.

One man in Ohio, sixty-eight years old, had in 1957 been waiting for three long years to receive the first payment on his pension. All he had been given by the union was one letter blaming the company for the delay and another letter asking him to verify his birth date.

All letters that came into the committee offices which concerned the income and the welfare of the writers and their families were of course given close attention, and if the staff could offer any solutions, they did so. Almost always, however, the condition was beyond our authority and was a matter for local agencies to take up.

One of the most pathetic cases was that of a man in his late seventies, who had finally decided it was time to retire after a long lifetime of hard work. He applied for his pension only to discover that the fine print in the contract limited pension funds to men who had a single employer during ten preceding years. He had changed jobs a few years before, while retaining his union membership.

It was perfectly obvious to all who read the letters that a distressingly large proportion of the complaints and pleas about benefits and welfare funds stemmed directly from criminal malpractices in local unions and in internationals, just as it was clear that many of them were the results of inefficiency, mismanagement, and neglect upon the part of both management and union officials. In either case, the dire straits of the rank and file were not to be ignored. It is as much a crime for union funds to be grossly mismanaged as it is for them to be purloined; the end result is the same—workers are cheated of the pension and welfare funds that they have worked hard to build to their credit.

Why did they have to write letters to a Senate committee? Why didn't they simply take the matter up at a union meeting? Most of them explained that they were afraid to protest. Other men had tried it, they said, and were either brushed off or beaten up. A St. Louis teamster wrote that his local meetings had no democratic procedures whatever. *If you stand up to talk,* he said, *he just points a finger at you and says to sit down and shut up. You'd better do it, if you know what's good for you.*

The shame of this kind of treatment of decent union members is redoubled when one considers why a man joins a labor union in the first place. If it is his free choice, he does it because he seeks to improve his conditions of employment by seeking an honest agency to bargain for him, to represent him in his dealings with his employer (which more often than not in our complicated economy is a huge corporation), and to safeguard his interests in all matters pertaining to his livelihood. Instead of achieving these ends, far too often he finds that he has simply gained another boss, and too frequently that second boss uses force and violence to keep the union member at heel.

There were other areas of abuse that roused the indignation and often the wrath of the committee.

One that was particularly irksome to most of us was the regular practice of many unions of levying assessments upon their members, irrespective of an individual's political views and his philosophy of government, and the use of such funds to aid in the election, or conversely, the defeat of candidates for public office whom local officials or the international union wished to support or oppose. There is no reason on earth why union members should not be interested in political affairs, just like any other citizens, and no reason why they should not be just as vitally concerned in the election of the officers of government who will make and execute the laws of the various states and of the nation. If they wish freely to band together as union members and in free association support or oppose certain candidates, then they are only exercising their rights as citizens. To force them to do so, however, by discrimination against them in employment, or by threatening them with the loss of their livelihoods, is wicked, coercive, and criminal.

There were thousands of letters which objected strenuously to this kind of pressure. The writers protested against not only the periodic assessment, but also against the practice which compelled them to contribute or to pay a fixed percentage of their wages for political campaigns in which they had no particular stake or interest, or in which they held opposite viewpoints from those of the leaders who levied the assessments. One man wrote from Chicago, enclosing the receipt given him for a political "contribution" and saying simply: *I don't like to make an issue of it with the union, Senator—but I like to pick my own political candidates. If I make an issue of it, I might kill my livelihood.* Another man wrote unhappily about his opposition to forced political assessments, saying that he told his business agent that he would pay if he had to in order to keep his job, but that he deeply resented the use of the word "voluntary" in describing his payment.

Still another prime subject of an astonishingly large number of letters sent to the committee was the pressure that is put upon the operators of small businesses of various kinds to pay tribute to unions just to stay in business. Typical of these blackmailing practices is the one where the owner-operator of a truck that carries produce from rural areas into urban centers is forced to belong to the Teamsters in order to drive his own vehicle within the city limits. The only alternative is for him to hire a union driver to take over the wheel at the city line and drive his truck into town.

Some of the following excerpts from letters of operators of small businesses show just a few of the multiple evils of "featherbedding" (the practice of requiring unneeded workmen or forcing the slowing up of work) and allied extortions:

Carbonated Beverages: [The driver is a Teamster] but he is not allowed to unload or assist in unloading by the local of the same union in the terminal cities. . . .

Beverage Distributors [Six small outfits in Brooklyn]: Independent operators, men who are in business for themselves, and normally operate without any helpers, delivering soda, beer, and seltzer to homes, are being forced to join the Teamsters Union . . . or they will lose, not only their total investment . . . but their only means of making a living.

Seafood Distributor: I am a small jobber in the Smoked Fish line. I have no help of any kind since my route is a small one & does not require help. In spite of this, I have been approached and threatened many times by Local 635 of the Sea Food Union, stating that if I don't join their union, I will be put out of business.

Small Retail Store: One of the things I've had enough of was Teamsters Local #70 at Oakland and their Un-American, Un-Constitutional racket of forcing truckers to hire unwanted, unneeded helpers.

One letter written anonymously told us that a man who owned a garage and operated it by himself would probably have it burned if he didn't join the union.

Once again it must be said that there are thousands of other examples in the files—one that comes to mind concerns a team of hard-working brothers who move heavy machinery in Illinois. The three brothers put in long hours each day at their enterprise. Their union helpers, however, want to work only from nine to four, since they travel daily to the job from Chicago to Waukegan, receiving expenses for the trip. The partnership wants to employ Waukegan men, but the union will not permit it. One of the brothers wrote to the committee: *They don't do a thing all day but stand around and argue among themselves. We'll have to go out of business if it keeps up.*

The partnership had a sensible solution—enlist Waukegan men in the union and use them on Waukegan jobs, calling upon the Chicago local for extra men whenever they might be needed. The suggestion was abruptly rejected. So the brothers of the partnership, requiring a crew of five or more men for most of their contract work, have to wait until the imported employees arrive from Chicago before starting the day's work, and have to quit when the Chicagoans start for home.

That is a sorry reward for old-fashioned American industry and enterprise, always so highly respected in this nation, when men of vigorous energy have to fight in this fashion to hold on to the product of their resourcefulness.

Another subject covered in a multitude of letters was the practice of trusteeship for local unions of the big international brotherhoods. At the outset, it should be made clear that there is nothing wrong, in principle, with the placing of a local union in the hands of a trustee appointed by the international union, under proper circumstances. There are sometimes very good reasons for doing so, when certain serious problems arise at the local level. Trustees appointed by the international may be the only effective agents in the restoration of a troubled local union to good standing. The problems to be solved may involve dishonesty, jurisdictional disputes, fiscal inefficiency, or almost any kind of poor leadership that results in unfavorable treatment of the rank and file. The international's proper role in such cases is to step in to restore order and to police the local until its members are again able to run it for themselves.

Trusteeship is a serious step; local affairs should be in a critical state for it to be taken. In the interests of the democratic process, the trustee should be removed and replaced by local autonomy as soon as possible. That is the principle upon which trusteeships have traditionally operated in the labor movement. The actual practice in some unions like the Teamsters and the Operating Engineers was revealed to be quite another matter entirely. In those two organizations particularly, the trusteeships have been frequently used in power grabs, in stamping out vocal opposition, as a shield for corruption, and as a weapon for all kinds of foul practices.

A typical example of how trusteeships can be used to insure dictatorial control was heard in the testimony of Barney Matual, of La Salle, Illinois, who had been a Teamster official during the period from 1936 to 1959. Hoffa, as president of the Central Conference of Teamsters, proposed to merge five locals and place them under the control of a convicted extortionist named Virgil Floyd.

The membership of four of the five locals, however, voted against the proposal, 694 votes to 7 votes, and decided to merge into one big local, excluding the fifth local which was headed by Virgil Floyd. The membership of the new local, Teamsters #46, thereupon elected Barney Matual president.

Almost immediately the new local was put into trusteeship by Dave Beck, under the control of Teamsters' vice-president John T. O'Brien. (In a later chapter, the reader will learn from committee testimony how this man O'Brien received a percentage of the dues paid by the members of his own local in Chicago.) Matual objected strenuously to the trusteeship. He was called to Dallas, Texas, to meet with Dave Beck. As he arrived at his hotel, he met Jimmy Hoffa and Einar Mohn in the lobby.

Matual testified that Hoffa told him: "Barney, I get what I want." The next day, Barney Matual went to a meeting with Dave Beck, armed with a briefcase full of records to show that the local was in good shape and needed no trustee. He never had a chance to open the briefcase. He faced Beck, Hoffa, O'Brien, Mohn, and Richard Kavner, another Teamster official. Hoffa declared that Matual had negotiated a "sweetheart" contract. Matual denied it. Hoffa jumped up and cried, "Are you calling me a liar?"

Dave Beck stepped between the two men and said to Matual: "I am going to give you a trusteeship if I have to spend fifty thousand dollars, one hundred thousand dollars. You are going to have a trusteeship because my boy Jimmy knows what he is doing."

A long fight ensued. This is one of the few that Hoffa lost. Barney Matual took the teamsters in his local into District 50 of the United Mine Workers. Matual testified forthrightly about his attempts to maintain democratic procedures in his local against the pressures of dictatorship by means of a trustee's control. His disclosures drew praise from all the committee. Senator Frank

Church of Idaho, who had succeeded Senator McNamara, seemed to express the sentiments of all committee members when he said:

SENATOR CHURCH: Mr. Chairman, it seems to me . . . that this witness's testimony indicates how very difficult it is for the rank and file to deal with those in command of the Teamsters International. So often we hear it said, "Why don't these working people rise up and throw the rascals out?" Well, that is much easier said than it is done. I think this story exemplifies that fact very well.

I want to commend the witness for the way he stood up for his rights and for the rights of his people. In the long run, the best work will be done by men like the witness, who are determined to fight for their rights and the rights of the people they represent and are not going to let themselves be shoved around. I think we owe this witness a good deal in coming here today and giving us his story.

At an earlier hearing, Hoffa was asked if he knew the circumstances of the trusteeship of Local #46. His answer was: "Not enough to talk about it; no, sir." Subsequent to Barney Matual's testimony, John T. O'Brien took the Fifth Amendment on this same subject when he was interrogated about it.

Another sordid incident, which illustrates the cynical manipulation of trusteeships for the benefit of favorites, took place in Minneapolis. A disreputable character named Connelly was tossed out of control of a Minneapolis local of the Teamsters by a trustee, leaving the union practically penniless upon his departure. He didn't stay away long, however. It was testified that Hoffa promptly fired the first trustee and then appointed another who immediately put Connelly back in his job as leader of the local. Connelly was under indictment for extortion and for dynamiting. Later, he was convicted of extortion and sentenced to two years' imprisonment, while he was still head of the local. *The Teamsters paid fifty-four thousand dollars in legal fees to defend him.* He was also convicted as a conspirator in the dynamiting. Incidentally, this same Connelly was elected secretary-treasurer of the Minneapolis local with a total of 135 votes, cast at a meeting which twenty people attended!

In the Operating Engineers, trusteeships were used similarly. The convicted extortionist Joey Fay was trustee of a local while he was serving a term in Sing Sing Prison. From his prison cell, he exercised sole control of the local under the ironclad authority granted him by the parent body.

One local of the Operating Engineers was kept under trusteeship for the incredible period of thirty years. One of its members might have started his working career on heavy machinery in the first year of the trustee's reign, and finished his career within thirty years without ever having had the right to vote for a single officer or a single bylaw, and without ever having seen a financial statement of his own union.

In the Teamsters, at the time of the Select Committee's investigations, trusteeship quite evidently was used as a device to control any locals that showed signs of independence or of rebellion against the thugs and gangsters who surrounded the international officers. In effect, in some instances a trusteeship was regarded and treated as a license to steal most anything that wasn't red-hot or nailed down.

The Committee received stacks of letters from members of locals which had been in trusteeship for years. The writers complained that they had never voted for officers, never attended a meeting, never had heard of an audit of the local union's books, and were never given any opportunity to present their grievances. In those instances where such trustees were crooked and corrupt, and where they exercised autocratic control over the local, only they could say how many tens of thousands of dollars they had stolen, and they weren't talking—they were Fifth Amendment addicts.

The startling facts on Teamster trusteeships were detailed to the uninformed president of the international by the former Senator from Massachusetts in one of the early hearings, at which Dave Beck was still attempting to answer some questions without taking the Fifth Amendment:

SENATOR KENNEDY: Mr. Beck, how many locals are there in the Teamsters? There are about eight hundred?

BECK: Senator, I would say about nine hundred and some, and maybe nine hundred and eight or nine hundred and ten.

SENATOR KENNEDY: Now the records we have gotten from the Teamsters organization shows that about twelve per cent of those are in trusteeship. Does that fit with your memory? It says in 1957, one hundred and eight locals out of eight hundred and seventy-six were in trusteeship, which is twelve per cent.

Now, looking at the steelworkers, out of two thousand nine hundred and twenty-five, eighteen were under administration. Of the IBEW, one thousand seven hundred and eighteen locals, nine were under trusteeship. United Mine Workers, three or four hundred locals and one was under trusteeship. The machinists, AFL, twenty-one hundred locals, and about four were under trusteeship. Of the IUE, four hundred and thirty-nine locals, none were under trusteeship. . . . Can you tell me . . . why you feel it is not possible for the members to run their own affairs and why it is necessary to keep some twenty-seven or twenty-eight [locals] in trusteeship for longer than five years when no other large union comparable to yours has any comparable experience?

Dave Beck answered the Senator's question at great length, or attempted to, but he failed to furnish any sensible reason why tens of thousands of Teamsters were deprived of all their democratic rights and privileges as union members. In summary, the committee found that wherever trusteeship was used by an international union to any considerable degree, i.e., more than a handful of locals under the management of trustees, then it usually followed that those trusteeships were being used by the international as cloaks for dishonesty, corruption, and the quelling of honest insurgency by the decent rank and file members. Conversely, the committee found that when the principle of trusteeship was sparingly and judiciously used by the international, the purpose in almost every instance was to clean up a bona fide undesirable local situation.

In addition to permitting venality on the local level, the abuse of trusteeships was discovered to have a very real effect upon the control of power in the international. For example, in some unions the trustee is empowered at his discretion to appoint officers to run the local. He also appoints the delegates who attend the national convention. With 112 locals in trusteeship just a few years ago, the Teamsters conventions were stacked with delegates who had no loyalty to anyone but the president who appointed the trustees and who kept them in power. Here is how one Teamster delegate named James Clift testified about his selection as a delegate.

MR. KENNEDY: Were you elected as a delegate?
CLIFT: I will be.
MR. KENNEDY: You will be elected?
CLIFT: Yes, sir.
MR. KENNEDY: Do you have a meeting scheduled to elect you?
CLIFT: Yes, sir.
MR. KENNEDY: When is that scheduled?
CLIFT: Tonight.
MR. KENNEDY: How do you know the membership—it is four o'clock in the afternoon in Washington—is going to elect you tonight in Detroit? And what kind of a democratic process is that?

Clift explained that he was nominated by the executive board of the local, and Senator Mundt asked him if he had nominated himself. Clift said he didn't think so. He was immediately corrected, both as to the nomination and the supposed election that same evening. It turned out that Clift had made the motion many months before that he and other officers of Local Union #337, including Hoffa's betting partner, Bert Brennan, be *elected* as delegates to the international convention. The membership had no say at all.

Since the selection of convention delegates in a number of Teamster locals is predetermined by such autocratic methods as described above, it should not be greatly surprising to anyone who knows the facts that Hoffa has been able to forge his way to greater power.

Happily for the union movement, and particularly for those members of the rank and file who have been held in bondage under the device of corrupt trusteeships, the new labor law adopted by the Congress in 1959 * established some strict regulations for the imposition and administration of trusteeships, as well as penalties for violation. The law has not been in effect long enough for the Congress to assess all of its weaknesses, some of which are already apparent and will be discussed later in this work.

Under adequate law, however, whether it be the Landrum-Griffin Act or some stronger statute, it should never be necessary again for a union member to write a bitter letter like the one from Chicago that told the Committee: *I have been a member of this union for 23 years, and have never been informed of the date of a meeting.* We had many similar outbursts; one man wrote simply, *I do not even know the names of the officers, if there are any.*

The avalanche of correspondence the Committee received stands as a tribute to the American workingman, to his integrity and his deep-seated and true knowledge of the principles upon which his country was founded and has endured and prospered. Unhappily, however, in the main it does not warrant the belief that there are enough of the rebel leaders and rank-and-file mem-

* Public Law 86-267, the Labor-Management Reporting and Disclosure Act of 1959, known as the Landrum-Griffin Act.

bers working ceaselessly and courageously to cleanse their unions of the corrupt elements that are too often in control.

The great majority of the letters revealed the fear of their writers to take up the battle, as well as the natural inclination to stay out of controversy or conflict and thereby not risk losing their job security and union benefits. The tremendous cascade of anonymous letters attested to the lack of willingness and capacity for struggle.

On the other hand, the letters and the telegrams in the files give clear and sharp summaries of what the labor union member wants from his union. Since the demands came in such tremendous volume, they actually comprise what is probably the most accurate poll of America's working force that could be taken.

What are the things that the labor union members have asked for?

First and foremost, and perhaps surprisingly to those labor leaders who think that a man who has written a letter to a Senate committee is a traitor to the cause of organized labor, the members want unionism. They ask only that it be honest, aboveboard, and dedicated to the interests of the rank and file. They want the thieves and gangsters barred from leadership, and they insist upon an end to conditions that, for example, permit a racketeer to control their economic destinies from his prison cell.

They believe that every American should have the right to work in the field of his choice and his talents, without coercion and without the forced payment of tribute in order to get and to keep a job.

They say that they have the right to know the uses to which their dues and fees are being put, and they demand the opportunity to look at the accounting of their pension and welfare funds. They want the books of their local unions and of their internationals subjected to the scrutiny of certified public accountants who are responsible to the state and federal governments, and not just to the union bosses alone.

They insist upon the right to vote for their officers in regularly scheduled elections, and they ask for secret ballots and the opportunity to compete in elections with their own slates of candidates whenever that may be necessary.

They have the right, they say, to cry out against alliances with Communists, against gangster control, against brutality and cynical struggles for power that have the effect of slashing into their economic well-being.

One great value of the flood of letters was to furnish a "live" file, as the committee investigators called it. Every letter we received was a check against every other from a similar source about comparable conditions. These cross references proved invaluable to the staff, furnishing leads to possible witnesses or informants, to the well-covered trails of racketeers who were muscling into various locals and regional councils, and to the type of criminal activity that was rampant in particular areas. In effect, when investigator Alphonse Calabrese began to trace the threads of crime that enmeshed the taxicab drivers' local in Chicago, he knew at the beginning of his work that there were dozens of letters in the file that cried out for justice. These cries were directed at Joey Glimco, a well-known Chicago Teamster official.

The job of investigating, however, was far too complex in most instances for the staff to do more than check the file for leads before embarking on arduous field work. There was one case, however, that was different from all the rest. The first notice of it arrived in the morning mail, in an envelope like most of the others in the huge sack that was dumped daily on the reception desk in Room 101 of the Old Senate Office Building. The envelope was addressed to the committee, like the majority of the others in the sack. There was no outward evidence that its contents were a time bomb that was ticking away the few quiet hours that still remained in the careers of two greedy labor officials who were gleefully draining a union of its life's blood, the rank and file's money.

CHAPTER 6

Greedy Hands in the Till

T HE letter was clearly and neatly typed, on legal-size
white stationery. It had no date, no return address, no
salutation, and no signature. Its first paragraph was direct and
simply written: *April 25, 1952, United Textile Workers (AFL)*
convention ended at Miami Beach, Florida. Convention Expenses
and the meeting of the executive council Expenses (which did not
include any expenses for delegates attending the convention) in-
cluded an outlay of $29,255.17 of UTW funds at Miami . . .

Then it went on, paragraph after paragraph, detailing to the
last penny the entire tale of the calculated and at times frantic
manipulation of a small and prosperous union's treasury for the
personal luxurious accommodation of its two national leaders.

This communication was remarkable for several reasons. Its direct simplicity did not vary in two and one-half single-spaced
pages. It gave names, places, and amounts of money, check numbers, and indorsements. There was no overt outrage to be read
into its objective language. There were no cries of indignation in
any paragraph. It did not even suggest that the Senate Select
Committee should launch an investigation. It merely stated the
facts.

The letter created excitement in an office that was almost sur-
feited with new sensations. It passed from hand to hand among
the staff, from counsel to investigator. Comment upon it might
have been used as a model for discussion in a workshop on crim-

inology. One investigator identified the make and model of the typewriter that had been used; another classified the paper; and a third attempted a tentative analysis of the identity of the writer. The envelope was examined carefully. Scarcely anyone on the staff recognized the name of the union: United Textile Workers (AFL). Quick research and a few telephone calls resulted in some preliminary figures. The union was a small one, with a national membership totaling only fifty thousand or thereabouts, and it had an annual income of about one million dollars, which came solely from the dues of its members. In an era when big unions had more than a million members and treasuries of gross values in the hundreds of millions—so large sometimes that several accountants might labor for weeks to determine the true financial status of some of them—obviously the UTW was only a small dark recess deep within the house of labor. Let us consider, however, the scurryings and scratchings that went on in the darkness.

Had the letter used vehement language; had it made shotgun charges against union officials; had it borne the usual signs of instability or revenge for slights; had it been less objective and more impassioned, it might regretfully have been laid aside because of the tremendous pressure upon the committee's staff to complete and prepare for hearings the widespread and mushrooming investigations that were in varied stages of progress during the spring of 1957. The letter was so concise and so detailed, however, that Robert Kennedy was sure it wouldn't take a good investigator more than a few days to check out the authenticity of the information.

With the approval of the chairman, Mr. Kennedy gave the letter to Al Calabrese, telling him to look into the affairs of the United Textile Workers. Almost immediately, Mr. Calabrese reported shock at the depth of the corruption that his preliminary investigation disclosed. Furthermore, the detailed statement in the anonymous letter was based upon solid facts. These are disclosed in the record as follows:

The two top international officers of the United Textile Workers were Anthony Valente, president, and Lloyd Klenert, secretary-treasurer. Their union careers had followed the typical pattern: both had been young workers in the textile industry and had quickly become active in union affairs. Valente started to work in a textile plant at the age of thirteen, while Klenert became a textile worker in a yarn dyehouse in 1929. Both men joined the international union in 1933 and soon became officers of their locals. Their rise to power in the international took only eleven years. Both were elected to the union's top jobs in 1944.

Once they had consolidated their power and had the union firmly in their grasp by means of provisions in the constitution that in effect made them dictators, Valente and Klenert proceeded to misuse the international treasury. (It might be more accurate to reverse the order of names to Klenert and Valente, since the hearings showed that Klenert was apparently the leader of this pair, while Valente was cast in the role of the follower.)

The door to the union treasury was wide open to them. The organization had a twenty-two-man executive council composed of twenty vice-presidents and the president and the secretary-treasurer. The council was supposed to be guardian of the funds, but the salaries and expense accounts of the vice-presidents were the sole responsibilities of the president. Therefore any control of the twenty men over the affairs of the two top officers was purely mythical. Any member of the council who might have objected to the conduct of the president and the secretary-treasurer could have and would have been immediately fired out of hand. A three-person committee of the council supposedly audited the accounts. This is the way the chief auditor, one of the trustees, testified to the auditing procedure that was followed:

George Emerson: One of them takes the checks, and I take the stub, and the other one takes the vouchers, and they call out the name of the check and the amount that is on it, and I check it against the stub. The name is also there, and Mrs. Hamme has the vouchers and she opens it like that, sitting at her table like this, and if the amount is correct, and there is no question about it, and if it is a routine thing, we go right on through.

When asked if the committee ever questioned Lloyd Klenert about vouchers, Emerson said they had done so two or three times: "This is a lot of money; let's talk with Lloyd about it."

MR. KENNEDY: Did he explain it all?

EMERSON: He did.

MR. KENNEDY: Have you ever refused any of his vouchers, ever turned them down?

EMERSON: Have we ever refused any of them? No.

Now let us consider what this efficient auditing committee accepted from Lloyd Klenert, who spent more than $60,000 of the union's money on personal purchases for himself, his family, and his friends. Different amounts were charged to the union in various ways—for example, he pocketed a $783 discount on a 1955 Lincoln automobile purchased for him by the union. He charged personal items on his Trip-Charge credit card, amounting to $1,776. His best efforts on his own behalf, however, were in the "paid-out" accounting of hotel bills that he ran up in a three-year period from 1954 to 1957. (Union records prior to 1954 were destroyed by vote of the executive council, an action not surprising when viewed in the light of Klenert's and Valente's difficulties with the Internal Revenue Service in 1954.) For the benefit of readers who do not frequently travel and stay in top-notch hotels like those Klenert frequented, the "paid-out" figures on a hotel bill indicate that cash was disbursed to the visitor or C.O.D. packages were paid for by the hotel's desk. Morton E. Henig, committee investigator, described Klenert's procedure thusly:

MR. KENNEDY: Now, on those hotel bills at each one of these hotels, did Mr. Klenert make it a practice of having payouts or C.O.D. packages delivered to his hotel?

MR. HENIG: Yes, sir; he did. He would purchase in Washington, he would make purchases at certain stores in Washington, and have the item delivered to the hotel, on a C.O.D. basis, and the hotel would pay for the merchandise, a suit of clothes or a coat, and put the charge on the union's bill, which was in turn paid by the union, the entire bill. The same was true just about every place we were able to check, Mr. Klenert would buy a number of things and have it delivered to the hotel and the bill would go to the union, and the union would pay the entire bill, including the personal items.

In this manner, by the "paid-out" technique, Klenert ran up a total of $30,036 during the three years in question. The records for previous years had, of course, been destroyed. So there is no way ever to expose and bring to light the total that he may have pilfered from his union members since he moved to the top in 1944. Valente was not so avaricious on personal purchases, according to the records. His personal bills for the three-year period amounted to $1,400, including a $600 discount on a 1955 Lincoln for himself.

Investigators Calabrese and Henig ran into some trouble at the union's headquarters when they wanted to check out the astounding hotel bills run up by Klenert and Valente, as indicated in the anonymous letter. The international office had the paid bills, all right, or at least the upper section of each one—the part that gives the name and address of the hotel, the name of the guest, and the amount of the bill. The detailed statement section on the lower part of each bill had been neatly detached. "We need only the upper part for our records," said the Klenert-Valente team. It was necessary for the investigators to obtain duplicates from each hotel. The duplicates told an incredible story of luxury at some of the nation's finest resorts.

Where did Klenert stay? He chose carefully: the Vanderbilt in New York, the Ambassador in Atlantic City, the Beverly Hills in Los Angeles, the Boca Raton Club in Boca Raton, and the Princess in Bermuda. In Miami Beach, where he was wont to stay for long periods at the height of the season while his membership was working diligently in the factories in less temperate climes, he was a welcome guest at the Balmoral, the Eden Roc, the Roney Plaza, the Blue Bay Motel. His bills in seventeen hotels during a three-year period cost the union $86,364.46 in the membership's hard-earned dues money. Of the total sum, the "paid-out" items on the bills amounted to $30,036.31. These items were divided into the following major categories: cash advances, $12,644.93; C.O.D. packages, $14,107.75; golf fees and cabanas and solariums, $971.04; miscellaneous, $2,312.59. There is no way of determining what Klenert did with the cash advances. The cash-on-delivery items, however, were carefully checked. Incidentally, Klenert told the committee in his testimony that all these outrageous expenditures were justified by a 1948 resolution of the executive council which authorized expenses in the following language: ... *as they may deem to be necessary which would maintain the dignity and prestige and appearance of the international president and secretary-treasurer while engaged in work for the international union as part of their legitimate expenses ...*

Now let us look at some of the items that were necessary to maintain "the dignity and prestige and appearance" of the secretary-treasurer. One could easily substitute the name "Dave Beck" for "Lloyd Klenert," although the latter's greed is possibly multiplied many times over because he had only about a million dollars a year to play with, while Beck had many millions.

The contents of the packages that were delivered in unending streams to hotel desks were intriguing in their variety and in their incongruity with the public image of a dedicated union leader. Here are just a few, with their prices:

Milk stool	$ 5.50	Four pieces of luggage	$168.15
Corkscrew	25.20	Handbag	49.50
Sport cane	15.00	Portable typewriter	84.27
Magnavox TV set	277.59	Eleven sun suits	46.87

RCA color TV set	$566.50	Six handbags	$181.69
Two toy dogs	16.66	Hosiery	39.53
Toy airplane	9.95	Three swim suits	27.11
Phonograph brush	17.85	Six suits	821.33
Radio	39.98	Five pairs of shoes	92.45
Zenith radio	93.76	Three golf balls	3.87
RCA radio	84.27	Thirteen record albums	143.26
Another RCA TV	125.00	Candy	26.58
Lady's umbrella	7.50	Scarf	9.27
Air conditioner	321.86	Children's clothes	20.55
Two dolls	11.90	Linens	83.28
Diaper service	26.00	Sheets and pillow cases	65.66
Blue-and-white dress	35.00	Eleven handkerchiefs	28.33
Blue dress	71.95	Beauty salon	35.00
Beige dress	100.00	Jakari game	3.95
Skirt and sweater	99.65	Cigarette case	10.00
Two skirts	25.90	Picture frames	34.00
One white dress	92.65	Doll	8.00
White dress	56.65	Photo album	9.95
Navy dress	135.00	End table	24.95
White dress	89.95	Hassock	61.20
Two brassieres	3.61	Caddy	10.00
Lingerie	18.44	Sweater, size 36	28.79
One brassiere	12.50	Black coat	200.00

One of the more startling items that Klenert charged to the rank and file was a "golf lamp" at $49.50. The committee staff speculated whether this item was for hunting lost golf balls at night. Another bizarre charge to the dues-payers was "trampolin lessons" at a cost of $40.00. It should be remembered that Klenert took his wife and children on many of his jaunts, and their expenses were charged to the international union, as were those of a "friend," who had no connection with union affairs.

The most outstanding account of all was for the hit Broadway musical show *My Fair Lady*, for which Klenert purchased tickets costing $2,564.65. The ticket agencies' records showed that this

amount covered twenty-four visits to the same production. Klenert
was a music-lover, apparently.

MR. KENNEDY: For this three-year period, could you tell the committee what the charges were to the union for the theatre tickets
that Mr. Klenert purchased?
MR. CALABRESE: Yes; the charges were $11,411.

These speculations of Klenert and Valente turned out to be small
operations, however, in their over-all scheme to build up their
"dignity and prestige and appearance." To live properly as the
kingpins of the United Textile Workers, these two operators
needed houses worthy of them. They found what they wanted in
Rock Creek Hills, Maryland, an area convenient to union headquarters in the city of Washington. There were two houses;
Klenert selected one costing $52,500 and Valente took the other,
which cost $42,500.

The problem, of course, was how to pay for them with union
funds. They figured it out in short order. They took ninety-five
thousand dollars from the treasury and deposited it with a title
company which then paid out fifty-seven thousand dollars to the
builders and sent the balance to a life insurance company as full
payments for the mortgages on the two homes. Thus the ninety-
five thousand dollars was fully expended. It had been borrowed
by the union from a Washington bank. Klenert and Valente had
second thoughts, however. They returned those funds to union
accounts by having the title company void its checks. Then they
negotiated another loan, from another bank, for one hundred
thousand dollars. Thereupon they approached George Meany,
president of the A.F.L., for still another loan for one hundred thousand dollars for "organizing expenses." (Meany didn't like their
account of the union's finances and turned them down, pending
a complete fiscal report. They immediately backed away from
that kind of probing by the A.F.L.) In the meantime they were
practicing a bewildering sleight-of-hand act with the various large

sums that they were depositing and withdrawing, seemingly without rhyme or reason.

They had the assistance of the title company and its executive officer in an exchange of trail-covering letters which mentioned, for the benefit of auditors, that the two union chiefs were negotiating for a future headquarters for the international. The affair was completed finally, with Klenert and Valente paying fifty-seven thousand dollars in union funds for their houses and assuming thirty-eight thousand dollars in mortgages.

At one point, Klenert tried to justify these acts of taking union money by stating that the union was under organizational attack from a rival outfit in the C.I.O., and that he thought it was a good idea to "hide out" some money as a defense fund. Senator Goldwater questioned Klenert as to his reasons for such strange transfers of the union's money on a "layaway" basis:

KLENERT: . . . We were hiding this money, Senator.
SENATOR GOLDWATER: I know that.
KLENERT: We were hiding the money.
SENATOR GOLDWATER: Why did you put it under that rock? Why did you not put it under the other rock?
KLENERT: Because it appeared that this rock was the better façade than the other rock.

The money moved around the rock pile so rapidly and so bewilderingly that no committee of three members of the executive council could have possibly tracked it down without the aid of trained investigators, like those of the committee staff who tackled the job after the reported theft. Even then, the committee accountants labored long days before they straightened out the jigsaw puzzle of what they began to call "the hundred-thousand-dollar swindle."

Another factor in the maze of fraud was furnished by Klenert's use of "organizing" funds at the same time. The sum of fifty-seven thousand dollars, which represented the identical amount of the down payment for the houses, was withdrawn by Klenert for "the Canadian situation," and the "New Jersey situation," and the "North Carolina situation," as well as "organizing expenses" in New York, Pennsylvania, Massachusetts, and the Midwest. Klenert was asked how he spent the money in Canada. He said he paid seventy-five hundred of it to a man named "Jacques," who furnished fifty men to the union to aid in an organizing fight. He testified that he didn't know Jacques' last name, nor did he know anybody who knew him, nor did he know how to get in touch with him, nor had he received signed receipts for seventy-five hundred dollars in cash because Jacques gave him "the horse laugh" when Klenert asked for a signature.

There are in the record dozens of other examples of chicanery by these two betrayers of a union's trust. It was estimated that in the brief period of three years for which records were available to the investigators these officials had misused $178,000 of the United Textile Workers' money, and that they succeeded in milking the union, in one way or another, of an amount equal to 18 per cent of its annual income in an average year.

Their fall from security resulted in their frantic and avaricious efforts to cover their fiscal adventures by loans secured hither and yon, while at the same time keeping the luxurious houses they had purchased. They made the mistake of asking George Meany for money. He asked for a financial report. Klenert supplied one which Meany questioned vigorously. Klenert then said he would justify the report down to the last three-cent stamp. They tried to shy away from Mr. Meany thereafter, but he kept insisting on a proper financial report, and he testified before the committee that he had good reason to doubt them, because he had heard "rumors" from certain bankers and lawyers that the two officials had used union funds to buy houses for themselves. In the meantime, the two miscreants were racing around trying to borrow enough money to "square away" the treasury of the Textile Workers.

Shortly after the hearings were concluded, the AFL-CIO directed the United Textile Workers to correct internal abuses, eliminate corrupt influences, and remove and bar from office the men responsible.

Klenert and Valente went out, but even to the end, they had their hands in the till. The AFL-CIO appointed a monitor on the textile union's affairs, who discovered that when these two operators resigned, they took with them a union arrangement for long-term severance payments of $104,000. Thereupon the AFL-CIO expelled the union from the Federation. This relatively small organization would probably find existence difficult as an independent, so it quickly managed to restore its integrity and to pledge compliance with the parent body's code of ethics. This done, the United Textile Workers were reinstated in the AFL-CIO.

This case should stand as an object lesson for the leaders of labor in America today, and for those members of the rank and file who are deeply concerned with maintaining honesty in their unions. The amount of money involved in the manipulations of Klenert and Valente may be comparatively small when one considers the testimony about the looting of the treasuries of great unions, but the pattern of greed was a familiar one to the committee, and Klenert and Valente pushed it to the extreme limits.

It seems axiomatic to conclude that in this case, as in several similar investigations, the corruption at the top began to rot away the structure of the union in direct proportion to the loss of democratic processes at lower levels of the organization. Consolidated in power, this pair first took pains to insulate themselves from any rebellious action by the rank and file by changing constitutional provisions so as to give them full control over the economic destinies of the executive council. Once any prospect of revolt was eliminated, the avarice was allowed to race unchecked. All the essentials to successful looting of a union treasury were present—an apathetic membership that evidently made no serious attempt to restore the principles of democracy within the monolithic organization; an executive council that abjectly approved the wild fiscal forays of Klenert and Valente; an accountant who closed his eyes to glaring malpractices; and finally, financial institutions and their executives who apparently violated all ethical standards of their quasi-fiduciary functions. All these puppets who danced to the tune played by the scoundrels at the top contributed to the scandals that almost destroyed the United Textile Workers of America.

It is likely, viewing the affair in retrospect, that if Klenert and Valente had been allowed to continue their looting, the union would have been a hollow shell that would have ultimately collapsed, tearing down with it all the benefits that its members had worked arduously to attain for themselves. George Meany acted properly in taking steps to clean the union of its taint of corruption. Eventually he succeeded in doing so, but the main surgeon in removing the malignancy from the union was the writer of the anonymous letter who sat calmly at a typewriter and tapped out the step-by-step disclosures of fraud and swindle and then dropped it into a mailbox to send it on the mission that brought the labor-leader careers of Lloyd Klenert and Anthony Valente to an ignominious close.

At the outset, we considered the apathy toward crime and criminals upon the part of the representative citizen who quite humanly believes that wrongdoing on a national scale is perhaps of sensational interest but has little to do with his daily life. We have thus far looked at the hidden costs that are added to every single item of freight that is carried in the nation's trucks—costs added by the racketeers in the Teamsters. We have heard the outcry from anguished union members about the gangsters who have been plundering their treasuries. We have seen in the preceding pages the destructive effect upon the textile union of the actions of two greedy men; and let no reader view that kind of looting with complacency. The costs were passed on indirectly in one way or another to the consumer, and paid in the purchase prices of his clothing and his linen and other household fabrics.

Those examples, however concrete, may not be direct enough

to satisfy the skeptical. Let us therefore take a look at the dinner table. Whatever food a housewife serves to her family is paid for directly out of the family budget, and all prudent housewives are aware of the rising cost of living, which has been spiraling upward since the acceleration of the American economy brought about by the Second World War.

During the Select Committee's hearings in the spring of 1958, housewives in metropolitan New York and its suburbs were paying unnecessary higher prices at the butcher counters every single week as they did the family shopping. A pair of operators named Max Block and Louis Block, brothers, whom our investigators quickly tagged as the "Butcher Blocks," had a throttling grasp on the metropolitan area's locals of the Amalgamated Meat Cutters and Butcher Workmen of North America. The Blocks were men of many titles. Max Block was a vice president of the international union, president of the metropolitan district council, and chief executive officer of both big New York locals. His brother Louis was formerly president of one of the locals and administrator of the welfare and pension funds of that local after he withdrew as president in favor of his brother.

The butchers' union has been a responsible labor organization for many decades, and the committee was gratified to see that its hearings on the betrayal of trust by one pair of officials were answered promptly by the international union in remedying the shocking conditions that were exposed. The Blocks were thrown out of the union with commendable speed once their records in the New York area became known—records of activities that related an odious tale.

There were two sets of hearings in which these brothers played principal roles. The first group of hearings served to reveal the improper actions of the largest retail organization in the world, the Great Atlantic and Pacific Tea Company, popularly known as the A & P, which knowingly entered into a deal with the Block brothers and other officials of the Meat Cutters Union. The A & P operates forty-five hundred stores in the United States and

Canada, and in 1958 its consolidated income was more than $4,700,000,000. Its eastern division has been plagued with labor difficulties for many years. The testimony discloses that the Block brothers offered a solution, and the titanic food chain accepted it. The deal between company and union served to shove more than ten thousand A & P employees into the union in disregard of their collective bargaining rights. They were given no choice.

The A & P stores, for their share of the bargain, received a five-year guarantee of the existing forty-five-hour working week, while having only one union to represent all their store clerks—a union, moreover, that was evidently wide open to "sweetheart" contract proposals.

The union, on the other hand, received a gift of ten thousand dues-payers that it probably would have lost in an aboveboard election for bargaining agents. The extra income for the Meat Cutters' Union treasury amounted to about five hundred thousand dollars per year. The Select Committee in its report to the Senate stated that there was competent and uncontradicted evidence that the A & P and the union committed a "long series of overt acts in furtherance of the aims and objectives of the deal, a great many of them violative of both the spirit and the letter of the National Labor Relations Act . . ."

The A & P, of course, defended itself through its attorneys by saying that it was forced into a position from which it was unable to extricate itself. This contention was denied by the evidence which overwhelmingly supported the conclusion that the food chain knowingly and deliberately accepted the deal offered by Max Block, and that its supervisory personnel coerced its employees into membership in the Meat Cutters Union by threatening them with loss of their jobs, loss of seniority, and loss of their pension rights. It was either join the union, or else.

In spite of the honorable reputation of the international union, the Select Committee reported that the record of the New York area locals was reprehensible and indefensible.

Max Block, Louis Block, and the members of their family

treated the two huge New York locals as medieval tyrants treated their baronies. They had absolute control over the economic destinies of the rank and file. The testimony showed that they removed, for their personal enrichment, a total of $241,000 in salaries and expenses during the three-year period from 1955 through 1957. They expended another $293,000 in questionable fashion during the same period.

The Block brothers owned a country club in Connecticut. The system here was a simple one. Some companies that employed meat cutters invested in the Block brothers' country club and by coincidence they received exemptions from paying into the pension funds of the two locals. Operators in the meat business could apparently procure "sweetheart" contracts with the union by lending money to the country club or by buying bonds of the club issued by the Blocks. Louis Block pressured the Connecticut General Life Insurance Company, which held all union welfare and pension business, into taking a $350,000 mortgage on the club.

Max Block made a deal with Food Fair Stores—a great chain of supermarkets—to gain preferential prices for himself in purchasing a new issue of stock. Food Fair was given deferment on pension fund payments. Max Block also induced Food Fair and other large firms to purchase packaging supplies from his son-in-law. Food Fair, after repeated requests from Max Block, bought five hundred thousand dollars' worth of paper and cellophane products from the son-in-law, in spite of testimony that his prices were not competitive.

In mid-Manhattan, there is a restaurant where patrons may get a fine steak amidst ornate surroundings. It is known throughout the nation as the kind of steak house that serves the best meat, done exactly to the diner's specification. It is the Black Angus Restaurant, and it was owned by the Block family. Its prices are high, but the Blocks had a fine method of keeping expenses down. Union vehicles and personnel were used in a pickup and delivery service that kept the great refrigerators full of prime beef. The meat itself came directly from the meat warehouses of a huge New

York food chain in an "accommodation" that, so far as we know, no other restaurant ever enjoyed. The chain sold the Black Angus a total of thirteen hundred thousand dollars in meat during a six-year period.

The union paid ninety-five thousand dollars for annuities for Max and Louis Block, and for two other officials. The union bought so many automobiles for the Block family that it was difficult to straighten out the devious financial transactions relating to each car (the Blocks followed the practice of selling union automobiles and pocketing the proceeds). At one time, Max Block had two Cadillacs and his country club had a Chrysler, all bought by the union.

To show the record clearly, and to convince the skeptical, if any remain so, how the Block combine treated the union treasury, the union members, and the companies that held union contracts, I recite these bizarre financial dealings of Max and Louis Block as revealed in committee hearings:

Checks drawn to "cash" totaling $86,507.02.

Payments of $26,705 to Max Block for "expenses" without vouchers.

A check drawn to cash for $2,000 to be paid to both the Republican and and Democratic parties in New York State. (Those organizations never received the money. Max Block couldn't remember what he did with it.)

Trips to Florida: Mr. and Mrs. Max Block, at a cost of $9,372.65.

Cigars, flowers, fruit, lingerie, telephone bills, etc.—$6,491.35.

Hotel bills for persons having no connection with the union—$9,301.82.

The case was typical of control by a dictatorship. The Blocks first stifled the democratic process, then solidified and perpetuated themselves in office. The Select Committee's exposures resulted in

the resignations of the Blocks and other officials of the Meat Cutters Union and their subsequent troubles with the Internal Revenue Service. The international union cleaned up the mess, and
it is to be hoped that henceforth, throughout the New York area,
families can buy with confidence that there is no one in the
shadows siphoning pennies to support such a grotesque empire
of avarice. It is a certainty that in cases like this one, as well as
the others that have been detailed, there are ultimately only two
contributors to the greed of men like Max and Louis Block, Lloyd
Klenert, and Anthony Valente. One of them is the American citizen who must hand over the money to pay for the hidden costs in
the items produced by the union members who are the bond
servants of these men. The other contributor is the union member himself, who unhappily is forced into the position of paying
double the amount—he lost it from his union treasury and he lost
it from his pocket in the marketplace.

PART TWO

PART TWO

CHAPTER 7

Crime Convention at Apalachin

A MONG the rolling hills of New York State, in the area along the Pennsylvania border that is known as the Southern Tier, the law is quietly and efficiently enforced by state and local police who generally work with little publicity or fanfare. The region is a calm rural part of the state, relatively distant from the big cities that are commonly considered the breeding places of organized crime. Police action against criminals rarely furnishes streamer headlines for the newspapers in the area.

The committee records set forth the following remarkable story.

The investigative curiosity of one state police sergeant stationed in that peaceful countryside uncovered in 1957 one of the most notable crime stories of the century—significant because its repercussions have been felt throughout the international circles in which the modern criminal syndicate operates. The story furnished new and startling evidence of organized crime in America, showing that it is linked in a ruthless and potent conspiracy.

Sergeant Edgar D. Crosswell took official interest in a prosperous local resident named Joseph Barbara as early as 1944, when Barbara, proprietor of the area's Canada Dry Bottling Company franchise, refused to prosecute one of his employees who had been caught stealing gasoline from the company's tanks. Gasoline was a valuable commodity during the years of rationing in World War II. In the course of his investigation of the theft, Sergeant Crosswell was surprised to discover that Barbara carried a revolver, not an ordinary custom for law-abiding business executives in the Southern Tier. The sergeant decided to check out the bottler's background.

The results were more than interesting. Barbara had been arrested for murder in Pittston, Pennsylvania, in 1931. He was arrested in a murder investigation in Scranton, Pennsylvania, in 1933. He was convicted in Utica, New York, at a time when sugar was in short supply, for illegal acquisition of three hundred thousand pounds of sugar, an amount so large that it could only have been destined for bootlegging purposes. Sergeant Crosswell made up his mind to keep an eye on Barbara's activities over several years. For a long time, he found very little to indicate that Barbara was anything more than the soft-drink bottler that he appeared to be. However, Crosswell was persevering and tenacious. Any man who packed a gun in his district was a man to watch.

Finally, Crosswell picked up another indication that Barbara was leading a double life. He discovered that the bottler met in 1956 with a group of well-known gangsters in a hotel in Binghamton, New York, where Barbara paid the hoodlums' hotel bills. Every man at that meeting had an extensive criminal record and was identified in one way or another with well-known big city gangs.

On the night of November 13, 1957, Crosswell drove his patrol car into the parking lot of a motel in the town of Vestal, New York, to make a routine investigation of a bad check charge. By conversation with the motel manager and by checking the registrations of cars parked there, Crosswell discovered that Joseph Barbara was apparently having another meeting. He had registered some guests at the motel, which was near his imposing hilltop home at Apalachin, New York. These friends were unsavory types whose appearance and automobile registrations showed them to fit into the same underworld categories as Barbara's earlier guests at Binghamton.

A few friendly visitors do not, however, warrant police investigation, but Crosswell's nagging suspicion persisted. Unaware of the Pandora's box he was about to open, Crosswell got permission from his superior officer to pay a call at Barbara's house the next morning. As he told it in his testimony before the Senate Select Committee, "We drove in and everybody started running in all directions."

The Barbara house, except for one main road, was well isolated ordinarily, but at that time the secondary roads were cut off from the main roads by a washed-out bridge. The state police set up road blocks, called by radio for assistance, and then began to haul in the runners. Crosswell said that the fugitives who took to the woods or puffed along the dirt roads around the Barbara place were mostly dressed in silk suits, white-on-white shirts, highly polished and pointed shoes, and broad-brimmed hats, the conventional garb of well-heeled underworld characters.

The men who took to the woods in frantic flight when the black-and-white state police cars appeared were not in such fine array when they were rounded up in the dragnet that swiftly spread throughout the area. "Some of them lost their hats," said Crosswell, "and they were full of cockleburs and their shoes were scuffed up." The police officers were still not fully aware of the nature of the gathering they had interrupted. At the outset, they simply followed normal police procedure—a group of men started to run at the sight of the law, and the officers naturally gave chase.

It soon became apparent, however, that the dragnet had made a fabulous haul of criminal figures of national and international repute. Fifty-eight men were picked up on the Barbara estate or in the immediate surrounding countryside. It is likely that at least a few made good their escape before the roadblocks could screen all the area's traffic. Of the fifty-eight who were caught, fifty had records of arrests, thirty-five had records of convictions, and twenty-three had served time in prisons or jails. The prosperous bottler of Apalachin had as his guests eighteen men who had been arrested or questioned in one or more murder cases.

The names and faces of the visitors to Apalachin formed a veritable rogues' gallery that included the notorious Vito Genovese, who ranked among the top hoodlums in the nation; his lieutenant Mike Miranda, with multiple arrests—twice for homicide—and whose name was prominent on the international list of the Federal Bureau of Narcotics; Big John Ormento, with multiple narcotics convictions; the late Joseph Profaci, arrested many times in Italy and in the United States—an established figure in gangsterdom. Another visitor was Carmine Lombardozzi, whose activities as a strong-arm man along the waterfront were bared at committee hearings, and whose arrest record has the following notations: homicide, burglary, unlawful entry, disorderly conduct, abduction-rape, carrying a concealed weapon, policy operations, and common gambler.

There was outward respectability in the roundup, also. The big surprise that popped up when the net was hauled in was John Charles Montana, of Buffalo, New York, who only the year before had been named "Man of the Year" in that city as recognition of his civic interests and enterprise. He had many friends in high places in government and industry. He was caught at Apalachin by the state police while he was trying to unsnag himself from a barbed-wire fence at the edge of a dirt road near Barbara's house. He told New York officials an astounding story of how he happened to be at Apalachin, and he later testified to the same incredible tale at a Select Committee hearing. He said that he had just stopped that day at the home of Barbara, an old friend, to have a cup of tea while his new Cadillac automobile had its brakes and windshield wipers repaired by Barbara's mechanics. He didn't know anything about any gangsters' meeting, he said, and his arrival was purely coincidental—a spur-of-the-moment decision taken during a business journey to Pennsylvania.

But Montana's traveling companion on the New York highways that day was Anthony Maggadino, who had been arrested in Italy for falsifying passports, for clandestine activities, and for homicide. He had been denounced for robbery, rape, and extortion. He had violated United States immigration laws. It is small wonder that the committee members heard Montana's testimony with amazement and complete distrust. However, Montana was the only Apalachin visitor among those who testified before the committee who did not at any time take the Fifth Amendment. His course was apparently taken because of his civic honors. He was probably trying desperately to patch the rents in his cloak of respectability.

The meeting of the gangsters at Barbara's house was only one of a long series that criminals have held through the years at various places in the United States. There was one of major importance in Cleveland in 1928, and another in the Florida Keys some years later. National experts on organized crime testified to police knowledge of others, held in key cities throughout the nation. The crime convention at Apalachin was different from all the others in that it was exposed and became a tremendous national news story.

The meeting gave to millions of Americans their first clear knowledge that we have in this country a criminal syndicate that is obviously tightly organized into a secret brotherhood, which none of its members dare to betray, and which has insinuated its tentacles into business and labor and public life at high levels, such as those reached by citizen-of-the-year Montana. The story had been revealed previously by enterprising prosecutors and investigators, and the existence of the criminal combine had often been publicized by capable writers, but prior to the Apalachin meeting there had always been a large skeptical audience for the tales of syndication. Such a thing could hardly exist in America! Since the Apalachin convention, however, all doubt has been dispelled.

The members of this criminal combine have made vast fortunes in bootlegging, narcotics, prostitution, gambling, and extortion. They have placed strangleholds on certain businesses that they have managed to infiltrate in some cities, such as some segments of the garment industry in the northern states and of the trucking organizations that service it. One of the most significant results of the examination of the backgrounds of the Apalachin visitors was the revelation that twenty-three of them were directly connected with labor unions or with labor-management bargaining groups. It was no coincidence that the names of these men and their cronies and associates kept cropping up during almost every investigation that was made into improper activities in labor and management. Hundreds of honest, decent union officials throughout the country, and perhaps millions of their hard-working members, are daily subjected to the manipulations of these racketeers and their henchmen.

These men with the life-long criminal backgrounds claim to operate legally and honestly in reputable business enterprises. Of course, most of them took the Fifth Amendment on almost every question asked them by the committee beyond the response of giving their names and addresses. There is no way therefore of determining from their own testimony, or lack of it, what they regard as legal and honest business enterprises.

John Montana was one exception to the string of grim Fifth Amendment artists, with his fantastic story of trouble with his new Cadillac and how he felt impelled to delay his journey to have Barbara's boys fix his car while Mrs. Barbara served him with a steaming cup of tea on a chill November day.

The single other exception was Thomas Lucchese, well known to police of two continents by his colorful alias, "Three-Finger Brown." Lucchese evidenced little interest in the nickname, which was given to him upon arrest in 1920 by a police officer who jokingly identified his prisoner, a man with a missing finger, by the name of the Chicago Cubs' famed pitcher of that era, Mordecai "Three-Finger" Brown. Under either name, Lucchese was twice arrested for homicide and served a prison term for grand larceny. Unlike the other mobsters who claimed respectable fronts but refused to talk about them, Lucchese at least answered some of the committee's questions, taking the Fifth Amendment on others. Every time Mr. Kennedy's questions touched upon the legitimacy of Lucchese's various business enterprises he took the Fifth.

Supposedly he was not an Apalachin visitor, but those who did

attend were his long-time associates. He was asked about his relations with them and with other criminals. The answer rolled out
monotonously and unchangingly: "I decline to answer under the
Fifth Amendment." In a long series of questions, he was asked if
he knew "Trigger Mike" Coppola, Joey Rao, Tony Bender, Frankie
Carbo, Jimmy Plumeri, Johnny Dioguardi, Vito Genovese, "Tony
Ducks" Corallo, Abe Chait, and finally, the late kingpin of them
all, the then exiled overlord of the crime syndicate:

Mr. Kennedy: We have information that you do know "Lucky"
   Luciano; is that correct?
Lucchese: I decline to answer under the Fifth Amendment.

Once the list of criminals had been gone through, Lucchese decided to answer some questions, and in view of information gathered about him by the committee's investigators, his replies were
astonishing, to put it mildly:

The Chairman: Are you a member of the Mafia?
Lucchese: No, sir.
Mr. Kennedy: Do you operate any of the illegal enterprises in
   New York City, such as illegal gambling, or narcotics, or any-
   thing like that?
Lucchese: Definitely not, sir.
Mr. Kennedy: Do you have any illegal activities in New York
   City at all?
Lucchese: No, sir.
Mr. Kennedy: None at all?
Lucchese: No, sir.

These replies were typical of the air of injured innocence that
some of the hard-eyed gangsters tried to assume. They were never
successful in carrying it off, for Lucchese and dozens of others like
him, just as powerful and just as ruthless, have for years corruptly
dominated the industries they have muscled into. The committee's investigators, as well as law officers from many agencies

everywhere in the country, have found in their enterprises the identifying stamp of the gangster—the record of violence, bribery, extortion, and corruption. In some sections of the vast garment industry in the northeastern states, for example, it is almost impossible for a manufacturer to conduct his business without trafficking with hoodlums. The record shows that he dare not hold out against them.

The manufacture and distribution of ready-to-wear clothing, with which so many of the Apalachin mob have been identified, is a highly competitive industry wherein many firms walk a narrow path between success and failure, and their balance along the way is sometimes determined by the delivery of a single big seasonal order that must get to the customer on time and in good condition. Since the mobsters control the trucks that move the merchandise, the manufacturer must deal with them or suffer the consequences, which may be slow and attenuating, like truck breakdowns or misdirected shipments, or which may be abrupt and final, like the spraying of a vial of acid through a truckful of $19.95 dresses.

As with Thomas Lucchese, however, a common trait of the syndicate criminal these days is his apparent respectability. The committee staff gave close attention to the business activities of the "delegates" to the Apalachin convention. While almost every one of them was known to be a criminal or the associate of criminals, most of them were the proprietors of supposedly legitimate enterprises, or were the employees of such enterprises. Some of the men of Apalachin operated in several fields at once. This accounts for the duplication of numbers in the following summary of their activities. Nine were connected with coin-operated machine firms and their distributing companies; sixteen were either in garment manufacturing or in allied trucking interests; seventeen owned taverns or restaurants; eleven were in the olive oil and cheese business, both importing and exporting; and nine were in building and heavy construction. Others had automotive agencies, coal companies, entertainment enterprises, funeral homes, horses and race tracks, linen and laundry services, trucking, taxis, waterfront firms, bakeries, and many other types of business. One of them was the leader of a dance band.

It is no coincidence that a close study of their records reveals that most of them had some connection, direct or indirect, with labor unions that were infiltrated by racketeers or with management that dealt with such unions.

The meeting at Apalachin caused detailed studies of the activities of the men who attended it, and these investigations contributed several other significant facts about the crime empire in America.

It cannot be considered a local meeting of men with similar interests and background, in spite of the fact that the site was only about two hundred miles from the metropolis of New York. This was not just a barbecue, where old friends gathered to chat about the good old days back in Sicily or on New York's East Side. While the majority of those who attended were from New York and its immediate environs, there were also visitors from Pennsylvania, Texas, Colorado, Massachusetts, California, Missouri, Florida, Cuba of pre-Castro days, Ohio, and Illinois.

What is more, study of telephone traffic among the principals and their associates all across the nation revealed that there had been widespread interchange of phone calls immediately prior to the meeting. Vito Genovese, Joseph Profaci, and Big John Ormento were among those who had been busy on the telephone in the days just preceding. For example, Ormento, then alleged to be one of the nation's top dealers in narcotics, who was long a fugitive from justice as a result of a narcotics indictment for which he has subsequently been convicted, had talked to racketeers in Canon City, Colorado, in Dallas, and in Detroit just before he went to meet his friends at Barbara's estate. The telephone communications among these men just before the meeting gave conclusive evidence of the national scope and significance of this surreptitious conclave of the high and mighty in the underworld's secret domain.

Sergeant Crosswell also exploded the plaintive tale told to him by some few of the more garrulous members of the conference— that they had arrived coincidentally with all the others on the same day simply to visit their ailing friend, Joseph Barbara, who was suffering from a heart condition.

MR. KENNEDY: Is there any way that you could tell or prove that the meeting was actually planned ahead and that these people all didn't just drop in to see their sick friend Joseph Barbara?

SERGEANT CROSSWELL: Yes. On the fifth day of November, 1957— that was nine days prior to the actual meeting—Barbara called the Armour Company in Binghamton, New York, and placed an order for prime steaks. The steaks that he ordered were their best cuts of meat and stuff that Armour in Binghamton, a city of eighty thousand, does not even stock. They had to send to Chicago after them. That was picked up on the thirteenth by one of Barbara's trucks and signed for by one of his caretakers named Blossom. The bill for the steaks was $399.10.

Since the raid on the Barbara estate went into action shortly after noon, at 12:40 P.M., and since Sergeant Crosswell testified that "a lot of the men ran from around the barbecue pit and around the corner and some ran for the house . . ." it may be safely assumed that a great many of those costly steaks from Chicago were never eaten by those for whom they were prepared. They most probably went up in smoke during the frantic race that ensued through the woods away from the law officers.

Another important factor in the national crime alliance is demonstrated by the interrelationships of the men at Apalachin, through blood and marriage ties and criminal associations developed through these links. Roughly half of the hoodlums attending the meeting were related by blood or marriage, and in the main, their police records paralleled their intergroup relationship. Gangsters' daughters married gangsters' sons, and in doing so, harvested a new crop of potential gangster relatives all across the country, from Brooklyn to Los Angeles.

One of the committee's investigators, George H. Martin, developed a chart of the blood and marriage ties that bind the criminal syndicate, and he testified at length about the discoveries he made in his research. A small portion of Mr. Martin's testimony shows how the birds of a feather flocked together in one particular section of the United States:

MR. KENNEDY: Can you give us two examples, possibly, in Detroit, where marriages in the families brought together a number of different leading hoodlum families?

MR. MARTIN: Well, Papa John Priziola had five daughters. We find that one of the daughters is married to Michael Polizzi, who, in turn, is the son of Angelo Polizzi. . . . Angelo Polizzi is the one particularly noted for criminal activities in the Detroit area. There was testimony . . . that he was involved with Joseph Barbara down here as a suspect in murders in Scranton, Pennsylvania. Priziola had another daughter who married Vincent Cammarata . . . Vincent Cammarata and Frank Cammarata are brothers. Both have records in the Detroit area. Frank Cammarata is the husband of Grace Licavoli, who is the sister of Pete Licavoli. The Licavolis had a wide range of influence extending down from Detroit into Ohio, across Ohio into Cleveland and as far east as Youngstown. . . .

MR. KENNEDY: And there are four or five members of the Licavolis themselves with police records, is that correct?

MR. MARTIN: Yes. . . . Going down the chart we find that Licavoli's wife is Grace Bommarito, the sister of Scarface Joe Bommarito, and his sister is married to Sam Zerilli, who is in turn the brother of Joe Zerilli. Rosalee Zerilli is married to Dominick Licavoli. You will note, too, that the Priziola connection juts down into the Toccos, and the Toccos into the Zerillis and the Toccos into the Melis. . . .

Investigator Martin's testimony covers several pages of the Select Committee's records, tracing family and criminal connections.

The meeting of the delegates to the Apalachin convention suggests a lawless and clandestine army, armed and determined, in a quiet but savage conspiracy against society—at war with the government and the people of the United States. If we were to anticipate the worst that could happen—the continued growth and eventual triumph of the conspirators—we might imagine the emergence of a culture in which honesty and integrity, liberty and justice, decency and morality all would be outlawed philosophies, to be discussed in whispers and taught to youngsters in secrecy. That culture and society would differ little in its essentials from those of the dictatorships that have so grievously plagued the world in this century. It is a fantastic image, perhaps, until one remembers the days when Adolf Hitler was dismissed as a paperhanging clown; when the Communist conspirators were pictured in editorial cartoons as ludicrous, bearded fellows who carried bombs.

The secret army of the criminals in our nation today is allowed to continue to wage war because our citizens do not affirmatively enlist in their own army in order to fight back. It is necessary to admit unhappily that the general public is not nearly so aroused and indignant as it should be. Instead, it is rather apathetic. Indeed, the evident slackening in moral standards throughout the nation during the past two decades definitely strengthens the criminals' position. A citizenry that too often excuses dishonesty by shrugging and saying, "Everybody's doing it," is not likely to rush to arms against men who make a career of wrongdoing.

The testimony of witness after witness at the series of hearings on the Apalachin meeting also made clear the tremendous size and tight links of the criminal network. It furthermore showed the concerted effort of the members of the underworld syndicate to become outwardly respectable by controlling industries and labor unions, while continuing their criminal acts. Their success has posed a national problem of disturbing import. It represents a real threat to everything that all decent American citizens hold dear.

There is no doubt that their power is growing. In spite of national publicity given to Senate hearings, and notwithstanding sporadic rashes of prosecuting zeal upon the part of local, state, and federal agencies, the menace increases. Their success is reflected in their expanding economic enterprises, most of which have respectable façades. It is also reflected in their outrageously arrogant operation of lawless activities almost in the fashion of legal corporate bodies. And finally, it is reflected by the infiltration of the top gangsters in the country into segments of labor and management.

CHAPTER 8

Crime Is a Major American Industry

THE men of the syndicate are a different breed from the Daltons and the Youngers and the James brothers of the last century's outlaw bands. They are different also from the hoodlums of the lawless second and third decades of this century —Jack "Legs" Diamond, "Dutch" Schultz, Vincent "Mad Dog" Coll, John Dillinger, "Pretty Boy" Floyd, "Baby Face" Nelson, and dozens of others who flared briefly in national headlines by blasting their way into infamy with firearms and crime. Those gangsters of another day were enemies of society in spectacular fashion with their Thompson submachine guns and their wild raids upon banks, armored cars, and other repositories of large sums of cash. Their injuries to the national well-being, however, when compared to those of the criminals of the 1960's, are promptly relegated to secondary consequence.

The patriarchs of the syndicate, the hard-eyed and impassive elder statesmen of the criminal empire, learned their business well during the turbulent decades of Capone and O'Banion, of Luciano and Lepke, of the Purple Gang in Detroit and similar mobs in a dozen other big cities. They are the survivors. Al Capone wasted away in prison; Dutch Schultz was assassinated; Louis "Lepke" Buchalter died in the electric chair; Luciano died in exile. Dozens of prominent hoodlums like Dillinger and Nelson and Floyd and the members of the Barker gang were shot down in battle with the FBI or else went to prison for most of their lives. The younger gangsters who escaped both guns and convictions garnered the lessons of those decades. The man who blasted away with guns and bombs in senseless and fruitless savagery was destined to pay for his insanity in one of two ways—he died in the electric chair, or he was riddled with bullets at the hands of police or of other gangsters. Robbing banks and payrolls was a dangerously stupid way to wrest an easy living in lieu of earning one from honest endeavor. When John Dillinger's score was totaled up in cash, and his ill-gotten gains assessed, it was found that that madman had little more than pocket money left. Furthermore, his brief and bloody career had been spent in alternate gun-flashing forays and long periods of hiding away from the sight of man. The new breed, our modern hoodlums, decided that was no way to live. It wasn't sensible; it wasn't businesslike.

There was a better way than violence. That was the considered judgment of the hardened survivors of the twenties and thirties. It was a modern world, and modern methods were needed. New techniques were in order. Most of these men had learned in grim conflict that a mobster who packed a gun and used it almost invariably finished his career by being a target for somebody else.

Besides, reasoned the leaders who survived, whenever guns might be needed for some fool who wouldn't learn the new ways of crime or for some veteran who had stepped out of line there were plenty of trigger-happy young hoodlums available at cheap prices. It could be arranged, they discovered, that gunmen would do the necessary killing efficiently, take the rap if need be, and even die in the electric chair or in the gas chamber without knowing who had directed that they be hired to pull the trigger. It could be done so neatly that the crime chieftain who had ordered an execution could be lying on Bermuda sands, basking in tropical sunlight, while a thousand miles away a gunman whose name he didn't know and whose face he had never seen was blasting the designated murder victim into eternity.

Organization was found to be the answer. Business methods,

tried and tested in industry, had to be studied. There were rules to be set up and followed by men who wished to succeed in the business of crime. The rules are unwritten, but they are indelibly impressed on the warped intellects of these willful and carnal men who, as a way of life, callously engage in a career of corruption and crime.

It will be remembered that the federal agents, who hadn't been able to pin any one of countless murders and other heinous crimes on Al Capone, were able to have him convicted and jailed with ridiculous ease for evasion of income taxes. So the men who ran the underworld began to keep accounts, and they hired graduates of our finest colleges and universities to be their financial watchdogs.

A good lawyer, and sometimes a battery of them, are today kept at hand. There are few shyster lawyers, who in the old days were just "mouthpieces" hired to hurry down to the jailhouse to post bonds when the boys were picked up. Nowadays they engage attorneys of reputation and accomplishment to explore the statutes that fill the law books—provisions that legislators have designed over the centuries for the protection of the rights of free men, but which nevertheless too often prove inadequate when manipulated or challenged by a shrewd lawyer. Even when a skilled attorney fails, and a criminal is sentenced to prison, he can frequently be kept on the streets and out of prison for many years by one appeal after another. Top-notch lawyers are expensive, but they are absolutely indispensible to the underworld.

Politicians and law enforcement officials are prime targets of the evil influence of organized crime. An entire metropolis can fall into the bag if a few key men are bought and controlled. In his heyday as a leader of the national syndicate, Frank Costello is reputed to have been quietly active at top levels in New York City politics. Many other examples could doubtless be cited. In testimony before a Senate committee in the spring of 1962, the Attorney General, while recommending legislation to permit wire-tapping for the control of crime, told of three cities corrupted by criminals:

ATTORNEY GENERAL KENNEDY: I can name the three areas now, Senator, where we have very strong information, one in the South, one in the East and one in the West, where the major political leaders and figures in those communities are being corrupted, and are on the payroll of some of our big-time gangsters and racketeers, and we cannot do anything about it. Now, if legislation like this was passed, we could move in on those areas.

Today's criminal rationalizes that if honest men can make fortunes in legitimate business by individual enterprise and hard work, then smart thieves should be able to live in splendor by coercive means and tactics adroitly employed in the same fields. There is rarely any need for violence. Quiet threats frequently suffice. When an obstruction of law enforcement is encountered, organized crime will often try the theory that "Every man has his price," find out what it is, and then pay it. That is simply regarded as good business for the syndicate, when it will work.

In summary, crime is an industry, and it is among the largest in the nation. As in all modern and successful industry, constant research and the adaptation of new techniques are necessary. Testimony at one of our committee hearings revealed that the Chicago mob had sent a team of experts to the city of Dallas to study the existing market possibilities for the syndicate's criminal operations. (The vigilant and efficient Dallas police force quickly discovered their presence and purpose, and just as quickly dispatched them back to Chicago.) Public relations are of tremendous importance. So are technological advancement and new scientific discoveries—pocket transmitters can send race results winging to the syndicate within seconds after the horses cross the finish line. There are new electronic devices to bypass the phone company's tolls. There are also new business machines that can, in a few seconds' time, tell the board of directors of a policy numbers racket whether it would be profitable to pay off bets on that day's "number" or whether it would be wiser to rig the operation so that another number, lightly bet upon in the day's play, should be the winner.

There are business traditions to adopt, also. For one thing, it is common practice in the field of commerce for the executives of an industry to gather every so often at a convention that is held in pleasant surroundings. Mutual problems are discussed and experiences exchanged, old acquaintances renewed, new developments in the industry debated, food and drink and entertainmnt provided. The Apalachin meeting was patterned accordingly.

The discovery and exposure of it, its background, and the wide publicity it received did more to reveal the presence, nature, and extent of the criminal conspiracy than anything that has happened since the racket-smashing trials in New York City in the 1930's and early 1940's when Luciano was sent to prison and Lepke was sent to the electric chair.

Representatives of the Federal Bureau of Narcotics and other crime-fighting organizations that appeared at our initial hearings on organized crime expressed the firm belief that the controlling organization of the crime syndicate in this country is the ancient secret society called the Mafia. Other competent observers are reluctant to pinpoint the direction so precisely, preferring the more general identification of a national network of allied mobs, one of the main elements of which is the Mafia group. Any suitable label such as "the syndicate" or "the organization" may be applied as needed. Anyway, it is established beyond any doubt whatsoever that a great segment of the American underworld, representing its top authority, is closely linked by nationality, blood, marriage, and background.

Former Commissioner Harry J. Anslinger, of the Bureau of Narcotics, told the committee that the underworld association, engaged in all kinds of criminal operations, probably totaled upwards of a thousand men possessing and exercising some ruling power and authority. His agents at that time had compiled a list of eight hundred members of the association. He said further:

These gangsters are not welded into a single unit. They operate all over the United States in separate groups, but are so interwoven personally that any one of the eight hundred men can telephone any other member of the group—wherever located—and arrange for the accomplishment of unlawful activities.

I wish to point out quite emphatically that their business is all done by telephone, and they are so well insulated through this medium of communications that they are virtually immune from investigation by law enforcement officers. Fortunately we manage to infiltrate by means of undercover operations, but these are long, tedious, and dangerous.

The early hearings on the Apalachin meeting brought out testimony that, whether or not the Mafia group exercised national direction of the crime syndicate, it was closely connected to top criminals throughout this country. Mobsters of other national backgrounds have always found it expedient and profitable to work with the Sicilians who traditionally make up the Mafia membership. It is probably true, of course, that sudden retribution would strike if they didn't.

The inquiry into the Apalachin meeting revealed with certainty that in the past few decades there has been a persistent effort by the mature leaders of the American criminal syndicate to achieve a surface legitimacy by infiltrating and controlling both labor unions and business organizations. The success of that effort in many diverse fields poses a very real threat to the future of our country.

They have arrogantly challenged the government and the decent people of the United States by their contemptuous conduct in the witness chair during the Senate hearings. They showed themselves to be a highly effective and efficiently organized enemy to all elements of decent society. They demonstrated that they are often above and beyond the law as it may be slackly enforced in many sections of the country.

They also exhibited a very sensitive vulnerability to the harsh light of publicity. They didn't like having the lights and cameras focused on their frozen faces. They glowered in sullen and helpless rage as their anonymity was shattered. Although their lawyers, one after another, made polite requests that cameras and lights be turned away from their clients, the committee remained firm in the application of its long-standing rule. Co-operative witnesses are usually entitled to and do have such requests granted. Fifth Amendment witnesses, however, are not regarded as co-operative. It does not seem as though the clicking of cameras and the glare or flashing of lights would serve to frustrate or distract them when in response to each question asked they simply read from a slip of paper the formula their lawyers have prepared: "I decline to answer on the grounds that my answer may tend to incriminate me."

Finally, during these hearings on the Apalachin crime conference and related matters, the mobsters unwittingly performed a major service to the country and a disservice to themselves. By their arrogance and contempt, they ensured that the attention of the committee's capable staff would be drawn to further penetration of the underworld, and they helped set in motion the slow but inevitable legislative and judicial processes designed to decimate their solid ranks by prison sentences and deportation orders in the years to come. They simply blundered into the bright lights, triggering for themselves many of the difficulties they have had to face in the years since Apalachin.

There was considerable testimony about the Mafia, which has long held the close attention of the Federal Bureau of Narcotics. This secret society of criminals is responsible for much of the international dope traffic. The Mafia had its birth and early growth in Sicily in the eighteenth century, when oppressed Sicilians banded secretly to fight their exploitation by the Bourbon regime that held power over the island. It continued as a clandestine organization long after the need for insurgency was gone. Its members soon turned their talents to extortion, blackmail, and murder, and these and many other crimes have continued with the secret society through the centuries. When Sicilians migrated to the United States in great numbers at the end of the last century and through the first two decades of the twentieth century, many of the new arrivals were members of or closely associated with the secret society. They used their malevolent powers over their fellow countrymen in the United States mainly for extortion and blackmail. Their supposed insignia gave them a common name in America, the "Black Hand." They were feared in Italian-American communities throughout the nation. Then came 1919, and the Volstead Act was the new law.

The prohibition era played a tremendous role in the transformation of the Mafia from a terroristic band of brigands into the prototype of today's criminal syndicate. This is no longer rooted strictly in Sicilian background, but in its many diversified manifestations it evidences the same code of silence, of ruthlessness, and of swift vengeance. The wild years of prohibition were tailor-made for the mobs that grew up in the Mafia tradition, and they took avaricious and savage advantage of the profits and the power that swelled in the production and distribution of bootleg liquor. Then they started to branch out. One of their principal sources of revenue became narcotics, another was prostitution, and a third was organized gambling.

Martin F. Pera of the Bureau of Narcotics testified to a decade spent studying the secret affairs of the syndicate:

... you could never appreciate the total activity of this group if you dissect it from one area and focus your attention only on one particular area. I don't think that enforcement agencies that observe their activities in one particular city can appreciate the network involved in this criminal conspiracy. I don't think they could appreciate the extent or the ramifications or what it costs the public, the loss of money to the public, and the extent of their criminal activity unless attention was focused on them from a national or interstate point of view.

Since that testimony, a great deal of national attention has been focused on them, and they don't like it at all.

Daniel P. Sullivan, operating director of the Crime Commission of Greater Miami, viewed the underworld alliance in the same fashion. "All of these people are very intimately associated with one another," said Mr. Sullivan, "and there is no question in my mind that they are operating on a national level and that they are highly organized."

He spoke at length about gangsters moving from their own lucrative operations into the field of unionism, where corruption and crime in the sleek fashion of the syndicate have become synonymous with some unions in recent years. He told about a shady character who had been asked why he'd moved from other enterprises into the union welfare field.

"Well, first of all," the scoundrel said, "when you have a checkoff system, you have a foolproof system of collections. It doesn't cost you money to operate. Secondly, if you run into one of these insurance companies or welfare outfits, you don't pay any money out and you take it all in. And thirdly, you have no inspection on the local, county, state, or federal level. So your funds are not audited."

There, in the words of a thief, is an express viewpoint as to why the field of unionism is attractive to racketeers.

Now let's take a closer look at some of these prominent mobsters connected with the syndicate. As was said earlier, all but two who appeared before the Select Committee took advantage of the Fifth Amendment.

Vito Genovese was the kingpin of those who appeared at hearings in the summer of 1958. He is now in jail, serving a long term for a narcotics conspiracy. Genovese is no stranger to jails. He has been in and out of them since his boyhood in New York City, on a variety of charges ranging from disorderly conduct to murder.

In 1934, Genovese fled to Italy to escape a murder trial in a gangland slaying. He became an intimate of Mussolini, for whom he performed various services, supposedly including arrangements for the murder of newspaper editor Carlo Tresca in New York, a crime that has never been solved. After the war, Genovese was discovered acting as an interpreter for the Allied Military Government in Italy and was brought home to face trial for the twelve-year-old charge of murdering Ferdinand Boccia.

Two witnesses who were to appear against him were then murdered, and Genovese was free to pick up his crime career again on this side of the ocean. He rose rapidly in the hierarchy of crime. When he appeared before the committee in the summer of 1958, he was considered one of the masters of the syndicate. He answered no questions beyond giving his name and address. He wouldn't even tell his birth date, claiming that to do so might incriminate him. There were many other matters to which he refused to testify. Most of them probably would have incriminated him.

Here are just a few samples of the subjects that Genovese refused to talk about: his American citizenship; black market operations in Italy; Apalachin; his membership in the Mafia; his income, which is supposedly enormous and is backed by an estimated fortune of thirty million dollars; his wife; the murder of Ferdinand Boccia; the murder of Albert Anastasia; his underworld associates, such as Joe Profaci, Tony Bender, Frank Costello, the late Charles Luciano, and Joe Adonis. He kept silent on his support for and friendship with Mussolini.

Vito Genovese was a top-ranking hoodlum when he appeared; he still is, even though he is behind prison bars. He looked the part, and even his smoked glasses could not conceal the hard, cold eyes. His studied arrogance and deliberate malevolence seemed to have more effect upon committee members and staff than most of these criminals could produce. Certainly Genovese roused more sharp, biting inquiries than the majority of his colleagues in crime. The record fairly bristles with the image of an evil figure. These following exchanges were typical of the afternoon during which Genovese was in the witness chair:

THE CHAIRMAN: Are you a citizen of the United States?
GENOVESE: I respectfully decline to answer on the ground that my answer may tend to incriminate me.

THE CHAIRMAN: Did you ever do anything in your life that you could tell about that wouldn't incriminate you?
GENOVESE: I respectfully decline to answer . . .

Then Senator Ives determinedly took up the question of Genovese's citizenship, sternly examining the sleek gangster.

SENATOR IVES: I would like to carry this thing out and find out why the witness declines to say whether he is an American citizen or not.
GENOVESE: I respectfully decline . . .
SENATOR IVES: Are you ashamed of being an American citizen?
GENOVESE: It might tend to incriminate me.
SENATOR IVES: Do you mean being an American citizen would incriminate you?
GENOVESE: I respectfully decline . . .
SENATOR IVES: I don't know how that would work. Maybe your counsel can explain it, but I can't see anything incriminating about being an American citizen. If anything, being an American citizen might do you some good.
GENOVESE: I respectfully decline to answer.
SENATOR IVES: I didn't ask you a question. I am telling you something.

The committee's objective was to give every witness a fair hearing, but the record of Genovese's brutality and cold-blooded ruthlessness was enough to turn anyone's stomach as it was read into the record during the course of the afternoon. The chairman's indignation erupted after the detailing of the extermination of one witness in the Boccia murder.

THE CHAIRMAN: Do you operate on that . . . basis of killing everything that gets in your way?
GENOVESE: I respectfully decline . . .
THE CHAIRMAN: Can you give an answer to any question at all without incriminating yourself?

GENOVESE: I will have to hear the question first.

THE CHAIRMAN: All right, I will ask you. Did you ever do any decent thing in your life?

GENOVESE: I respectfully decline . . .

To all who watched his performance, Vito Genovese seemed to be, above all the others of his kind, the epitome of evil.

The others came, however, in their dark clothing and with sleek, freshly barbered appearances—all of them seemingly cast from the same mold, all of them having the same cold and hard and depthless eyes.

There was Mike Miranda, lieutenant to Vito Genovese. He, surprisingly, answered some questions—but they were not questions designed to draw information from him. They were simply queries about his ability to read, to look at a photograph:

THE CHAIRMAN: Mr. Miranda, do you recognize yourself in that photograph? [The picture was of Genovese and Miranda outside a New York City bar.]

MIRANDA: I got no glass. I don't see.

THE CHAIRMAN: Where are your reading glasses?

MIRANDA: I got none. They are at home.

Senator Ives was also able to draw an answer from Mike Miranda. The witness had to confer with his counsel before giving a reply to the query:

SENATOR IVES: I would like to follow that up with a question. I would like to ask the witness if he has any respect for the government. That is a question.

MIRANDA: Yes, sir.

Mike Miranda was at Apalachin, has always been associated with Vito Genovese, has a long arrest record, including two charges of murder, but he has never been convicted. He is included on the Bureau of Narcotics' list of international drug traffickers.

There was Joseph Profaci, one of the old-timers in the syndicate. He answered some questions, too, a few of them—about his ability to speak and comprehend English.

MR. KENNEDY: Mr. Profaci, we had a talk yesterday, a nice conversation, did we not? Didn't we have a little talk in the office?
PROFACI: I decline to answer.
MR. KENNEDY: Mr. Profaci, your English was so much better yesterday. What has happened in the last twenty-four hours?
PROFACI: I don't catch your words right.

Profaci told Mr. Kennedy that if the chief counsel would be patient, he would "catch" the words. Bob Kennedy lashed out immediately:

MR. KENNEDY: I don't have to be. Yesterday you spoke very freely and easily. Your accent has gotten so bad today. What happened overnight, Mr. Profaci? You understood and answered all the questions I asked you yesterday and spoke very easily, with very little accent. What has happened since?

This was a pattern repeated time after time. They spoke well and fluently in the corridors and in the committee's offices, to the staff and to their associates and attorneys. In the witness chair, however, they evidently lost the powers of hearing, speech, and understanding.

At any rate, Profaci soon took up the wearisome pathway where all the signposts are labeled: "I decline to answer . . ." Here are some areas of questioning in which he declined: Apalachin; the marriages of two of his daughters; his business enterprises in olive oil and in clothing; his ties with union officials, including three specific locals of the Teamsters; his arrests for rape in Sicily, for theft in Sicily, for complicity in the Boccia murder, for possession of weapons at the great Mafia meeting in Cleveland in 1928, for forgery in Brooklyn, and his two convictions for violation of the Pure Food and Drug Act. He also was silent on his associations with the rogues' gallery: Luciano, Costello, "Joe Bananas" Bonanno, Paul "The Waiter" Ricca, Genovese, Ormento, Lucchese, the Dioguardi brothers, and Anastasia.

Let's look at one more; the record is filled with Fifth Amendment declarations, but all were preceded by questions that were based upon careful probing by trained investigators. The Fifth Amendment artistry of James Plumeri, alias "Jimmy Doyle," was an unbroken string of sullen responses in the following areas: his nephews, the Dioguardi brothers; his eight arrests, including one charge of murder; his business enterprises, centered in the garment industry—both trucking and clothing factories; his labor union links; his prize-fighting interests; his associations with the self-same list of gangsters. Plumeri did answer two questions toward the end of his examination; he said he had no children and he gave his wife's maiden name.

In this manner the members of the syndicate paraded contemptuously before the committee, day after day. Their silence added nothing, but their very refusals to answer tended to confirm the accuracy of the tremendous mass of information that had been gathered by the committee's investigators from scores of sources. The groundwork was firmly in place—upon it would be built the story of the syndicate's infiltration into many avenues of our society, and particularly into those business and labor organizations that offered greedy gangsters a fast dollar without much effort or danger.

CHAPTER 9

Arson and Murder Were the Weapons

WHENEVER the committee's staff launched an investigation, the word spread among the men of the syndicate and their allied underlings as swiftly as a crown fire blazes through a pine woods. In the labor-management field particularly the criminals were vulnerable to the effects of diligent probes. Whenever the operations started, generally with field interrogations and subpoenas for files and fiscal records, their normal criminal activities usually came to an abrupt halt. Records were often destroyed or mutilated or conveniently misplaced, key witnesses took long vacations in faraway places, and sometimes the chief culprits made frantic, hasty, and ill-disguised efforts to cover up their misdeeds and corruption. That was a common pattern of behavior once the searchlights were focused on a particular racket. That wasn't what happened in Chicago, however, in the spring of 1958, when committee investigators were digging into the unsavory record of shakedowns in the city's restaurant industry. Instead, the crooks fought back in their own vicious fashion.

At midnight on May 13, 1958, Andrew Milas arrived on schedule at the Fireside Restaurant in Chicago, ready to put his crew of six men to work at the nightly task of readying this renowned dining place for the next day's business. Shortly after midnight, Mr. Milas was high on a stepladder, running a vacuum cleaner's hose across the ceiling to remove dust and cobwebs. His six assistants were scattered through the building, engaged in the dozens of chores that must be done in the quiet hours if the customers of the following day are to have the traditional excellent food and service of an expensive restaurant like the Fireside.

Mr. Milas happened to glance down from his ladder, sensing that someone was in the dining room with him. He saw a man in a black hood standing at the foot of the ladder, revolver in his hand.

"Get down from there," the gunman said.

Mr. Milas got down quickly enough, and he and his six-man crew were herded together by the man with the revolver, who was now joined by a companion, also armed and hooded. There was no violence; the hoodlums were polite and talkative.

"You guys are going to have to get another job," one of them told Milas and his staff. "This place is going up in smoke."

Most courteously, he then asked Mr. Milas if he could have a glass of milk, and the custodian said he could, telling him where the refrigerators were. After a time, Milas caught the pungent odor of gasoline. Then one of the guards waved the cleaning staff toward the door of the restaurant, telling them to go outside and line up against the wall of the building. He said they were to wait three minutes after the getaway car had departed, then run north to give the alarm.

"You're sure," the leading gunman said to Milas, "that there are only seven men in this place? I don't want to leave anybody in here."

Mr. Milas assured him that all the staff had been rounded up.

Outside the building, the seven custodians lined up as they were told to, while the two gunmen joined a third hooded man in a waiting car. The car roared away on Lincoln Avenue, and Milas and his companions took to their heels, running north. Some distance away from the restaurant, Milas testified, he looked back, "and there were windows about eighteen or twenty feet high, and you could see it all red."

The Fireside Restaurant became a charred shell, a total loss estimated at fourteen hundred thousand dollars. Not far away from the blaze, in a Chicago hotel, LaVern J. Duffy and James P. Kelly, investigators for the Select Committee, were working late that night preparing a report on the shakedown racket through which Chicago gangsters were extorting huge sums of money annually from the owners and employees of Chicago's thousands of restaurants. One of the files that Mr. Duffy was working on was labeled *Fireside Restaurant*. Its owner, Gustav Allgauer, had been very co-operative during preliminary interrogations.

Mr. Allgauer testified about the arson before the committee.

MR. KENNEDY: Was this after the committee started its investigation?

MR. ALLGAUER: Yes, sir.

MR. KENNEDY: How long had we been in your restaurant, do you know?

MR. ALLGAUER: I don't know. I think about six weeks before; wasn't it something like that, Mr. Duffy?

MR. DUFFY: We spent quite a bit of time going over your books, and you co-operated fully with us at that time.

Who did it we don't know—the crime has never been solved.

Whatever the reason for the arson, and whoever the arsonists may have been, there is no doubt whatever that the crime was a strand in the evil web that surrounded the restaurants and taverns of Chicago. In a double-barreled version of the old-fashioned "protection" racket, the gangsters used both a completely corrupted union and a co-operative management association to extort huge sums of money. Their methods were crude, simple, and effective. It was either pay up or take the consequences. What were the consequences? An investigator for the State of Illinois, John McFarland, testified that there had been forty major fires in Chicago restaurants during the eighteen months immediately preceding his testimony. "They are all similar in nature, and their origin seems to be the same, and they start out with an enormous fire immediately."

He added that he received little or no co-operation from restaurant owners in his investigations of the fires. Mr. Kennedy asked him the reason. "Well," said Mr. McFarland, "I think they are afraid to talk."

He then testified that normally, before the racketeers moved into the restaurant field, there were only one or two serious fires in Chicago restaurants each year.

Mr. McFarland's testimony concluded with word of another restaurant burning to the ground just a month before his appearance, when two gunmen entered it and spread gasoline around before applying a torch. The place was named—of all possible choices!—The Flame.

Arson alone was not the only thing that restaurant proprietors in Chicago had to fear. During nine days of hearings in July, 1958, which were concerned solely with the restaurant industry in Chicago, witnesses testified directly about a total of thirty-nine unsolved murders believed to be connected with the criminals who were under investigation. There were also endless accounts of beatings, assaults, slashed tires, stinkbombs, sugar dumped into gasoline tanks, and countless other acts of violence and vandalism.

The racket that was being worked by the leaders of the Chicago branch of the crime syndicate involved local unions of the Hotel and Restaurant Employees and Bartenders International Union, as well as the long-established and once-respectable Chicago Restaurant Association.

The record discloses that this is the remarkable pattern that was followed: the crime syndicate controlled the locals, and its hoodlums and attorneys were hired by the restaurant owners' association to handle "labor relations." Nothing could be simpler or more effective—the money flowed in from both directions at once.

First, consider the union end of the arrangement. If an owner knew what was good for him, he agreed to have his place unionized upon the first visit of the organizer. The workers were not consulted in this organizing drive; they rarely knew it was going on. The restaurant owner was told that the union wasn't greedy, a compromise figure would always be accepted. If the owner had forty employees, then twenty memberships would be given to the union. The owner paid the initiation fees and the dues for twenty names that he gave the organizer. That arrangement usually continued for years. It didn't make any difference to anyone concerned in the deal that, after a period of time, possibly ten or more of the twenty union members might no longer be employees. They might well be living in California or New York, might be in the army, might even be dead. Dues continued to be collected for twenty names. There were no sudden fires in the middle of the night, no beatings, no sugar poured into gas tanks, no tires slashed, no vandalism. In one startling bit of testimony, the committee discovered that a union member for whom dues were being regularly paid had jumped ship two years before in Greece and as a result had lost his American citizenship. But he didn't lose his union membership.

This shakedown racket worked really well. There wasn't much bookkeeping involved, nor any fuss and bother with union benefits, welfare, meetings, elections, and the other kinds of activities and responsibilities that attend legitimate unionism. This was a typically modern, streamlined racketeering operation. Only names and dues were important, not flesh-and-blood members. As a matter of fact, testimony from several sources proved that waitresses, waiters, and other restaurant employees by the thousands never even knew that they belonged to the union!

The testimony of William Scholl, who ran some ice cream parlors, tells of the callousness of this "union." Mr. Scholl had once paid initiation fees and dues for some of his employees, and after a few years the union stopped collecting. Mr. Scholl breathed a little easier; his protection had amounted to thirty-two dollars per month. Some time later an organizer called. He said the union wanted money. Mr. Scholl offered fifty dollars and was turned down. They settled for a hundred dollars in cash.

MR. KENNEDY: And did you submit any names of members at that time?

Mr. Scholl: No, I did not.

Mr. Kennedy: You just gave him the hundred dollars in cash?

Mr. Scholl: I gave him the hundred dollars with the understanding that I would furnish the names later.

Unhappily for Mr. Scholl, the local wasn't satisfied. A month later he was visited by James O'Connor, then president of Local #394. O'Connor wanted $500, but he settled for $220. Mr. Scholl testified that he paid for five employees. "They didn't care who they were; just any five."

The union made it even simpler for Anthony DeSantis, proprietor of the Martinique Restaurant in Chicago. Frank Trungale, of Local #394, didn't even ask for a list of names. He was content to show up every once in a while to collect a hundred dollars. No union memberships, no books, no dues, no fees. Just pay Trungale a hundred dollars every now and then.

Mr. Kennedy: But he did organize the waitresses?

Mr. De Santis: No, sir.

Mr. Kennedy: That was the end of it, then?

Mr. De Santis: That is right.

Mr. Kennedy: Nothing happened?

Mr. De Santis: No, sir; other than I would say in the period of the last six, between the last six and eight years when he approached me I have given him a hundred dollars on different occasions. It might be six or eight times.

There was a long parade of such witnesses, telling the same shocking tale of no written contracts, no negotiation of wages or working conditions, no evidence that their employees ever wanted a union, and in case after case no knowledge on the employees' part that they were union members.

The international union eventually acted, placing the crooked Chicago locals in trusteeship, while the racketeers all resigned their positions just before their appearances before the Select Committee, where they took the Fifth Amendment. The AFL-CIO ordered a cleanup of the union, and a special committee took over operation of all eleven locals in the Chicago area.

On the other side of the fence, the operation was just as smooth and ruthless. Members of the Chicago Restaurant Association contributed to a "voluntary fund" for use when labor difficulties arose. The record showed that in the six-year period between 1951 and 1957, more than eleven hundred thousand dollars was paid into this shakedown fund by restaurant owners. One-third of this money went directly into the hands of two attorneys who allegedly had close connections with the Old Capone crime syndicate. One of them, Abraham Teitelbaum, had served as counsel for Al Capone himself.

He was "labor relations counsel" for the Chicago Restaurant Association at fees totaling $125,000 per year. The other lawyer was Anthony V. Champagne, attorney for some of Capone's hoodlums, who also served as counsel for the association. He quit in a hurry, however, when Tony Accardo (who succeeded Frank "The Enforcer" Nitti and Paul "The Waiter" Ricca to the Capone throne) got angry with him about affairs in the association. The record of the hearings contains the allegation that Accardo had ordered Champagne's murder, but had been dissuaded by friends. It was reported in committee hearings that Teitelbaum was also in mortal danger because of association affairs—two thugs who were trying to muscle in on the shakedown racket formulated a simple and effective plan for getting Teitelbaum out of the way. According to testimony before the committee, they wanted to push him out of his office window.

The testimony disclosed that the job of these two attorneys was to settle labor troubles when they arose, as they did with regular and scheduled frequency. There was only one system of settlement followed, that of shakedown, bribery, and payoff. Teitelbaum and Champagne arranged the "settlements." The association's "voluntary fund" was perpetually fluid—the money poured into the fund from the restaurants and then out again into the gangsters' pockets.

Those two men were among the very few attorneys-at-law who appeared before the Senate Select Committee in its years of operation to take the Fifth Amendment. There were other lawyers who were less than candid in their testimony, or who equivocated on questions of ethics, and some few who apparently lied when they testified.

Teitelbaum and Champagne did not plead immunity under an attorney-client relationship. They repeatedly stated that they resorted to the Fifth Amendment on the ground that a truthful answer might tend to incriminate them. Certainly, throughout the nine days of intermittent testimony concerning their activities, the same fearsome list of names came from the mouths of witnesses who talked about the Chicago shakedowns: Capone, Jake "Greasy Thumb" Guzik, Tony Accardo, Nitti, Ricca, Murray "The Camel" Humphreys, Rocco Fischetti, "Machine Gun Jack" McGurn, Joe Aiuppa, Sam "Mooney" Giancana, Sam "Golf Bag" Hunt—who was so named because he used to tote a machine gun in a golf bag.

One of the most disgusting exhibitions the committee ever had to witness was the performance of one of Teitelbaum's hired hands, Louis Romano, who did "labor relations work" in the restaurant field.

When he was asked about murders he had been accused of, Romano lost his temper at Chief Counsel Kennedy and snarled: "Why don't you go and dig up all the dead ones out in the graveyard and ask me if I shot them, you Chinaman!" None of us understood the significance of the Oriental aspersion, but Romano was severely rebuked for his contemptuous performance. His period on the witness stand did evoke some dry humor. He was asked about his income tax returns for the previous four years, in which he made the outlandish claim that his total income in each year was six hundred dollars. He told the committee that he had lived in Coral Gables, Florida, on his savings. Senator Ervin took over the questioning at that point:

SENATOR ERVIN: I would like to suggest that Mr. Romano can be one of the greatest public benefactors in the United States . . . if he can just tell us how it is, in this age of inflation and high cost of living, a man can exist four years on an income not exceeding six hundred dollars a year.

ROMANO: Well, one reason is I buy very little food. Mr. Kelly [Committee investigator] seen me fishing. I catch a lot of fish for food. And I can eat it six times a week. If you want any hints how to cut down the high cost of living, there is a good one.

There wasn't much else during the Chicago restaurant hearings that was calculated to draw smiles. Those sessions were among the clearest examples in all the hearings of how the crime syndicate has infiltrated into legitimate business enterprises. The restaurant industry didn't do very much to bring glory upon itself, either; the investigations brought nothing but abuse on the one hand or equivocation on the other from the very people who should have been happiest to see these conditions exposed and ended.

The association was certainly guilty of improper conduct in its handling of labor relations, and was undoubtedly aware that its counsel, Abraham Teitelbaum, and his successor, Anthony V. Champagne, were funneling the association's funds into the hands of criminals.

Up to the very beginning of the hearings, the terroristic tactics were continued, and there is little doubt that fear was the compelling reason behind the industry's reluctance to co-operate. The committee called two waitresses as witnesses, Mae Christiansen and Beverly Sturdevant. During their interrogations, they were asked if anybody in Chicago had talked to them about testifying.

MRS. STURDEVANT: I was told not to come down to Washington to testify.

THE CHAIRMAN: You were told what?

MRS. STURDEVANT: I was told not to come down to Washington,

that I should get sick before coming down to Washington or
be sicker when I get back.

THE CHAIRMAN: Have you given the full information regarding
this to the FBI?

MRS. STURDEVANT: Yes, sir, I have signed a complete statement
with the FBI.

As results of the hearings, the AFL-CIO moved with speed to
clean up the locals in Chicago, and the union dismissed the officials who were guilty of running the brazen protection racket.

Unhappily for the causes of justice and decency, however, most
of the racketeers who raked in the big profits are still walking
the streets of Chicago and other cities. Their crimes have gone
unpunished. All, that is, but two of them—Paul "Needlenose"
Labriola and James Weinberg, who claimed to be close associates
of the syndicate leaders like Tony Accardo, and who tried to build
a rival organization to the existing Chicago Restaurant Association, supposedly with the mob's backing. They were the two
thugs who plotted to push Teitelbaum out of his own window.
Some weeks before our hearings got under way, their bodies were
found stuffed into the trunk of an automobile.

Just as murder and arson were used in the shakedown of Chicago's vast restaurant industry, they proved to be useful weapons
also in the racketeers' seizure of power in the concentrated, rich
garbage business in New York City. There was scarcely any dis-
cernible difference in the methods used—the hoodlums took over
the unions and strong-armed the industry's associations by the
same kind of double-barreled attack that worked so well in Chicago. This set of hearings was another clear illustration of how
the American criminal syndicate has managed to infiltrate both
labor and management in the same industry, employing modern
business methods and techniques to give a veneer of respectability
to its operations while at the same time making use of the terrorism and violence that has always characterized gangland opera-

tions in the United States. The garbage racket, like the Chicago restaurant shakedown, involved both unions and management, first in a subsidiary operation in a New York City suburb, and then in a major campaign in the metropolis.

The city of Yonkers, New York, where the streets and transportation lines are directly connected with those of New York City—Broadway in Yonkers is a northward extension of the big city's Broadway—decided by vote of its city council to end municipal cartage of garbage for the city's commercial enterprises and to turn that service over to private industry. The city's action promptly started a small war that raged for several years during the early 1950's—a war that certainly reflected the truth of one witness's statement to the committee that "in the garbage industry we don't get Harvard alumni and Yale undergraduates."

Teamsters Local #456 had jurisdiction in the city of Yonkers in Westchester County. This local, headed by a long-time union official named John Acropolis, began to organize the drivers and helpers of the garbage companies—principally an outfit called Westchester Carting. Before the men of Local #456 knew what was happening to them, Teamsters Local #27, from the Bronx in New York City, moved across the city line and dived into the garbage pile.

Before digging any farther into this malodorous mess, it is necessary to look at the interloping leaders. Joseph Parisi, secretary-treasurer of Local #27, since dead of a heart attack, was the owner of criminal record B56267 of the New York City Police Department. He was convicted of rape and served two and a half years in Sing Sing Prison; he was convicted of disorderly conduct and indicted for coercion, murder, felonious assault, robbery with a gun, and again felonious assault. He was charged with conspiracy with Charles "Lucky" Luciano and Louis "Lepke" Buchalter. He was the associate of many underworld characters, including several prominent in the national crime syndicate.

On the management side of the industry picture was Alfred

"Nick" Ratteni, the president of Westchester Carting Company. This sterling citizen had arrests for suspicion of burglary, grand larceny, assault, and robbery. On the latter charge he was convicted and sentenced to seven and a half to fifteen years in Sing Sing. In 1953, he was indicted for income tax violations and was then described by the Attorney General of the United States as a "cheap lieutenant of Frank Costello."

With that kind of gangster talent opposing them, it was small wonder that the Acropolis local soon found itself on the outside looking in, while the Parisi local took control of Yonkers' commercial garbage.

The Acropolis people fought back. They urged the formation of another firm, Rex Carting Company, under the sponsorship of the city's Chamber of Commerce, and soon the battle for jurisdiction was on again. Among the tactics employed by Parisi's local was the boycotting of all Safeway supermarkets in the vast borough of the Bronx, simply because one Safeway store in Yonkers had taken on the services of Rex Carting Company. When the garbage began to pile up in the alleys and parking lots of Safeway's large chain stores, the company quickly made peace with Local #27 and the Westchester Carting Company.

During the hearings the committee was presented with an affidavit by Katherine Embree of Yonkers, who owned a small garbage pickup firm. Part of her statement follows:

In the early part of 1950 I started to experience difficulty in the operation of the carting service because of opposition of one of the unions, Local 27, private sanitation unit. About February of 1950 I was approached by a man whom I later identified to be Nick Ratteni, who was the owner of the Westchester Carting Co., at which time Ratteni told me, "We better get together or one of us will be out of business."

Subsequent to that time I received threats over the telephone from an unknown person.

On March 19, 1950, at 11:55 P.M., two trucks that I owned and which were parked seventy-five feet apart on a lot at 509 Riverdale Avenue, Yonkers, New York, were sprinkled with gasoline and burned.

It is of interest to note that Westchester Carting Company employed an "efficiency expert," one Joseph Feola, better known to the underworld as "Joey Surprise." He had been charged with violations of the Sullivan law, felonious assault, homicide with a gun, murder in the first degree—this involved the shooting of one policeman to death and the wounding of another. He was sentenced to death in the electric chair for the murder, but his conviction was reversed and he later pleaded guilty to manslaughter, for which he was sentenced to seven and one-half to fifteen years in Sing Sing Prison.

The undercover war raged on in Yonkers, with Rex Carting and Local #456 trying to hold their own against the racketeering lineup of Westchester Carting and Local #27. It came to a head at the New York State Teamsters convention in Rochester in 1952.

The hard-pressed John Acropolis and the secretary-treasurer of his local, Everett Doyle, went together to the convention, where they ran into Bernie Adelstein, president of Local #27. There were harsh words spoken at the convention hall.

Mr. Doyle: Adelstein said to Johnny, "You are not that tough. Don't think you are too tough that we can't take care of you. Tougher guys than you have been taken care of."

Doyle and Acropolis went to their hotel. Joe Parisi came to their room.

Mr. Doyle: They got talking all over again about the private carting, that they wanted the Rex Carting, and no matter what happened they were going to get it. Acropolis got into an argument with Parisi and Parisi pleaded, "Gee, I don't want to argue with you no more." I think his words came out, "I am through arguing with you. I have a bad heart. I am not going to argue with you. There is other ways of taking care of you." And, "We can see that it is done."

Doyle then testified that Acropolis had given him a strong warning to be careful. "Don't park the car when you go home in a dark spot," Acropolis told his friend and colleague. "Make sure you park it out in front of your house and walk into the house."

John Acropolis didn't follow his own wise advice to be "careful." Three weeks after the Rochester meeting, he parked his car near his home in Yonkers and walked to the house, carrying in one hand his car keys and in the other a freshly cleaned suit that he'd picked up earlier that night at the cleaner's. It was about two-thirty in the morning. Somewhere between the car and the house, he met someone he knew, or at least someone who properly identified himself, because when Acropolis got inside his house he turned on the light in the parlor that he customarily turned on when he was accompanied by a friend. He was shot twice in the head.

THE CHAIRMAN: Was anyone ever apprehended for his murder?
MR. DOYLE: No one was ever apprehended.
THE CHAIRMAN: Are you personally still apprehensive about your own safety?
MR. DOYLE: Well, I don't know. You got to die some time, Senator. You can't live forever.

Westchester Carting Company, with its gangsters, and Local #27, with theirs, had solved the garbage transport problems in the city of Yonkers. Rex Carting Company went out of business a month after Acropolis was murdered. They sold out to Westchester Carting. Ironically enough, after the long and bitter fight between the two Teamster locals that ended in John Acropolis' killing, neither one of them eventually succeeded in gaining long-term control of the unionization of garbage drivers in the city of Yonkers. A company union was formed by Westchester Carting to represent its own employees after Local #27 abandoned the field.

Questioned about the reasons why Local #27 gave up the

lucrative jurisdiction after the death of John Acropolis, Bernie
Adelstein gave this explanation to the committee:

ADELSTEIN: I was reminded by our joint council and by Mr. Parisi
    that our jurisdiction, in their opinion, did not extend into West-
    chester County, and that 456 or the locals up there should
    organize the unorganized. We didn't do any organizational
    work up there at all.

There may have been another good reason. The Westchester
operation became small potatoes, considering the developments
back in their own bailiwick.

Vincent J. Squillante moved into the garbage hauling field in
the metropolitan area of New York City, and he needed co-operation to take over the management side of a fifty-million-dollar industry with the same kind of vicious in-fighting that had worked
so well on a smaller scale in the suburban city.

Who was Vincent J. Squillante? According to Joseph Amato,
agent of the Federal Narcotics Bureau in charge of investigation
of narcotics traffickers in New York City, Squillante was well
known to the bureau as a drug dealer and also as a leading figure
in the policy numbers racket and in dock racketeering. Mr. Amato
testified that Squillante was considered a leading figure in the
syndicate, particularly through his close friendship to the overlord of Murder, Inc., Albert Anastasia. Squillante was fond of
saying that he was Anastasia's godson, at least until the day that
Anastasia sat in a barber's chair in a New York hotel in 1957 and
was pumped full of bullets by a pair of gunmen.

It was in 1953 that "Jimmy" Squillante began to muscle into the
burgeoning industry of commercial garbage carting in greater
New York. He was hired as a "labor relations expert" by the
Greater New York Cartmen's Association, at a salary of ten
thousand dollars. Presumably his close alliance with Anastasia did
him no harm when he was considered for the job.

Within a year and a half, Squillante was executive director of the association, which had members from three of New York's five boroughs, and he was also the boss of the garbage haulers' groups on Long Island, in the counties of Nassau and Suffolk. The latter two groups, conducting large operations in the mushrooming suburban townships on Long Island, were informed that they had affiliated with the Greater New York Cartmen by a telegram from Squillante on January 25, 1955. They were merged, whether they wanted to be or not.

The pattern by which Squillante and his hoodlums took over the industry was exactly the same as that followed in Chicago's restaurant field, in that same city's taxi operations as dominated by Joey Glimco (which we shall view later), and in the garbage carting in the city of Yonkers. It must be said, however, that Squillante added certain refinements. The entire power grab went off much more smoothly. Squillante had the complete co-operation of the union involved—#813 of the Teamsters, a subsidiary of Parisi's #27, and the solid experience of the same Bernard Adelstein, who emerged as the president of Local #813.

In testimony to the fact that regional and national conferences on methods of operation—meetings such as that at Apalachin— are sure to pay large dividends to the hoodlums, it must be emphasized that Squillante's dictatorship of the garbage business seemed patently modeled on similar syndicate operations elsewhere in the country. It mantled the industry, unionism and private enterprise together. It would almost seem that the syndicate maintains a correspondence school in methods of corruption.

The garbage firms of Long Island weren't even aware of what was happening to them before it was too late to do anything about it. Contracts that these companies had with Local #813 were generally due to expire toward the beginning of 1955. The firms were mostly small, with a high proportion of family ownership and family operation of the several trucks they might own. John Montesano, partner in East Meadow Sanitation Service and president of the Intercounty Cartmen's Association, was an important witness before the committee. He appeared in two roles, both as representative of this type of small family businesses and as the unwitting gatekeeper of the door by which Squillante moved into the industry.

There were seven employees in Mr. Montesano's firm, and all of them were members of the union, as was Mr. Montesano himself. The others were his father, his three brothers, his two brothers-in-law, and one outsider. They all belonged to Local #813 of the Teamsters.

When the union contracts were due to expire, Mr. Montesano sought, on behalf of his membership, some aid in negotiating new contracts with the union. His lack of guile in the ways of rackets led him to accept the advice of a member of the association who had a long criminal record. He was introduced to Joey Feola, alias "Joey Surprise," who just a few years before was "labor expert" with Westchester Carting, during the period of the Yonkers garbage war, when John Acropolis was shot in the head. Mr. Montesano, unfortunately for him and for his law-abiding association, didn't have the faintest idea who Feola was, nor did he know about Feola's sterling leader, Vincent J. Squillante. Mr. Montesano agreed that it was a good idea that the less experienced Long Island group seek counsel from the Greater New York Cartmen's Association, which had fine offices on Madison Avenue and the knowledge of how to negotiate union contracts.

Once he was inside the door of Squillante's office, ushered by Joey Surprise, Mr. Montesano's career as leader and spokesman for Nassau County's garbage collectors was finished, although he wasn't aware of it. Within a few weeks of the initial meeting, however, Squillante was executive director of the Intercounty Cartmen, and his nephew, Jerry Mancuso—a man with a criminal record—was shortly to succeed him in that post. Honest business-men like the Montesano brothers were about to be thrown out on the street for opposing the dictatorship to which they had opened the door. Mr. Montesano told how Squillante took over in bitter testimony, which was followed by this colloquy:

THE CHAIRMAN: You didn't oppose him at this initial meeting?

MR. MONTESANO: At the initial meeting, no sir.

THE CHAIRMAN: You had employed him?

MR. MONTESANO: I had requested him to come down.

THE CHAIRMAN: To help you out?

MR. MONTESANO: Yes.

THE CHAIRMAN: And he came down and helped you out?

MR. MONTESANO: Yes; and he helped himself, too.

Once he had control, how did Squillante operate? There were several devices. The first of these required union membership of everybody in the garbage industry, whether they owned their own firms and trucks or whether they didn't. The second was the allocation of territories by decree from Squillante and his lieutenants.

The third was a kind of penalty clause in the form of "security payments" to keep association members in line. A man who quit the Cartmen's Association in disgust would shortly thereafter receive notice from the union that he had to pay three hundred dollars in "wage security" for every person in his employ, including himself, since he, like other owners, was a union member. In other words, a man who thought he could go it alone had to put up three hundred dollars with the union to guarantee that he would pay himself his wages. Once the security payments were made, it was an ordeal to get the money back when the union contract ran out. At the time of the hearings on the garbage industry, several witnesses had been completely unsuccessful in securing the return of their money. The use of this device was strengthened by the dictatorial tactics at union meetings, where the owners who showed up to protest union methods were denied any voice and any vote in their own union's affairs.

The "security" racket was flagrantly collusive. One operator who protested Squillante's raising of membership fees in the association was immediately notified by letter that he was expelled from the association for not attending meetings. *In the very next delivery of mail,* he got a registered letter from Local #813, telling him that he had to pay forty-two hundred dollars as wage security for his employees.

One of Squillante's major enterprises in the field of labor-management collusion was the formation of "whip" companies. They were used for the purpose implicit in the name, to whip offenders into line. Incidentally, they added magnificently to the personal plunder of Squillante and his friends. There were whip companies in New York City and in both of the Long Island counties. They operated with the full aid and backing of the union, although they paid nothing into the union—no dues and no assessments to pension and welfare funds. There were a couple of remarkable samples of whip company dealings revealed in the testimony.

The stores along the "Miracle Mile" in Nassau County were getting satisfactory service from a nonunion garbage firm until one morning in the spring of 1955, when pickets were strung out along the line of stores—pickets from Local #813 of the Teamsters. Union agents then visited the store managers, who described their shopping area as "the Fifth Avenue of Long Island," to suggest that the pickets would leave if the managers selected a garbage firm from a union-endorsed list. First on the list was the General Sanitation Company, the property of Jimmy Squillante. Most of the managers picked this firm, and none of them had the faintest idea that it was nonunion. They did only what the union's agents suggested. The prices were raised almost immediately; for at least one store, they went from forty dollars per month to twenty-five dollars per week.

In another instance, a man named Angelo Recchia, owner of Trio Carting Company, got into difficulty with Squillante and his cronies on a matter of rigged bids for garbage pickups at Mitchel Field. Almost immediately, Mr. Recchia was called by an executive of Sunrise Stores, Inc., with ten supermarkets on Long Island, to be told that he was finished as the garbage collector for the stores. A new outfit was starting the next day. This turned out to be

General Sanitation, Squillante's company. The business had been worth $750 to Mr. Recchia every month. John Montesano told what happened when Mr. Reccia ventured to protest this banditry:

MR. MONTESANO: . . . In one meeting, in particular, Squillante got very violent with him and he used very abusive language, and he just told Angelo, "Well, that is the straight of it," and that was the end of it. And Angelo had to sit down and keep quiet and be thankful he only took the Sunrise supermarkets.

When anybody started to protest, there was nothing to protest. Jimmy had the stores, and that was it.

So Mr. Recchia got whipped, and he stayed whipped. It is interesting to note that General Sanitation Company was headed by Nunzio Squillante, who was Jimmy's brother. In a lighter moment, Squillante is reported to have said that he founded the whip company to give his brother something to do.

In retrospect, it is surprising that so many of the Long Island garbage collectors fought against the criminal band that was arrayed against them. They did fight, however, evidently not connecting their own difficulties in the refuse business with those just to the northward of them, in Westchester County, where John Acropolis fought and was killed.

The men on Long Island, if they had known it, had just as good reason to be careful. There were sinister shadows behind Squillante. John Montesano, during an altercation with Squillante, received a phone call from a relative who was a very prominent figure in the Brooklyn underworld. Mr. Montesano resented interference from this racketeering relative, but he listened to the telephonic advice. "Don't you realize that they could put you out of business and they can hurt you in other ways?" Mr. Montesano replied heatedly: "If they can hurt me, let them hurt me." The relative cautioned him again, obviously with full knowledge of the men he was talking about: "Don't forget, you have got kids. . . . Sometimes they won't hurt you, but they will hurt the kids."

The threats weren't the only reason why the Long Island men should have shown caution. If any of them had knowledge of the underworld, the other reason would have been apparent in the appointment of C. Don Modica as "educational director" of the Long Island association. He attended meetings, made "suggestions," and generally stood around, as one member put it, like a "watchdog." He probably was. C. Don Modica had once been an instructor in the philosophy of education at New York University and so had earned the nickname "Professor," but he had also been jailed in Delaware for practicing medicine without a license and served time in Queens County, New York, for grand larceny. His importance to the garbage collectors of New York City and Long Island was not in his nominal job of conducting public relations for the Greater New York Cartmen's Association, where he edited a paper called *The Hired Broom*. (One issue contained a poem in which Modica declared that "Out of garbage, there grows a rose.")

His other occupation seemed even more innocent, but it certainly had sinister undertones. He was a tutor of children. On three occasions when John Montesano visited the cartmen's headquarters, he saw Professor Modica at the blackboard:

MR. MONTESANO: We went all the way to New York, and while we were there on three different occasions, I saw this young boy come in, and it seemed to me that the professor was tutoring him. That is the truth. He was tutoring him. . . . He had a blackboard and he had all kinds of symbols and numerals and different things. It didn't bother me at first, but after the third time I said to myself, "Who is this fellow?" I asked Beansie Fazula, "Who is this fellow?" And he turns around and tells me, "That is Albert's boy." I drew my own conclusions after that.

MR. KENNEDY: Just on the basis that it was Albert's boy? Didn't he say Albert who?

MR. MONTESANO: Well, it was common knowledge. I mean, after

a while I found out that Jimmy was supposed to be—this is later, after I got out of the organization.

MR. KENNEDY: Jimmy was what?

MR. MONTESANO: Linked to Albert Anastasia.

When Modica himself appeared before the committee, he took the Fifth Amendment after he identified himself and said he was a "teacher and writer." It was brought out, however, that other fond parents who had hired him to tutor their children were Willie Moretti, Sal Moretti, Vito Genovese, and Joe Adonis. He also taught "marine safety" during World War II at a shipbuilding corporation controlled by Albert Anastasia. While Modica was "educational director" for the Cartmen's Association, there were a startling number of phone calls from the offices of that organization to the home of Albert Anastasia. The Long Island cartmen were obviously on thin ice when they protested Squillante's dictatorship in the presence of the professor. They might have undergone a little "tutoring" themselves.

Vincent J. Squillante's greatest personal achievement came at a period of great personal crisis. He was in serious trouble and he extricated himself with remarkable dexterity by manipulating association funds.

The Internal Revenue Service had instituted a "crash program" against Squillante, serving notice that he had to pay back taxes, penalties, and interest by June 15, 1956. At the time, Squillante was under severe attack from the newspapers, notably the Long Island paper *Newsday*, which later furnished one of its fine reporters, Robert W. Greene, as a temporary staff member for the Select Committee. Squillante was also the target of the New York State attorney general's office, the New York City commissioner of investigations, the district attorney of Nassau County, and the district attorney of Manhattan, Frank Hogan, whose office and staff were always most helpful to our committee in all investigations involving New York City.

At any rate, Squillante was in serious trouble at the beginning of June, 1956. He rose to the occasion with an exhibition of executive ability that indicated how he had managed so easily to become the czar of a fifty-million-dollar industry.

First, he called a meeting of the Greater New York Cartmen's Association on June 7, 1956, only eight days before the Internal Revenue Service's deadline. He declared that there was an attack on the entire carting industry. He had the battle lines drawn and the defense forces marshaled.

JAMES KELLY (Committee Investigator): He stated that the only plan of defense was to engage the best legal service, the biggest legal mind. "We do not stand a chance otherwise," was his conclusion. He advised that the members had to be prepared to spend substantial sums of money in order to engage this type of counsel.

He advised that there had to be collective action; all members should forget their own individual problems and band together to meet the attack. He advised that each individual should not wait until he is touched and then attempt to defend himself individually. He called for action along the line of deciding what action should be taken to "defend ourselves."

The reaction was splendid, considering that there were only eight days to go before the tax collector jumped on Squillante. Each cartman pledged $250 for every truck he had wheeling through the city's streets. The money rolled into the association's account at the Royal State Bank of New York. The funds were earmarked, in the language of the meeting that decided to levy them, for these five purposes:

1. For the defense of the association and its members.

2. For the defense of Vincent J. Squillante (in any shape or form).

3. For the defense of any cartman, regardless of membership (if any), area, color, or creed.

4. For publicity, investigations, and research.

5. Toward any charities, for the benefit of mankind.

Once those rules were laid down, Squillante proceeded swiftly to use the money to take care of Purpose Number Two.

Within four days after the meeting, there had been deposited approximately $15,000 in the cartmen's defense fund. On June 14, the officers of the fund made out a check for $14,215.99 to the Royal State Bank of New York. Then the bank, also on June 14, made out a cashier's check in exactly the same amount—$14,215.99. The endorsement on this check, when it was placed in evidence, was written testimony to the ingenuity of Vincent J. Squillante: *Pay to the order of the Director of Internal Revenue, for 1948 and 1949 income taxes, penalties, and interest in full,* [signed] *Vincent J. Squillante.*

The total that was eventually deposited in the cartmen's defense fund was $57,855. Of this sum, Jimmy Squillante used $26,558.08, in order to pay his taxes, penalties, interest, as well as state taxes and penalties and the fees of his attorneys. Part of the defense fund was used to hire private detectives to investigate the Nassau County district attorney and his staff, who were at the time busily engaged in investigating Squillante.

The preceding pages are a summary of the record of corruption in the garbage industry in greater New York. It highlights the criminal activities of Jimmy Squillante, his relatives, and his associates, and the operations of Teamsters Local #813.

While running that local, Adelstein, according to testimony, caused the printing of 10,000 tickets for the local's annual dance in 1957, although the dance hall held only 1,750 persons. Every year enough tickets at five dollars each were sold to bring in as much as twenty thousand dollars. Out of these funds Adelstein bought himself an air-conditioned Cadillac, made payments on a ten-thousand-dollar annuity for himself, and purchased liquor in quantity from a store owned by himself and his wife. In six years of this kind of operation, Local #813 spent fifty-six thousand dollars without any supporting vouchers of any kind, and Bernard Adelstein had full control of this money.

It is significant to note that in five days of hearings on the garbage industry which were held by the Select Committee in the fall of 1957, witnesses testified about a total of fourteen murders with which the racketeers who figured prominently in the testimony were reportedly connected, and that figure of fourteen slayings includes none of those with which Albert Anastasia and his henchmen in Murder, Inc., might have been charged.

Action to clean up the garbage industry was taken by local authorities either before and during the committee's hearings, or shortly thereafter. Jimmy Squillante had pled guilty to federal income tax violations and was later indicted in Nassau County on three counts of extortion. Bernard Adelstein was indicted on two counts of extortion. Squillante has now disappeared, according to police, while Adelstein's conviction was reversed.

By all means it should be further pointed out that the International Brotherhood of Teamsters took no part in curbing the activities of Brother Adelstein, nor was the parent body concerned with the collusion between the union and the Greater New York Cartmen's Association.

Professor Modica was wrong. It was thorns, not roses, that grew out of this garbage.

CHAPTER 10

The Taxicab King of Chicago

I T is unhappily no mere coincidence that the bright investigative lights turned frequently toward the great city of Chicago. The ashes of another era have often burst into flame in that city, from which Alphonse Capone has long since departed, although his rule of a gangster empire and the carnage it wrought have not been forgotten. He and his gangland minions founded and dominated a kingdom of the greatest corruption and the most horrible violence that the world has ever known. Capone reigned by means of terror; his scepter was a Thompson submachine gun, his edicts were announced by bursts of gunfire or by the detonation of "pineapple" bombs. He and many of his associates in crime, his successors and heirs, finally succumbed to rigors of prison, to the bullets of rival gunmen or of officers of the law.

Those who survived him, however, could not forget that period of "golden days" when for a time they were above and beyond the law and utterly defiant of it. They saw the mighty Al take his fall because he sneered at the income tax laws; they learned a valuable lesson from that. The third decade of the century came and went, and with it went the gun-crazed killers of the depression years—the Dillingers and the Floyds and the Nelsons. They blazed briefly across the headlines before they fell to FBI bullets or died in execution chambers. Capone's heirs learned from that era, also. One after another, they found the smoother and more scientific pathways of modern crime and the techniques they use today.

It was still possible to reap the golden harvest as Capone had done, and at the same time evade many risks and penalties that astuteness and shrewdness could circumvent. The new rules were: stay in the shadows, duck the limelight, refrain from pointless violence, adopt modern business methods, maintain respectable business fronts, hire top-notch lawyers and accountants, and with ingenuity and skill devise new rackets of shakedowns, corruption, and extortion. Stay just inside the law if you can, but if you have to step over the line, hide your tracks. And if the so-and-so's down in Washington called you to testify, have your lawyer write out the customary "dodge" on a sheet of paper for you to read: "I decline to answer the question . . ."

Some of the most interesting testimony in the record concerns Joey Glimco, one of Chicago's present-day notorious characters, who was born in Salerno, Italy, in 1909. He was just past voting age when Al Capone went to jail. Glimco couldn't vote, however; he was refused naturalization on November 17, 1932, for want of good moral character. He applied for, and was again denied, naturalization on July 6, 1939, for the same reason. But he was persistent, and when he applied once more in 1943 he was granted citizenship, notwithstanding the fact that his police record in June, 1943, showed thirty-four arrests. He was then assistant business agent of the Taxicab Drivers Union of Chicago, Local #777, of the International Brotherhood of Teamsters.

With all his arrests, Glimco served no time in jail or prison. Among the charges against him were assault with an auto, larceny, disorderly conduct, vagrancy, murder, attempted murder, and robbery with a gun.

In a city like Chicago, with a record like Glimco's, it would not be very startling to find him seeking the company and counsel of the old-timers who had fallen heir to Capone's criminal estate. They obviously accepted him, for it would appear that Joey

Glimco might well have taught them a few new tricks of his own that they had not theretofore known.

At any rate, in the spring of 1959, when he appeared before the Senate Select Committee in his role as head of the Taxicab Drivers, Maintenance & Garage Helpers Local Union #777, International Brotherhood of Teamsters, the following men were named in testimony as some of those who were or had been his associates: Anthony Accardo, alias "Joe Batters," who was an heir to the Capone mantle; Paul DeLucia, also known as Paul "The Waiter" Ricca, another overlord of Chicago rackets; Louis "Little New York" Campagna, whose last will and testament was witnessed by Mrs. Joey Glimco; "Tough Tony" Capezio; Jake "Greasy Thumb" Guzik; Gussie Alex; and Murray "The Camel" Humphreys. When he was asked at the hearings if he knew these men or was associated with them, he replied under oath that to answer might tend to incriminate him.

The record reflects that once Joey Glimco was solidly established in unionism in Chicago, through his position with the cab drivers' local, he launched himself on a shameless career. Upon the death of William "Witt" Hanley, a Teamster leader who controlled the Fulton Street Market in Chicago, Glimco revealed himself as the new boss. He was indicted in 1954 on the charge of extorting money from poultry dealers in the market and was acquitted in March, 1957. The committee testimony disclosed that Glimco was charged with extorting $50 to $60 a week from one Nelson, a scavenger, who collected feathers from the Fulton poultry markets. The hearings further disclosed that another Fulton Street merchant, Sommers Cartage Company, paid some $24,069 to Glimco in a related arrangement and was permitted to operate in the solidly unionized trade with non-unionized employees. The money was collected by a "bagman" named "Big John" Mallec, who stopped at Glimco's union office once a week. When Glimco was absent, a secretary would take an envelope from Mallec and place it on Glimco's desk. Called to testify, the "bagman" took the Fifth Amendment.

In the operation of Teamster Local #777, Glimco had all kinds of deals working for him. The president of the union, Dominic Abata, was supposed to get $175 per week. Payroll vouchers attested to this amount. He actually received $71, and the rest was "kicked back" to Glimco, according to Abata. Five other union officials were required to give up part of their salaries, so that Glimco, who was actually paid $125 per week on the books, was receiving $608 per week from Local #777. To top it all, Dominic Abata testified that he was forced to pay income tax on $9,500 per year, although all he got was $3,500. Mr. Abata got out of unionism for a time to become a delicatessen operator. Abata said: "I batted absolutely zero against him."

In 1959, Mr. Abata came back to lead a rebel movement against Glimco which eventually resulted in the rank and file abandoning Glimco's local, although the national leaders of the Teamsters still stand strongly with Glimco. According to current news dispatches, Hoffa attributes all of Glimco's troubles to "bad headlines." He says that the rebels will perhaps last a year and then ask to return to Glimco's kindly mantle.

At this writing, the rebel group had won contracts with the city's two largest cab companies, and thereupon four taxicabs were dumped into the Chicago River and two others were burned. A Federal District judge called upon the FBI to protect drivers from "terrorism," and he promised to use his powers to ensure that the drivers' rights "be resolved by the court under law and order, and not by hoodlums and gangsters through lawlessness and brutality."

The hearings further revealed that all the local's officials were supposed to get a hundred dollars per month as expense money. They kicked it all back to Glimco—not just some of it, but all of it, according to testimony heard by the committee.

One of the most amazing tales of collusion between union and management was also revealed by Abata's testimony. The Yellow Cab Company and the Checker Taxi Company, during a period of twenty years, most of them while the local was under Glimco's management, had received from the union a total amount of $327,491.46 in rebates of union dues. The committee had never heard of such an astounding practice or transaction. This called for explanation. Mr. Abata said that he'd had nothing to do with it; he had been told by the companies that they needed this rebate in order to pay for the additional help necessary to operate the union checkoff system for payment of employees' union dues.

Investigator Al Calabrese explained to the committee how the system worked. The two cab companies used the checkoff of dues and transmitted the dues to the union in a lump sum. The union thereupon returned a certain percentage, either 7½ or 10 per cent of the total collected. The union members were actually paying back to their employers a part of their wages. The practice was stopped abruptly when the committee's investigators started to work on Local #777.

One effect of all the financial back-scratching in the taxicab local was to make the poor employees, union members all, knuckle under to these schemers. A driver named Louis Linzer was owed $180 by the union for six weeks of sick pay. After a long, patient wait he demanded his money. Glimco threw him out of the union. Then the Checker Taxi Company wouldn't put him back to work, because he wasn't in the union! Linzer was a brave man; he sued for his money and got it. He also got his job back by appealing to the Labor Board.

Another driver named Roy McDowell was owed sixty dollars in sick benefits. He went to see Glimco.

MR. MCDOWELL: . . . Glimco asked me what I wanted, and I said I wanted to get that sixty dollars that is coming to me. He said, "You are going to get a hole in your head if you don't get out here and stay away from here and behave yourself. You are not going to get it."

MR. KENNEDY: What happened after that? Did you ever get the sixty dollars?

MR. MCDOWELL: Yes; I got the sixty dollars through the Yellow

Cab Company. They paid it to keep from losing my wife and myself. My wife was radio dispatcher for them at the time.

The union official who was in charge of health and welfare funds of Local #777, and who should have paid Mr. Linzer and Mr. McDowell the claims they were entitled to, was an attractive young woman named Laverne Murray. She was Glimco's secretary. She came to the witness chair on March 12, 1959, and immediately took the Fifth Amendment when she was asked her occupation:

THE CHAIRMAN: Miss Murray, do you honestly believe—are you conscientious about that—do you honestly believe that if you told what your profession is, what your work is, what your livelihood is, that it might tend to incriminate you? Are you honest about that?

(The witness conferred with her counsel.)

MISS MURRAY: I do.

THE CHAIRMAN: You are? I am sorry for you. Proceed, Mr. Kennedy. It is pitiful, pitiful.

Laverne Murray was shown to be fully familiar with Glimco's operations and to be one of the beneficiaries thereof. For example, she held joint title with Joey Glimco to a house costing $44,000. The builder of this house in a Chicago suburb took the Fifth Amendment on all questions but his name and address. While Glimco took out an $18,000 mortgage, no records could be found of the remaining $26,000 cost. At the same time, the builder was the recipient of $85,325 in union funds for remodeling the offices of Local #777. An expert was put in the witness chair to testify that, with generous estimates, the office repairs and construction would total, including profits, $35,803. Since all participants in the affair took the Fifth Amendment and refused to explain it, about the only conclusion that could be drawn was that the union members paid $26,000 in dues money for Joey Glimco's house.

It was also shown that Laverne Murray had drawn a union check, in her own handwriting, to pay a hotel bill in Los Angeles. The check, for $1,045.65, was drawn upon the checking account of Local #777. The bill included flowers, photographs, and beauty shop services. The registration at the hotel was charged to "Mr. & Mrs. J. Glimco," at a false Chicago address. In the union records, the check was charged to "entertainment expenses." No doubt entertainment may have been involved. Miss Murray refused to explain her presence in Los Angeles as Mrs. J. Glimco.

By this time, the chairman's consideration had lessened, if not evaporated:

THE CHAIRMAN: Are you still working there at this office?
MISS MURRAY: I respectfully decline to answer....
THE CHAIRMAN: Well, if you are, you and Glimco and the whole gang ought to be kicked out, you right along with them.

According to the testimony, Joey Glimco, like many hoodlums in unionism, never used a bank account or drew a personal check. All his expenditures were in cash, and he sometimes went to great lengths to maintain the pattern, even to paying his insurance premiums through a third party. He spent the union's money, however, almost as if it were water from Lake Michigan.

For two and a half years, he kept an apartment at the Oak Park Arms Hotel at seven dollars per day, a total of $6,282.62 that was charged to organizing expenses of Local #777. The local paid one-third of the cost of a dinner for Jimmy Hoffa at the Hotel Fontainebleu in Miami, Florida, and the bill to Local #777 alone for this was $4,289.89. Three officials of the local went on an all-expenses tour of the Caribbean, and that cost the dues-paying members of #777 a total of $1,656. When Hoffa was tried on the charge of bribing John Cye Cheasty of the Select Committee's staff, Glimco and Oscar Kofkin, vice president of #777, lived at the same Washington hotel where Hoffa stayed, the Woodner, throughout the trial, at a cost to #777 of $7,094.55. (When Glimco was losing his rank and file in a rebellion, Hoffa returned the favor, going to Chicago and making thumping speeches for his pal Joey, telling the taxi drivers that it was all McClellan's fault that Joey was in trouble.)

The trial of Joey Glimco for extorting money from the merchants of the Fulton Street Market, according to the findings of the committee, cost the dues-payers of #777 a total of approximately $124,321.45 for attorneys and other legal fees and expenses for Glimco. He was acquitted. Not only that, but Glimco arranged for a private detective named Maurice Adler to investigate the police department of the city of Chicago! Glimco wanted to determine particularly whether the police had dug a tunnel under the offices of Local #777 so that they might tap his telephone. This gesture, seemingly fit only for a television script, cost the union treasury $3,840.

There were countless other examples in the record of the committee of Glimco and his aides siphoning off thousands of dollars of the members' money. There was violence whenever the men threatened rebellion. A cab driver named Everett Clark was beaten up by six men while in his cab at the Northwestern Station in Chicago. A Glimco henchman named Colling told Clark that he would "smear him up." Dominick Abata testified that one of the main reasons he abandoned unionism for the delicatessen business was because his wife was afraid that he would fall victim to the goons.

One taxicab driver was approached while waiting in line at Chicago's Midway Airport. He was shown the roof of a nearby building and was told it would be easy to pick him off from there. He never went back to the airport for fear that someone would carry out the threat.

There were gross malpractices in the administration of Local #777's insurance program, involving hundreds of thousands of dollars on "overwrite" commissions that passed between the Occidental Life Insurance Company and the Dearborn Insurance Agency, certain of whose employees revealed every evidence of collusion with the union in the distribution of the commissions.

Welfare and pension funds have been favorite targets for thieves in the corrupt unions investigated by the Select Committee. And far too frequently, management in the financial institutions involved has either closed its eyes to what was going on or else has quietly co-operated in the plundering.

Joey Glimco's ugly career in the union movement reached its nadir during the fight that began in 1959 for control of Chicago's taxicab drivers, a fight in which the decent working men flocked away from Local #777 to join an independent organization that promised them honest administration. Like a drowning man, Glimco thrashed wildly to save himself. One of his efforts, as the membership abandoned him, was to have Hoffa proclaim that Glimco suffered only from bad headlines, that Joey was a friend and colleague as well as a great union leader.

Another effort resulted in the publication of what was probably one of the most scurrilous "newspapers" ever issued in the United States. Its four issues carried the masthead, *Illinois Teamster News,* and it purported to be "The Voice of Those Who Toil in the Teaming Industry in Illinois."

It blazoned quotes of Thomas Jefferson: "No government ought to be without censors; and where the press is free, none ever will," and of Abraham Lincoln: "Let us have faith that right makes might; and in that faith let us, to the end, dare to do our duty as we understand it." In the light of those two renowned principles, let us examine the filthy nature of the material that Glimco refused to deny under oath that he had published under his warped concept of "freedom of the press."

This travesty of a newspaper was published four times during 1959 at the height of the bitter battle to release Chicago's taxicab drivers from Glimco's despotism. There were 19,339 copies of the paper printed; these were mailed to union members as well as handed out at rallies and to anyone who happened to be passing the distributors on Chicago streets.

What kind of "news" did it print? In the first place, it repeatedly struck below the belt to attack the dissident union members and their leader, Dominic Abata, who had returned from retirement to fight Glimco. It said that he was simple-minded, inept, devoid of judgment, and in one direct quotation, "an idiot." Mr. Abata and his colleagues were obviously considerably more able than Glimco would admit; the revolt was eventually successful, and the rebel faction now dominates unionism in the Chicago taxi industry.

Secondly, the newspaper praised the high moral qualities of Joey Glimco and Jimmy Hoffa. It held up for admiration Glimco's sterling citizenship, which was denied him twice by the United States, his brave fight for unionism, his martyrdom on behalf of the membership, his charities—not mentioning, of course, those private ones dedicated to the welfare of Joey Glimco.

Thirdly, it printed direct, personal, foul attacks upon the chairman of the Senate Select Committee.

Most importantly, however, in a desperate attempt to whitewash Glimco and the Teamsters, and to proclaim Joey as a saint who had been knifed in the back, the paper printed false and slanderous accusations about the motives of the U.S. Senate in authorizing the committee, and about the personal motives of the committee members in their roles as members of the Congress.

For example, here are some lies that the paper printed about the chairman and the Senators on the committee:

. . . the Arkansaw blot shouted the secret oath of the plotters . . . We must pass a law to stop Hoffa!
. . . heavy campaign contributors are putting the squeeze on exalted ward-heelers in Washington . . .
. . . the boys in the back room huddled . . . from the huddle came the infamous "McClellan Committee."
. . . for eighteen months the boloney was sliced . . .

The members of the Senate Select Committee, outraged though they were by such debased language, refused to lower the dignity of the Senate of the United States by getting down into the cesspool to wrestle publicly with the authors of this filthy rag.

Glimco and his man Barker were required to appear in executive session before the Committee, there to deny or affirm that they were responsible for this odious purulence.

Glimco was of course the instigator of the project, but the wielder of the poison pen, a man named George Barker, was listed as owner and publisher of the *Illinois Teamster News* in the application made to the Post Office Department for second-class mailing privileges—an application that the Post Office Department promptly denied.

We know about Glimco. But who was this George Barker, the "editor and publisher" that Glimco hired with thirty-six hundred dollars of union funds to disseminate such putrescence?

George Barker wouldn't tell the committee who he was, or what kind of person he made himself out to be, or why he was qualified as a newspaper publisher. He took the Fifth Amendment.

It would seem that a good qualification for employment by many high Teamster officials is that a man be an ex-convict. Barker was asked about his file #314491 of the Federal Bureau of Investigation. He was asked about his sentence to a term of one year to life in 1930, for burglary. He was asked about being sentenced again in 1933 to life imprisonment as an habitual criminal in the Illinois State Penitentiary at Joliet. We asked if his sentence was commuted to forty-five years in 1948, and if he had been paroled in 1949. He was asked if he had been again sentenced in 1951 to life imprisonment as a habitual criminal. He refused to answer any of these questions. The chairman pressed for answers:

THE CHAIRMAN: You are perfectly willing to be a witness against others, aren't you?

BARKER: I assert my privilege under the Fifth Amendment.

THE CHAIRMAN: When you can hide behind the privilege, you are perfectly willing to be a witness against others. Isn't that correct?

BARKER: I assert my privilege . . .

THE CHAIRMAN: When you do that don't you think that you are kind of a moral coward, when you go out and publish a statement like that and not have the guts to walk in like a man and admit it and say why you did it?

The chairman turned away in disgust. Senator Ervin took up the interrogation of Barker.

SENATOR ERVIN: I would like to ask a question. It has been charged that you tendered a plea of guilty in Illinois to having broken and entered some twenty churches and stolen some twenty poor collection boxes. I wish you would tell the committee whether that is true or whether that report is true.
BARKER: I assert my privilege . . .

There before us sat a man who would not deny that he qualified as one of the meanest thieves in the world—a robber of poor boxes. We turned from him to his employer, who immediately took the Fifth Amendment.

THE CHAIRMAN: Would you employ a known criminal, a known burglar to write and publish such articles as that?
GLIMCO: I respectfully decline to answer . . .
THE CHAIRMAN: Don't you think anyone who would do such a thing and then refuse to acknowledge it is a moral coward?
GLIMCO: I respectfully decline . . .

The Chicago *Daily Tribune* had dug up Barker's record. Its reporter, Sandy Smith, who was given a foul nickname in the *Illinois Teamster News,* confronted Joey Glimco with Barker's prison photograph.

"What's this—a stir picture?" Glimco asked. "I knew Barker was kinky, but I didn't know it was this bad."

Then Glimco, the long-time associate of Capone mobsters, made this incredible statement to the reporter: "I don't want ex-cons around the union. I'll get rid of this guy. I need him like I need a hole in my head. He'll stink me up."

So George Barker, after a fashion, made his mark as one known criminal to whom the doors of the Teamsters Union were finally barred because his criminal record had been exposed. It was a distinction of a kind, for Glimco and his Teamsters Union are not known often to have turned their backs on murderers, extortionists, rapists, thieves, and assorted felons of every description.

There is a brief postcript to this incident. A few minutes after the executive session of the committee adjourned, Barker followed the chairman into another room near the hearing chamber in the Senate Office Building. Barker offered his apologies for what he had published, saying: "Senator, I am sorry I done it. I didn't know about your troubles. If I had known it, I wouldn't have done it. Anyone who has had as much sorrow as you have shouldn't have had a thing like that done to him. I'm really sorry about it, but don't put me back on the witness stand. I just can't swear to it."

As a corollary to the Glimco investigation, the committee also looked into the affairs of Teamsters Local #710, in the city of Chicago, of which John Timothy O'Brien, as secretary-treasurer, was the czar. He had held that office since December of 1922, and had been elevated to the post of second vice-president of the International Brotherhood of Teamsters. It should be remembered that he is the same John T. O'Brien, who, in 1957, loudly proclaimed that he would like to be the knight in shining armor who would lead a crusade to clean up the Teamsters in the wake of the outrageous conduct of Dave Beck. In a short time, however, he did an about-face and linked himself with Jimmy Hoffa. When he testified before the Committee, he was asked what steps he had intended to take to clean up the Teamsters.

O'Brien: I respectfully decline to answer because my answer might tend to incriminate me.

The Chairman: What does a cleanup campaign mean in the

Teamsters? Clean the members out, get their money? Is that what you mean by a cleanup campaign? It looks as if that is what has been going on.

Just what had been happening in Local #710 in Chicago? Let us see. In the first place, for two and a half years the Senate Select Committee heard countless stories of corruption, chicanery, violence, murder, embezzlement, dictatorship, and almost every crime in the book, all within the field of unionism, and of some groups on the management side that, either through voluntary agreement or coercion, participated in those crimes. The committee members thought they had already heard most everything up to March 19, 1959, when the story of the funds of Local #710 was told in full detail. What they now heard seemed absolutely incredible. There was no complicated sleight-of-hand with funds, nor any attempts to camouflage the disappearing money as "entertainment expenses" or "organizing funds," "defense funds," or something else. John T. O'Brien and the other officers just took it. They did have a name for the practice; they said they were paid "commissions" on the dues collected.

Let's look at how it worked. Of every four dollars in dues paid by some fourteen thousand members of the local every month, ninety cents was set aside to be divided up among O'Brien, Frank C. Schmitt, president of the local, and Michael J. Healy, vice president. From every member in every month, there came ninety cents, of which O'Brien was to get 45 per cent, Schmitt 35 per cent, and Healy 20 per cent. How did it work out over a seven-year period?

Let's start with Healy, the Number Three man. The poor fellow was only getting 20 per cent of the rakeoff. In seven years of salary, commissions, bonuses and vacation funds, he rolled up a total of $230,889.87.

Frank C. Schmitt, President, grabbed, in that same seven-year period, a total of $333,925.22.

Finally, the boss of the outfit, John Timothy O'Brien, the

would-be "great cleaner-upper" to follow Dave Beck, took in seven years the grand total of $471,286.11.

There were also payments of $100,174.77 to Frank Brown, retired president of the local.

The total for these four men in seven years, as "commissions" they took from the regular monthly dues of the membership, which varied above and below the fourteen thousand figure, was $1,136,275.97.

SENATOR CHURCH: . . . They take the Robin Hood story and turn it right around. Instead of robbing the rich and giving to the poor, they are robbing the working people and making themselves rich.

I think it is the most shocking disclosure. I just wish that all the working people could know of it in the same detail that it has been brought to light in these hearings this morning.

That was March 19, 1959. At that time, as has been said, John Timothy O'Brien was second vice-president of the International Brotherhood of Teamsters. He no longer holds that post. *He is now first vice-president of the International Brotherhood of Teamsters.* That was a deserved promotion, no doubt, by International Teamster standards.

CHAPTER 11

Said the Pieman...
"Show Me First Your Penny"

THE efficiency of modern methods of racketeering has been demonstrated in the lucrative fields of Chicago restaurants and taxicabs and in the garbage industry in New York. The hoodlums studied their lessons well, used their enforcement weapons sparingly, and were able to plunder honest union members and honest businessmen almost at will. In effect, the hoodlums used the trappings of respectability, disguising their evil deeds by giving themselves some of the labels so common nowadays in corporate structures—calling themselves "educational directors" and "labor relations counsels" and "efficiency experts." They used credit cards and expense accounts and electronic business machines to give their stealing the aura of rectitude and responsibility.

The sleekness of their operations did not go altogether unnoticed in the labor union movement. Many among the most reputable of labor leaders were shocked to observe what was going on. The AFL-CIO set up its strong ethical practices code in an attempt to stop the crooks. Forthright union leaders were appalled at the waves of extortion, kickbacks, briberies, "sweetheart" contracts, and criminal activities of all kinds that rocked the foundations of a certain minority of American unions.

Since the end of World War II, labor leaders like George Meany, president of the AFL-CIO, and others have taken strides in repairing and maintaining the integrity of the labor union movement. They threw some unions out of their councils; they advised others to correct corruption immediately or suffer the same penalty; they seemed to be ready to clean their own houses. Some of their measures have been effective. Some have not. From evidence given before the Select Committee, there are some unions that have hardly lifted a finger to throw out the racketeers that infest them. The notorious example, of course, is the Teamsters.

In assessing the multitude of facts presented over the past several years both the Senate Select Committee and Permanent Investigations Subcommittee have been keenly aware of the dangers of generalization. Much that is shameful and unsavory was uncovered about the behavior of certain elements in both labor and management. This kind of information was necessarily spotlighted, but this has never been done with the intention to reflect on the great majority of the labor unions and businessmen of this nation of whose integrity we have always been firmly convinced. For example, it is our observation that most of the country's labor unions are operated by dedicated men whose lives have been spent honestly and productively in the cause of unionism.

The gangsters worked hard to corrupt many unions, but there were some that needed no gangsters. Their leaders were able to observe and then emulate the racketeers' methods. They did the job of corruption by themselves, without any help from outside. They probably started by looking enviously upon the shadows of unionism where the gangsters burrowed and tunneled. Then these so-called labor leaders began to move slowly but surely toward that periphery of crime; they were not appalled, but instead, they were attracted.

Just as the mobsters put on the pressure to force their way into decent unionism, securing one beachhead after another, so some union leaders studied the tactics and procedures of men like John Dioguardi and Jimmy Squillante, and they perverted the Biblical words of Luke: *Go, and do thou likewise.*

To put it another way, the gangsters had always carried an aura of evil, and they were clever enough to cloak it with a veneer of virtue; on the other hand, there were union leaders who came to office garbed in the honored traditions and just practices of generations of predecessors, and they made use of them to cover up crime and injustice.

To round the picture of gangsterism under the guise of unionism, therefore, we should take a look at what went on behind the façade of one of America's oldest and most respected labor organizations: The Bakery and Confectionery Workers International Union.

In the city of Chicago in 1955, one of the local unions that bargained for the makers of the city's bread, bagels, spaghetti, macaroni, biscuits and rolls, pies and pastries, and dozens of other products, including candy, was Local Union #100, led by Gilbert Mann, who had been an officer of the local for eighteen years. Mr. Mann was sixty-nine years old in 1955 and had been in the bakery industry for fifty-seven years. On January 21, 1955, he walked into his office and discovered that he was out of a job. The international union had charged him with certain offenses. They involved financial matters, and to tell properly the story of the Bakery Workers Union, it is necessary first to discuss the charges against this elderly man who had been a union member and officer since boyhood. The charges were prepared by the union's attorney and put to Mr. Mann as he sat before the Select Committee. He answered each as it was asked.

The first charge of those that cost him his job involved the drawing of his salary in advance. He admitted that he had done this once, with the approval of his executive board.

The second charge concerned his car. He admitted that the union bought him cars from time to time, eleven of them in eighteen years, but that he signed a document which provided that upon his death or removal from office, the ownership of the car reverted to the local union. The purchase of cars for union executives is a general practice throughout the country.

He was charged with setting up an illegal health and welfare fund with a Chicago firm. He answered that it was not illegal; that it was a fund for that company only and run by the employees, and that the local had nothing to do with it.

He was accused of using union funds to pay large motel and hotel bills, which included bills for liquor. He said that he did spend money during negotiations, and he cited some examples.

Perhaps Mr. Mann, after so many years in office, was somewhat careless in managing the local; perhaps his long stewardship was not a marvel of meticulous administration.

This must also be said about the affair, however—Mr. Mann came before the committee and spoke freely, while the man who threw him out of office at the point of a gun took the Fifth Amendment.

Here is the way Mr. Mann told the story:

MR. MANN: Well, conditions were that I came into my office on January 21, 1955, and one of the vice-presidents, George Stuart, was there with an auditor, who told me he would like to ask me a few questions . . .

He was sitting behind my desk with a gun. It was my gun, he had taken it out of the drawer, left there by my brother while he was in the hospital . . .

He told me that I must resign and he showed me a telegram from the president of the Bakery and Confectionery Workers International Union where he had been placed in trusteeship . . .

So far, except for the gun, the case of Mr. Gilbert Mann looks pretty much like an ordinary union problem, to be settled by the international with the imposition of a trustee upon the local until its affairs are straightened out. The trusteeship, a device whereby an international union may take over the management of any of its locals that run into difficulty, is certainly not a rare practice in unionism. However, the case of Gilbert Mann deserves closer attention. Let us once again take up Mr. Mann's testimony:

MR. MANN: . . . He just told me I was through. He promised me
fifteen weeks of pay, and I told him that I had no money and
that I owed on my home, fourteen hundred and some dollars and I said I would like—or I think that I gave the union
service and I have organized every one of these shops and I
have been here for eighteen and a half years and I should have
some kind of compensation.

But he said he would give me fifteen weeks' pay and give
me an insurance policy for the rest of my life, health and welfare. Well, I felt that was that, and so he took the keys out of
my overcoat and took my car and sent someone home with me
and that was that.

I had no right to trial, and I had no right to nothing and I
was broke and I had to live. I applied for my social security,
which was ninety-eight dollars and fifty cents, and he came out
to my home on Sunday and he said he would take a mortgage on
my home and reduce my payments, and I could not meet them
on seventy-eight dollars a month and he said the union would
probably take care of it.

Asked about the salary for fifteen weeks, Mr. Mann testified
that he never received it. Asked about funds for pension and welfare, Mr. Mann testified that he never received them. Asked about
the payments on his mortgage, Mr. Mann testified that he was
unaware that the $50 he paid each month on his mortgage found
its final resting place in the personal bank account of George
Stuart, international vice president and trustee of Local #100.
Asked if he had ever received anything from the Bakers Union
after eighteen and a half years of service, Mr. Mann testified that
officers of several locals had taken up a collection and given him
$376, and that he was very grateful for it. All those years, and
Mr. Mann had no savings or income, and he was booted out of his
job and forgotten, excepting for his regular monthly payment of
$50 into Stuart's personal bank account. Compare Mr. Mann's con-
dition with Dave Beck's affluence in the city of Seattle, where,

before he went to prison, he managed to scrape by on his pension of $50,000 annually from the Teamsters.

Sad? Perhaps. Pitiful? Maybe.

Well, as Al Jolson used to say, "You ain't heard nothin' yet."

What happened in Bakers Union Local #100 *after* Gilbert Mann was bounced into the street? George Stuart was the trustee for that local, and for Local #300 in Chicago. The rest of the story is set forth as it appears in the record of the committee.

Stuart set up an organizing fund of $10,500 to unionize the Salerno Biscuit Company. Most of the fund disappeared, and there are no known reports to the international concerning such an organizing drive. Not only that, but George Salerno, president of the company, said that he'd never heard of any attempts to unionize his employees. It was a pretty quiet drive.

Local #100 also appropriated $13,100.18 for a joint organizing venture with Teamsters Joint Council 43. That money went for new Cadillacs for Stuart and for the international president, James G. Cross, of whom much more later. A few months later, the union bought another Cadillac for Stuart. He traded it in for a Corvette and put the price difference in his pocket. The year before that the union had bought him a Buick for $2,396.80, and again, a year previously, he'd been given another Cadillac for his devotion to duty and the sacrifices he'd made in taking over the trusteeship. Sacrifices, surely—he had to make frequent trips from Kansas City, where he lived, to Chicago in order to collect the loot.

There were lesser matters that came under Stuart's position of trust and responsibility: $278.17 for an air conditioner ordered for the union offices, but somehow shipped to Stuart's home in Kansas City; $780 for a pearl necklace and earrings; $470 for a cocktail set and two pairs of gold cuff links; $450 for three suits and an overcoat; $539.32 for a bed and high-fi phonograph; $2,591.48 for cameras and equipment. He had a free hand with gifts, also—all paid for by the union.

Bad enough? Perhaps. Crooked enough? Maybe.

But let's go a little further. Let's take a look at James G. Cross, president of the Bakery and Confectionery Workers International Union.

Before studying the man himself, it would be wise to examine his union. It was founded in 1886 and had a long and distinguished history as one of the oldest and most firmly established labor unions in the nation, with 319 locals and a total membership of more than 160,000 in 1956. Small in comparison to giants like the Teamsters and the Steel Workers, the United Mine Workers, and the United Auto Workers, it nonetheless is a very important union. Its membership supplies a large part of the nation's bakery products.

The union once had a splendid record for integrity in the safeguarding of its members' interests. As late as 1952, James G. Cross, the secretary-treasurer of the international, wrote in the Bakers and Confectioners Journal this statement of union principle:

Our organization retains the basis of pure democracy, even more so than the Nation itself. We vote directly for the candidates, where in the Nation we vote for electors pledged to vote for certain candidates. We maintain more democracy than many labor unions who elect their officers by the votes of the delegates at their conventions.

Four years later, in 1956, when Cross was president, the fate of the "basis of pure democracy" might have been foretold in Psalm CIII: *The wind passeth over it, and it is gone; and the place thereof shall know it no more.* For on the floor of the San Francisco convention of the union, James G. Cross used his power to help destroy any vestiges of the democratic process that might have remained in the organization since he took command from former president William Schnitzler in 1953. Formerly, international officers had been elected by secret ballot of the rank and file. In 1956, they were nominated and elected on the floor by the delegates at San Francisco. Secret balloting was called a "definite waste of the membership funds." (Mark those words well!)

The constitution of the union was changed at the convention to prohibit challenges of delegates to future conventions.

Robert's Rules of Order was cast aside as the guide to questions not answered by the constitution. Cross was quoted on that ruling: "Parliamentary procedure was made for Senators, not bakers."

It was agreed that salaries of international officers were to be fixed henceforth by the executive board instead of the rank and file; three-quarters of the executive board had their own salaries fixed by the president. You scratch my back, and I'll scratch yours!

Immediately after the adjournment of the convention, the executive board boosted Cross's salary from $17,500 to $30,000. Cross then gave varying increases to the executive board.

Finally, the delegates gave Cross the sole right not only to select international representatives, but to remove them. Again, it should be pointed out that they comprised 75 per cent of the executive board. The entire operation was reminiscent of the United Textile Workers, where Klenert and Valente completely controlled the same kind of board by power over their economic destinies.

The power grab was a personal triumph for the man who had started his association with the union as a pan greaser and fruit cook. Now he stood alone at the pinnacle, and his word was law to the multitudes below him.

He had the power, and he used it.

There had been attempts to protest against the dictatorship. A delegate from New York, Joseph G. Kane, was one of the protestors. It didn't do much good. "Every time we got up we got booed," said Mr. Kane, "practically off the floor . . ."

Being known as a dissenter was dangerous. Early in the morning of October 21, testified Mr. Kane, Cross and Stuart and two men named Gardone and Mykalo came to his room at the Olympic Hotel in San Francisco. They got into the room through a friendly telephone call from Stuart. They proceeded to beat Kane up, or in his words, "President Cross decided to give me a working over, which he did."

International vice-president Stuart seems to have been fond of guns; he held one at Kane's back while the four men marched him to the Fielding Hotel, where they went to the room of another protester, Louis Genuth:

MR. KENNEDY: Was he beaten up?
MR. KANE: Beaten up by both Cross and Stuart.
MR. KENNEDY: Did you go anywhere else?
MR. KANE: Well, George showed the gun again and moved us along to the Cliff Hotel, where we went to the room of Mr. and Mrs. Nathan Ehrlich, and both of them were beaten up.

The victims got a few licks in while the Ehrlich beatings were going on, because Mrs. Ehrlich managed to get the phone off the hook, whereupon the male victims piled into the goons.

"I hit Cross once," Mr. Kane said. "That was enough." Senator McNamara asked if Cross went down. "He picked up a bottle to hit me," Mr. Kane testified, "and Ehrlich took the bottle out of his hand, and after that he ran down the steps."

A San Francisco grand jury went into the matter. Cross said that he hadn't even been in the fracas; he hadn't been there. The grand jury did not return an indictment, but declared that the case was rife with perjury.

Cross told the committee: "I was asleep in my room."

The committee heard testimony that once the dictatorship was established at San Francisco, James Cross proceeded along a wild, if rather brief, career as czar of the nation's bakers.

In the year 1956, he received $17,500 in salary. His expenses, paid by the union, reached the astounding total of $39,682.55. Of this amount, $9,667.39 was directly billed as travel and hotel costs. The remaining $30,015.16 included all other items. There was a total of $25,102.10 for entertainment, dinners, birthday parties, gratuities, and personal expenses, but there were no bills or receipts of any kind for the vouchers he cashed. The committee took a close look at some of his jaunts and jollities.

He went to Portland, Oregon, from Washington, D.C., in October, 1955. That cost the dues-paying members $962.53 for two days in Portland and one night in Los Angeles.

He went to New York for the merger meeting of the AFL-CIO. That cost the members $4,069.75 for a ten-day trip, including $214 for twenty-two Rose Bowl tickets which he bought in New York, and a $130.13 item for a hotel room which was used by the executive board, Cross said, for playing poker. He went to Miami for six days in February, 1956, and that cost the membership $2,980.15. He drove his car to Florida for that visit, and the motor journey cost the members an additional $1,079.58. He took a six-day trip to London and Paris (on union business, of course) in 1956, accompanied by his wife and daughter. That cost the members $4,261.48. He went to Florida again in January and February, 1957—that state must be jammed in midwinter with union officials all on union business at the height of the season—and that cost the working bakers a total of $4,431.17. The last item included a hotel bill of $331.31 for accommodations for Elsie K. Lower.

Who was Elsie K. Lower? Cross told the Select Committee that she was a union organizer. She told the committee that she was a union organizer. She had various names: Kay Lower, Elsie K. Lower, and Mrs. E. K. Thorpe.

She admitted to the committee that she had done very little organizing indeed. She had been to Van de Kamp's Bakery in Los Angeles once or twice and said that one visit was to apply for a job. Then she admitted that she had talked to only one employee in all the months that the union was paying her bills. He was the head baker, "a very good friend of mine."

MR. KENNEDY: Can you give us his name?
KAY LOWER: I can't even remember. He is a Mexican fellow. He is married to a woman named Margie. That is all.

She had made one or two visits, had talked to the head baker, and she couldn't remember his name. She was a union organizer.

Now let us consider how well informed she kept her employer of that visit to one bakery.

James Cross testified that Kay Lower was in Portland, Oregon, where the union paid her bills, to report to him on the Van de Kamp organizing campaign. She was in Miami on two occasions to report on the Van de Kamp campaign. She went to New York City with him to talk about the campaign. She was with him in Ottumwa, Iowa, to discuss the same matter, and in Denver, Colorado, for the same reason. The union paid for airline tickets and all expenses for these reports to Cross.

There were telephonic messages, also, between Kay Lower in Los Angeles and the international union's offices in Washington. There was about twenty-three hundred dollars' worth of phone calls that the members paid for so that she could report to Cross about what the head baker said.

Cross explained to the committee that when these phone bills were protested by Secretary-Treasurer Curtis Sims, he put his personal check for twenty-five hundred dollars into the treasury to pay for the phone calls. He wanted to explain why he did this, when she was simply reporting on union matters:

CROSS: The daily newspapers had already smeared me with a relationship which was not true, and rather than have the organization exposed, I remained silent and took the blame and returned the check.

Finally, Cross told the committee that Kay Lower no longer held her position as union organizer.

Curtis Sims, who protested the phone bills, wasn't neglected by James Cross. The counsel for the union, an attorney named Herman Cooper, testified that at Cross' request he had prepared a document that suspended Secretary-Treasurer Sims, before Mr. Sims' charges against the malpractices of James Cross had been placed before a meeting of the executive board. Senator Ervin commented with a quotation from a seventeenth-century English poet named William Browne:

SENATOR ERVIN: To my mind, it is sort of similar to the Lidford
    Law. . . .
COOPER: I am unfamiliar with that, sir.
SENATOR ERVIN: Listen and you can hear about it.
COOPER: I will be happy to learn.
SENATOR ERVIN: You may not have heard of it, but you seem to
    be familiar with it. "I oft have heard of Lidford Law, how in
    the morn they hang and draw, and sit in judgment after."

There were other matters of paramount interest to the committee and to the public in the affairs of the bakers' union. For
example, as disclosed by the hearings, Cross moved into a threatening strike situation in Chicago and perpetuated a substandard
contract with Zion Industries, Inc., against the wishes of the union
members who worked for Zion. They had to get along with the old
contract, because Cross prohibited a strike against Zion. It was not
incidental that Cross had been obligated to the ownership of Zion
Industries (Martin Philipsborn, Sr., and his family) for a total of
$112,700 in mortgages and loans.

There is every reason to believe that James G. Cross and his
henchmen almost destroyed the venerable union which, although
no giant, had enjoyed seventy-two years of progress in the American labor movement.

The Bakers Union tottered and almost fell with the impact of
the body blows from Cross. The AFL-CIO threw the Bakers out of
its organization because of the corruption that Cross brought into
the union. A rival labor group was formed within the AFL-CIO,
and tens of thousands of members of the Cross union went grate-
fully into its membership. The original union was reduced to a
shell of itself. It did not die, however, as well it might have after
Cross and Stuart and their cronies had departed.

The damage was severe, and it has taken years to repair. At a
Cleveland convention earlier this year, some good evidence was
shown that the union is on its way back to integrity. The delegates listened to a rousing speech by the self-designated savior

of the labor movement, Jimmy Hoffa. He urged them to affiliate with the Teamsters as a subsidiary of that titanic organization. Hoffa is busily engaged these days in trying to build a combine that will be able to challenge the AFL-CIO. He approaches many of the unions that have been tossed out of labor's councils for corruption or Communism. The delegates at the Bakers' convention turned him down flatly with a thumping two to one vote. Then the delegates elected officers. The remnants of the Cross machine were defeated by another two to one vote, and a reform administration was elected. The new officers immediately announced that they would seek reconciliation with the dissident bakers and confectionery workers who had flocked to the new union set up by the AFL-CIO, and then they would petition to be returned to the ranks of decent unions in the house of labor.

PART THREE

CHAPTER 12

Punishment Without Crime

MUCH of the record of the two-and-one-half years of hearings on criminal activities in the labor-management field was necessarily devoted to the crimes and to the criminals, as they were detailed by witnesses whose testimony was corroborated by overwhelming evidence that was gathered, evaluated, interpreted, and submitted by the committee's staff. The ugly record of corruption that drew no punishment still heavily outweighs the unhappily slender file of convictions and sentences that have been handed out in the federal, state, and local courts of the nation. The guilty scoundrels who have avoided just retribution are still free because of many varied reasons—statutes of limitations that prevented prosecutions, apathetic or venal officialdom, the inadequacy of laws pertaining to their violations, brilliant legal maneuvering, lack of witnesses through fear or bribery, cynical misuse of the Fifth Amendment, outright perjury, and dozens of other factors that frequently operate to give aid and comfort to criminals in our free society.

The record of crime without punishment bulks large in the history of the Select Committee, as it does throughout the nation in these critical decades. Side by side with the accounts of multitudes of unpunished crimes, however, are fixed indelibly some hundreds of pathetic stories of the abuses, indignities, and outrages that were piled upon the innocent. There have been thousands of victims of the criminals—millions if we count all the union members whose union treasuries have been robbed. These victims directly suffered injustices and injuries without ever knowing why they were singled out for punishment. Among them were unwitting and guileless workingmen, businessmen who were powerless to protect themselves, and citizens who were struck by hardship, savagery, and violence without ever having had any connection with unions or management. Some of them were people who never saw their tormentors and never even knew their names.

If one were to file these cases separately, that file might well be labeled *Punishment Without Crime.* As in the days of the bootlegging barons, when violence was spewed from careening cars in a lethal spray of bullets from submachine guns, so in modern racketeering many innocent victims have been struck down, sometimes in the literal meaning of the phrase, without even knowing what had hit them.

There was a fourteen-year-old boy in Los Angeles who was a dutiful son—he tried to carry out the instructions of his father, a bakery owner. He was told to carry baked goods into an establishment that was being struck by the Bakery Workers Union. The goon squad beat him severely. As a witness described it, ". . . Frank Gordon went up to the boy and started pummeling him, and Mr. Nelson ran over to the car and grabbed the blackjack and went over and hit him on the head. They did not quite finish the boy . . ."

The manager of a Florida hotel was another victim. He had the misfortune to take as guests the Teamsters' prize roughneck, Barney Baker, and his sidekick, Tom Burke. The manager somehow made the mistake of arousing the antagonism of the two goons. The results were a disgusting illustration of vicious cruelty. A witness told the story: "Well, he was an old man, and he wasn't really too capable of running the hotel, and they didn't like the way he treated them. Mr. Burke said that he could have him fired, and he did, in a few days."

Getting the old man released from his job wasn't enough for

these two hoodlums. They had to work another trick on him before their taste for sadism was satisfied. Burke said that he would fix the old man's car for him. Shellac in the crankcase will ruin the motor of any vehicle. The witness concluded the story: "Pretty soon I heard the car would not go, and it was backfiring and everything, the poor old man."

In Scranton, Pennsylvania, a man named Anthony J. Ruby wanted to build a new house. He shopped around for good bids and then hired a contractor named Edward Pozusek, from nearby Wilkes-Barre, to come to Scranton with his crew and equipment to put up the building. Soon enough, representatives of the Scranton Building Trades Council showed up on the job, asking Mr. Pozusek: "Who the hell allowed you to come here to Scranton to build?"

Mr. Pozusek told the committee his reply: "Mister, it so happens I am American born, and I am allowed to earn a living in any part of this country as long as I earn it legally." He was given an ultimatum: "Well, you can't do that in Scranton. You will just pick up your tools and get the hell back to Wilkes-Barre where you belong. You are going to get trouble over here, and you are looking for it and you are going to get it." What was the difficulty? Mr. Pozusek's carpenters and laborers weren't union men.

Mr. Pozusek got his trouble, and so did Mr. Ruby, the owner. The partially finished house was blown apart by dynamite.

Scranton is a fine, progressive city whose businessmen and decent citizens deplored the reign of terror conducted by some of the city's unions acting in concert. Here are some of the acts of violence that went unchecked and mostly unpunished before the goons were stopped by outraged civic action: a contractor who opposed union demands had sugar poured into the fuel tanks of his heavy equipment; a dairy concern had kerosene dumped over the milk and butter in one of its trucks; a nonunion driver had his windshield smashed and his truck stoned; a construction company that employed only forty-five people was picketed by three thousand men, some of whom were armed with guns, clubs, and iron rods. The vehicles of this firm were sabotaged; wires were pulled out of motors, tires deflated, and trailers were uncoupled and dropped to the ground. One nonunion driver was hoisted out over a bridge railing and was shown "the bottom of the river."

These acts of violence were all committed in the name of unionism, and their victims were almost always innocent people who had no power to protect themselves against the goon squads.

In the hearings devoted to organized violence in Tennessee and adjacent states, the committee heard investigators LaVern Duffy and James McShane testify to 173 separate acts of labor violence, of which only eight had resulted in court action of any kind.

Let us consider a few of them—a few picked at random, for a thorough examination would take an entire volume. A taxi driver was hit with a beer bottle and then beaten with a motorcycle chain; a truck owner-operator was beaten so severely that he was laid up for at least two years; a truck driver was ambushed on the highway and had his elbow blasted away by a shotgun. These three men had committed no crimes, either in the eyes of the law or in the eyes of society. They simply maintained their American rights of independent thinking and dissent.

Dozens of trucks in Tennessee had their fuel tanks contaminated with sugar and sirup; tires were slashed; the number of dynamitings was literally beyond count.

Bob Caldwell, who drove a truck in Knoxville and didn't want to join a union in order to keep his job, went to a ball game one night. His car, parked outside his house, was blown to bits. What crime had he committed to be punished so severely? All he had done was assert his right to earn a living as he chose.

There were scores of other acts of violence, turned up in sickening detail by Investigators Duffy and McShane and graphically described to the committee, but let us just pick one more that happened in Tennessee—the case of a businessman who had not only committed no crime but didn't even know that he had made a serious mistake in the eyes of the Teamsters. All he had done was hire a nonunion driver on a temporary basis. The victim was Frank Allen, terminal manager for the Terminal Transport Company in Nashville. He was visited by W. A. Smith, widely known in the hoodlum circles of the Teamsters as "Hard-of-Hearing Smitty." Smith was assistant business manager of Teamsters Local #327, and was notorious for his viciousness in an organization where brutality is commonplace.

MR. ALLEN: I thought they were leaving at that time, and I stood up at my desk and was looking at some papers on the desk, and then I looked up and Mr. Smith, W. A. Smith, was right in front of me. He said something to the effect, "Take your hand out of your pocket," and then he hit me across the face.

MR. KENNEDY: Then did he continue to hit you?

MR. ALLEN: Yes; the first blow knocked me—I didn't know too much what I was doing.

MR. KENNEDY: Senseless?

MR. ALLEN: Senseless, in a manner, yes; and he continued to hit me. I was trying to avoid the blows.

THE CHAIRMAN: What condition were you in when he left?

MR. ALLEN: I was in pretty bad shape. My nose was bleeding. He struck me across the side of the face and the nose, and I was bleeding from a cut over my eye. I was very dizzy and sick at my stomach . . . The doctor sewed my eye—above my eye— and then later on that afternoon I went to a hospital. I was X-rayed, and there were several bones broken. My nose was broken on that side. I stayed in the hospital about one week.

Shades of the Gestapo and the storm troopers of Hitler's Germany! It turns a man's stomach to read it again. Another man who was beaten viciously by Smith and his goon squad lost his mind as a result of the bestiality. Smith was convicted and sentenced to a term of two to ten years.

Naturally, the reader tells himself, when news of the actions of this depraved person reached the marble palace in Washington, W. A. Smith was summarily fired from his job as a Teamster official. Think again! Remember that this was the man that Hoffa said he needed to "kick the hillbillies into line."

Nine months after the testimony about Smith's foulness, Hoffa was asked if he hadn't thrown this brute out of his union.

MR. KENNEDY: . . . he has just been sentenced from two to ten years and he is still business agent of Local 327, and you haven't taken any steps against him?

HOFFA: You are right.

Nineteen months after the testimony about Smith's foulness, Hoffa was asked by Investigator Duffy if he had thrown Smith into the outer darkness, and Hoffa's comment was that Smith had "negotiated a number of favorable contracts for the union."

Men are scarred for life, punished without ever having committed any offense, maimed and broken by a debased man, and Hoffa's Teamsters pay the costs of his trial.

At the moment of this writing, Hoffa stands charged with fraud in the so-called "Sun Valley" scheme to sell building lots in Florida to guileless Teamsters who had hoped to retire there in their old age. Some of the men who bought the lots, and their wives and families, believed that they were making a wise investment because they were told, "Jimmy says it's a good deal."

On and on the record goes, chronicling the chicanery—one of the favorites was the extortion of money from employers for testimonial dinners and lavish gifts for union leaders. This is one of the penalties that many men must pay because they are forced to do business with union racketeers.

Another example of how innocent people suffered punishments without reason is found in the story of Mike Singer, Teamster official in Los Angeles. Singer was once sent to Hawaii as personal representative of Hoffa; he took his girl friend with him, and the union paid her expenses. In an organizing maneuver in Honolulu, Singer cut off the milk supply for the islands for two days. Think about the babies, the young people, the infirm who depend upon a daily supply of milk for their health and well-being. Singer's Hawaiian efforts, however, as the committee heard, were only incidental to his main occupation of harassing and intimidating businessmen on the mainland.

In the city of Los Angeles, a voluble man named Morris Gurewitz was in the rendering business for twenty-three years. This is not the most pleasant occupation in the world, since it involves buying kitchen greases and processing them, as well as dealing in chicken feathers and in the offal that is discarded by poultry packagers.

Mr. Gurewitz ran a modest business reasonably well until he ran into the racketeering tactics of Mike Singer, business agent of Teamsters' Local 626-B. The first time Mr. Gurewitz met Singer was when a picket line was thrown around his plant and the union leader came upstairs to talk about a union contract.

"Unfortunately," Mr. Gurewitz told the committee, "I am one of these ulcer babies, and I couldn't take it much more, and so I said, 'Well, let us get this thing over and we will get a suit of clothes out of the deal and forget it.' And so we finished the deal, and I bought Mr. Singer and Mr. Grancisch a suit of clothes, which cost me about $350, which I couldn't afford to pay for."

That wasn't Mr. Gurewitz's last dealing with Singer, who took over the grease business entirely. When Mike Singer called a meeting of the industry in Los Angeles, the owners of the grease companies all attended, or else they might find that they were out of business for several weeks as a punishment. Mr. Gurewitz graphically described his race to attend one of Singer's frequent meetings: "I traveled seventeen miles to my home because I couldn't go up there with the stinking clothes I had on. I take my clothes off in the back room when I get home, and my wife threw some food on the table, and I gobbled that up after I had showered and rushed back and got there at seven-fifteen, I think, that evening, and this particular man was sentenced to six months. He was completely out of business and he is out of business to this day."

That was the method by which Mike Singer kept the grease dealers in line with trials during which he was both judge and jury. But Mr. Gurewitz's troubles didn't end with $350 tailor bills and threats to close down his business. He discovered that he was to be one of the generous donors of a fine new 1959 Oldsmobile to Mike Singer.

Mr. Gurewitz's contribution, he was told, was to be $1,000, and he paid it with a check for $334, another for $333, and a third for $333. Other grease dealers put up large amounts until there was enough to purchase a brand new car, for which Mike Singer offered his own 1955 Oldsmobile in trade, being allowed $1,100 as a down payment. To add the grossest insult to the meanest kind of injury, Mr. Gurewitz saw Singer riding in the new car about two weeks before he was visibly surprised to receive it at a testimonial dinner given in his honor. Jimmy Hoffa was the guest speaker at the dinner. Mr. and Mrs. Gurewitz had to buy tickets to the dinner to watch Singer happily receive the gift for which the money had been extracted from the dinner guests. As Mr. Gurewitz told the committee, ". . . that was the highest-priced squab my wife and I ever ate in our life."

The story should have ended there, but it didn't. Committee Investigator Pierre Salinger, now press secretary to the President, took up the financial trail of Mike Singer's new Oldsmobile:

MR. SALINGER: This automobile was totally wrecked in Roanoke, Virginia, on January 8, 1959. At that time, the driver of the automobile was identified as Mrs. Pat Harrington, who gave the address 507 North 19th Street, Montebello, California, and described in the insurance reports as a friend of Mr. Singer's. . . . There is a statement made by Mr. Singer to the investigators for the insurance company that, "This vehicle originally cost him five thousand six hundred dollars.". . . As a result of the accident

and the total loss thereon, the insurance company made out a
check to Mr. Singer in the amount of four thousand six hundred
and ninety-eight dollars . . .

Singer was later indicted by a Federal grand jury and convicted under the criminal provisions of the Sherman Antitrust Act.

Another favorite extortion racket, which operates in the guise
of a legitimate business enterprise, is the solicitation of advertising
for various obscure journals and newspapers supposedly representing the interests of good unionism. The committee heard
advertising salesmen for such publications, who testified that
their sales message was little short of direct gouging of money
for worthless advertising, cloaked in polite and businesslike language, but leaving no doubt about the veiled threat. One such
advertising space salesman knew the name of the labor organization he was working for, but he had never met anyone connected
with it, nor did he know its aims and purposes.

Gangsters and goons were endlessly at work, the committee
found, in almost every area of union activity, persecuting people
who were unable to fight back. Whether smoothly, like the bag-
men who picked up contributions for testimonial dinners, or
violently, like the goons who pushed a St. Louis taxicab into the
Mississippi River, they dealt out punishment with complete disregard of decency. They drove small businessmen to the wall with
exorbitant demands; they insisted on kickbacks of all kinds and
shakedowns of every imaginable type. They dealt in "sweetheart"
contracts that the union members were never told about, and
secondary boycotts that put men out of work for weeks and
months at a time.

All of these activities are crimes that generally went unpunished, but sadly, they are also "punishments without crime"—
penalties and suffering for innocent folks who had no recourse.

On September 14, 1959, President Eisenhower signed Public
Law 86-257, officially known as the Labor-Management Reporting
and Disclosure Act of 1959, popularly known as the Landrum-

Griffin Act. It was a well-intentioned step upon the part of the Congress to put an end to the abuses reported in sickening and malodorous detail by the Senate Select Committee. It was a partial answer to the cries for justice raised in the two hundred thousand communications received by the committee—an answer that may correct some of them, and may deter many criminals from committing others.

The Labor Reform Act should have some favorable consequences on the social, political, and economic life of the nation, if it is properly enforced with the kind of vigilance and vigor that is needed against the corrupt forces who seek to circumvent it. At best, however, it is only a single step toward the goal of eliminating corruption on the titanic scale that the committee revealed. While its passage was a victory for honesty in unionism, not enough time has gone by to determine its maximum effectiveness. It should have been stronger, more resolute, with strict enforcement provisions.

It must be admitted that the Congress showed very little taste for the job of stepping into an area that labor itself declined to do much housekeeping in, and during the first session of the Eighty-sixth Congress most legislators continued to approach the issue of labor reform timidly, haltingly, and seemingly without determination and firmness of purpose. One gained the impression that many men believed that if they closed their eyes, the criminal activities that demanded correction would somehow fade away and disappear.

There were certainly members of Congress who wanted a very mild bill, or better still, no bill at all. There were a few who insisted on a measure so strong it would have no chance of passage.

The majority of the members of the Senate and of the House of Representatives, however, wanted to pass a law that would be fair to both labor and management, as well as a law that would correct the evils that the investigations had chalked up against both of them. In summary, we worked for a bill that would provide the needed remedies, and most importantly, would restore integrity and justice to the labor-management field wherever they had been denied or destroyed.

In the meantime, as is customary in Washington when important legislation is being considered, intense lobbying activities and all manner of pressures were brought into play in a sustained attempt to influence the Congress to lean strongly one way or the other. On the one hand, the National Association of Manufacturers and the Chamber of Commerce of the United States were trying to focus attention upon some of the more prohibitive proposals, which would result in an attractive position for management. On the other hand, the AFL-CIO was stressing the virtues of the "do-it-yourself" philosophy of cleaning up the corruption and eliminating iniquities. Some unions, notably the Teamsters, turned tremendous artillery on any and all suggestions for labor legislation. They wanted none, and in colossal arrogance the Hoffa crew said no reforms were needed.

Members of the Congress were told that if they were too harsh in their judgments, they could expect political reprisal from labor at the polls in the 1960 elections. They were also told that if they supported a mild bill, they could look forward to union votes in their next campaigns.

There was a long period of uncertainty. No one could be sure whether Congress was going to yield to the powerful pressures, or whether it would resist intimidation, face up to its duty, and enact the kind of law that was needed. There was a strong factor in favor of the passage of a resolute measure—the wide and voluble popular support that came from people in all economic and social strata of the country.

The Labor Reform Act that was finally passed, however, is not as strong as it should be. Well-intentioned though it may have been, it is far from adequate. It is not sufficiently strong to stop all venality in the labor movement or in the business firms that deal with unions. Even without the advantage of the passage of time needed to judge the law's effectiveness, it can be said that it is not strong enough to do the job that must be done.

Nonetheless, if its provisions are correctly interpreted and applied as Congress intended them to be, then the crooks and the racketeers will have a tougher row to hoe. They will no longer be able to abuse power and betray trust with the arrogance they displayed in the past. If the law is observed, and if it is properly and vigorously enforced, the gangsters will have to leave the labor movement; the pickings will be too slim for their greedy appetites and the penalties too great for their sufferance.

Let us consider one section of the law, that dealing with the procedures for the imposition and administration of trusteeships, as well as the penalties for violation.

The law provides that every labor organization which assumes trusteeship over any subordinate labor organization shall file with the Secretary of Labor within thirty days, and semi-annually thereafter, a report signed by the president and treasurer, as well as by the trustees, which contains the following information:

1. The name and address of the subordinate organization.

2. The date of establishing the trusteeship.

3. A detailed statement of the reason or reasons for establishing or continuing the trusteeship.

4. The nature and extent of participation by the membership of the subordinate organization in the selection of delegates to represent such organization in regular or special conventions or other policy-determining bodies and in the election of officers of the labor organization which has assumed trusteeship over such subordinate organization. Each individual signer of such reports is held under the law to be personally responsible for the statements made in it which he knows to be false.

The penalty for violations of any of the requirements is ten thousand dollars, or one year in jail, or both.

That sounds strict enough, and it should effectively correct one of the greatest grievances of the committee's correspondents over the years. When abuses occur, the regulations should stop them immediately. But will they? At least one veteran observer of cynical perjurers and callous owners of poor memories doubts that many individual signers of such reports will be held "personally responsible" for false statements. The enforcement provisions in that section and throughout the law are simply inadequate to do the job properly.

The Landrum-Griffin Act was, however, a step in the right direction. But it is imperative to remember that the foes of labor reform are politically powerful. They are militant in opposition to the execution of the law. They make every effort to hinder and obstruct its enforcement, to impair its effectiveness, and to discredit its probity. There are big unions with great resources whose publications have made continuing and unrelenting attacks upon the law. They seek to prejudice the public and rouse their members by means of false slogans and labels.

Even though the law isn't strong enough, it is a just and fair measure. Yet it has been called "anti-labor" and a "union-busting" act. Its enemies say it is a "killer." They may be right—it was intended to be a killer of some racketeering practices.

Its provisions make it an "anti-" law, all right, but it is not "anti-labor."

If it is executed with strength of purpose, it can be "anti-" a few other things:

Anti—gangsters, goons, racketeers, and hoodlums.

Anti—theft, embezzlement, shakedown, blackmail, and extortion.

Anti—arson, acid assault, vandalism.

Anti—violence, brutality, cruelty.

Anti—dictatorship, boss rule, oppression, exploitation.

There are few pieces of legislation, however, that are effective only in their negative approach. The positive measures are just as important. In this law they are probably the strongest provisions, if they are enforced. They are the rights that follow:

The right of union members to equal treatment, to free speech, and to free assembly.

The right to invoke the protection of the law, to be free from arbitrary and unjust union discipline, and to be free from threats or acts of violence.

The right to participate in the nomination of union officers, to participate in deliberations of union business, and to vote in elections by secret ballot for union officials.

The right to control the use of union funds, to inspect records, and to receive copies of collective bargaining agreements.

The right not to be harmed by other people's labor disputes, to seek the redress of grievances, and the right to be free from domination by convicted criminals, crooks, and Communists.

Those are the Bill of Rights provisions in Title One of the law, and they came directly from the work of the Senate Select Committee. These provisions are the targets of the opponents of the law, as are the secondary boycott regulations in Title Seven of the Act and those provisions against organizational picketing, hot cargo contracts, and the "no man's land" section.

There are labor leaders who contend that the intent of the law is punitive. They say it is vindictive, repressive, and restrictive. They are wrong. The record proves it. The provisions are not punitive; they are protective. They are not vindictive; they are vindicative. They are not repressive; they are progressive. They are not restrictive; they are restraining, but only to the extent necessary for the establishment of equality, freedom, and justice.

The claim by some labor bosses that the Bill of Rights provisions were never needed is completely put to shame by the record as revealed in the volumes of evidence before the Senate Select Committee. Almost every evil imaginable is to be found indelibly written in the twenty-thousand-plus printed pages. It is a source of personal pride to be the author of the Bill of Rights Title in the Labor Reform Act.

The reason for writing the Bill of Rights section is found in the answer to this question: "Why should any citizen of this great country of ours be compelled to leave the rights, the freedoms, the protections guaranteed to him by the Federal Constitution outside when he enters a union hall—any union, anywhere and any time? Why shouldn't these rights and protections serve and attend him when he is at a union meeting?"

The Labor Reform Act was intended to safeguard the working-man's rights and privileges, as well as those of businessmen and citizens in all fields of endeavor. Strict enforcement is vital to the law, and it should be provided. It's a good law; it only needs more teeth.

CHAPTER 13

Three Years of Arduous Labor

THE tremendous volume of work that went into three years of Select Committee hearings is best demonstrated by some facts and figures that highlight the long and arduous effort to provide information upon which the Congress might base its legislation in the labor-management field. It should be borne in mind that the statistics relate only to the Select Committee, which functioned from January, 1957, through January, 1960, and not to the Senate Permanent Subcommittee on Investigations, which has its own records and statistics.

There were 270 days of public hearings, 1,526 witnesses, and a volume of testimony that is an amazing tribute to the work of the committee members and the capable staff—46,150 pages in the typewritten record, and 20,432 pages in the relatively small print to which the testimony was reduced in government records. There were 343 witnesses in three years who took the Fifth Amendment, roughly one witness of every five. The staff grew prodigiously as the volume of work piled high; it reached a peak total of 104, including clerks and stenographers and personnel borrowed from other government agencies. The work week grew as the effort mounted—nights and weekends belonged to the job.

Consider some other figures that demonstrate the work done in three years: 128,204 photostated documents; 2,500,000 miles of travel by plane, train and auto; 253 active investigations; 8,000 subpoenas; 19,000 field reports; 90,000 index cards on individuals and corporations.

A single book like this one could not attempt to cover, for example, the myriad details of the 253 active investigations carried out by the staff. Three years of steady operation provided far too little time to give intensive hearings to more than a small fraction of all the cases in the files, yet none of the investigations were fruitless. Even those cases that never reached the hearing stage provided rich corroborative detail upon which the committee based its recommendations for legislation. There were many cases that will not be discussed in this book, which were gathered in detail and did prove to be of tremendous value.

In Scranton, Pennsylvania, the committee heard details of a calculated reign of terror controlled by the leading officials of two of the city's key labor groups—the Teamsters and the Building Trades Council. These two groups sanctioned, directed, and often participated in acts of intimidation and property destruction against the citizens of their own city. There were several convictions in a dynamiting case, all of the culprits being union officials. There was violence of many kinds, together with its usual corollaries—conflicts of interest, lack of disciplinary action by the international unions involved, lack of action by the local officials in cleaning their own houses, and, inevitably, apathy in the local rank and file with its resultant evils of rigged elections and multiple voting. Fear of beatings and other violence of course contributed to the membership's failure to act against corruption.

And, as the committee reported to the Senate, "One final fact should be recorded in the Scranton story. Not one of the union officers or members convicted in a court of law after a trial by jury has been subjected to any sort of disciplinary action by their unions to this day ... [but] were feted at a testimonial dinner designed to raise funds for their defense in the dynamiting conviction."

The case of the New York City "paper locals" of the Teamsters

Union brought to the fore the suave, smooth, and polished figure of Johnny Dioguardi, who one day in the corridor of the Senate Office Building turned into a snarling image of vicious rage as he punched at a photographer who sought to take his picture. Hoffa helped Johnny Dio in order to help himself; he aided Dio in trying to take over the campaign to organize the New York taxi drivers, and he supported Dio and Anthony "Tony Ducks" Corallo in their attempts to grab control of Joint Council #16 of the Teamsters. It was quite evident that this was done in order to back Hoffa's climb to power in the international. Dio and Corallo had brought forty hoodlums into the labor movement with them— men with records of 178 arrests and 77 convictions for crimes that included theft, narcotics trafficking, extortion, conspiracy, book-making, stinkbombing, assault, robbery, accessory to murder, forgery, burglary, and other felonies.

It was during the hearings on the New York "paper locals" that Hoffa had his longest and most astonishing losses of memory, when he was forced to sit and listen to tape recordings of phone calls between himself and Dioguardi concerning their collusive drive to capture Joint Council #16. In one committee session, Hoffa pleaded loss of memory a total of 111 times.

In commenting on these seven phony locals, the committee said, ". . . working by themselves, such racketeers as John Dio-guardi and Anthony Corallo present a dangerous enough prob-lem, but when they have the backing of top officers of the nation's largest union, particularly James R. Hoffa, now its general presi-dent, the situation becomes one for national alarm."

The International Union of Operating Engineers was an ex-ceedingly nauseating example of dictatorship and corresponding corruption. The hearings examined the affairs of five big locals that govern the economic welfare of the men who run heavy equipment on construction projects in the areas of San Francisco, Long Island, Philadelphia, Newark, and Chicago. It didn't seem to make any difference which local the committee had under scrutiny; all of those examined were evidently rotten to the core. The following findings were the most important turned up by the investigations:

Democracy was practically stamped out. Only 46 per cent of the 280,000 members could vote, and the privilege may not have done them any good at that—rigging of elections was common.

The abuse of the principle of trusteeship was flagrant and wide-spread. Two Chicago locals were under trustee management for about thirty years. Such locals had their treasuries systematically looted.

There was much collusion between union officers and management executives, all to the disadvantage of the rank and file.

Conflicts of interest were prevalent, with union officials openly entering business contracts with management.

The usual fiscal malpractices common to unions in which corruption is deep-seated were outrageously evident in the Operating Engineers, with vast sums going for extravagant entertainment and luxurious living for union leaders.

In sixteen years of dictatorship, William E. Maloney, czar of the Operating Engineers, became a wealthy man. He had the advantages of a yacht and several chauffeured limousines; he had luxurious homes in Miami and Chicago; he had the use of a splendid apartment in Washington. Maloney never came to testify, although he was repeatedly asked to do so; he claimed ill health, and shortly thereafter he retired on a pension of fifty thousand dollars from the union. One of the deals he would have been asked to testify about was his relationship with Stephen A. Healy, head of one of the country's largest contracting firms. Mr. Healy appeared and took the Fifth Amendment when asked to explain what he did with more than two hundred thousand dollars in company funds which were listed as a nondeductible business expense.

Consider Maloney's income tax returns. During the period 1950 through 1956, they reported earnings of some $388,000 in salaries and expenses from the union. That is an astronomical figure for any labor leader, no matter how rich his union, but the committee investigators testified that the true figure was some $742,000, and that Maloney had understated his income by more than $353,000.

Then there were the DeKonings, father and son, who handled Local #138 on Long Island as their private property, ruthlessly smashing opposition, often with violence. Members who objected to tyranny were faced with expulsion and loss of their jobs. Both DeKonings were indicted on about one hundred counts of extortion and coercion; the father served a jail term, the son was placed on probation with the stipulation that he stay out of organized labor for a year. After the year was up, he was again president of the local.

The Detroit overall supply industry gave the committee one of its prize packages in demonstrating how thoroughly a group of gangsters can dominate a single commercial field. Some of the most infamous figures of the Detroit underworld were the financial backers of the Star Coverall Company. They didn't have to work alone to grab the business of honest enterprises; they had the active aid and comfort of Herman Kierdorf, ex-convict in the employ of the Teamsters. They all used pressure to insure a swift rise in a highly competitive industry. Kierdorf's intimidation of Detroit car dealers to force them to use his racketeering coverall service was brazenly continued even during the time that he was called to testify before the Select Committee, and it continued after he returned from Washington.

Unhappily, supposedly honest businessmen in Detroit were glad to go along with the racketeers, since Kierdorf promised them that they would not have to do business with the union. The committee, in reporting on these hearings, stated that "it is this type of activity by so-called reputable businessmen that prevents a cleanup of union racketeering and a halt to further underworld encroachment on legitimate business."

A startlingly similar case, but one of much greater magnitude, was discovered in the extensive investigations and hearings on the coin-operated machine industry, commonly referred to by the staff as "the juke-box case."

In dramatic sequence, witness after witness testified that a national industry had been heavily infiltrated by racketeers. From thirteen different states in the nation, the committee heard that the underworld controlled tremendous segments of the coin machine business, and the names that appear in the record are the same names that were repeated again and again during the Apalachin hearings. In one city after another, the hoodlums muscled in—and the names were familiar ones by that time to the Senators on the commitee: Eddie Vogel in Chicago; Longy Zwillman and Gerardo Cetana in New Jersey; John Vitale in St. Louis; Joe Salardino in Denver; Frank Zito in Springfield; Jake Guzik in Chicago; Meyer Lansky, "Buster" Wortman, Jack Dragna, Frank Costello, and Carlos Marcello. Every new witness brought familiar names and stories of familiar methods—intimidation and violence.

Assistant Counsel Arthur G. Kaplan, an expert on the coin machine field and its racketeering elements, told of investigations in at least eighteen cities:

MR. KAPLAN: . . . One of the very significant characteristics of the entire industry is the permeation of racket figures in it. No matter where you go, you are almost certain to find that leading operators in various areas are hoodlums, and they are people with racket connections and they are people with police records . . .

MR. KENNEDY: Is it also correct that probably the top hoodlums and racketeers or members of the underworld in the United States over the past twenty years have been in the coin-operated business?

MR. KAPLAN: I think we could establish almost every major racketeer.

In its findings, after two years of continuing investigations and several weeks of hearings, the committee made sixteen major points about the coin machine industry, declaring it dominated by gangsters in certain areas, pointing out that labor unions and their officers dealing with the field are either corrupt or spineless, and finding widespread apathy on the one hand and collusion on the other in respect to law enforcement officials, who have in many areas served to help drive out of the industry the honest businessmen who refused to pay tribute to the racketeers.

The committee emphasized these points by saying that "with notable and few exceptions, the efforts of honest employers, employees, labor officials, and public officers have not contained or restrained the spreading control of these mobsters, nor the increasing threat they pose to the legitimate merchandise vending business, which as yet seems to be comparatively untainted."

This far along, it is probably child's play for the reader to guess which union and its officers were mentioned most prominently throughout the involved hearings about gangster methods and tactics in the coin machine industry. Probably only one guess is necessary. The correct answer: The International Brotherhood of Teamsters.

There were extensive hearings on Nathan Shefferman and his labor relations outfit and its tie-ups with the truckers' union. There were outrageous disclosures about Local #707 of the Teamsters in Philadelphia—during a long series of hearings it was testified that a group of greedy, unscrupulous officers had grabbed control of the local and held it tenaciously, by means of intimidation, threats, and physical violence. It was further shown that these men beat down any democratic forces that threatened revolt, using terror and brute force, and that they proceeded to drain the union treasury of large amounts of cash.

There were important and extensive hearings on secondary boycotts employed by labor unions—again principally the Teamsters —and on the "hot cargo" clauses in Teamster contracts with employers. These hearings, the committee was pleased to observe, led directly to the provisions in the Landrum-Griffin Act dealing with the evils resulting from application of these two procedures in labor affairs.

The committee also went deeply into the twin problems in New York City that involved the great metropolitan daily newspapers, and the record showed: (1) the exposures of gangster infiltration and dominance of the newspaper and magazine distribution business by influencing union officials; and (2) reported payoffs made to union officials by news publications who sought union peace by yielding to shakedowns and extortion. (Once more the venal coalition was revealed: hoodlums, collusive management, and union leaders, all working together.)

Finally, there was another group of hearings that temporarily threatened the accord and close-knit structure of the bipartisan committee. These probes, centered on the activities of the United Auto Workers, AFL-CIO, were principally concerned with the Kohler strike in Wisconsin, the strike against the Perfect Circle Company, and the activities of Local #12, UAW, in Toledo, Ohio, and its leader, Richard T. Gosser. In the reports and findings submitted to the Senate, there were strong separate views. One set of reports and findings was approved by Senators Kennedy, Ervin, Church, and McClellan. Another set of reports and findings was submitted by Senators Mundt, Goldwater, Curtis, and Capehart. In addition, the four Democratic members split two by two to prepare and submit separate views on the Kohler and Perfect Circle strikes; one set of separate statements was reported by Senators Ervin and McClellan, another set by Senators Kennedy and Church.

In summary of this problem of diverging opinions, which often provided warm discussions during executive sessions, the chairman of the committee was impelled to make a separate statement to the Senate, which is repeated here so that the reader may understand that all of the three long years did not proceed in perfect harmony and concord.

SEPARATE STATEMENT OF SENATOR JOHN L. MCCLELLAN

As chairman of the committee, I think it proper for me here to state that the foregoing UAW-Gosser investigation was conducted by the Republican members of the committee and their counsel; also that the subsequent executive and public hearings were held at the request of Senator Curtis. All subpenas for witnesses and documents requested by him were issued by the chairman.

The witnesses, however, were not examined by the regular members of the staff, nor were the Democratic members of the committee made acquainted by Senator Curtis, or other Republican members of the committee, with the nature of the testimony that was to be presented. All documentary evidence which had been procured by Senator Curtis and by subpenas issued by the Chair was withheld and kept secret from the Democratic members and the regular staff of the committee until actually presented at the hearings.

Thus, this particular investigation was conducted by the Republicans and the hearings thereon were held for their accommodation. Therefore, they are entitled to all credit and chargeable with all blame for the adequacy or inadequacy and for the character of the record made, which record now speaks for itself.

Senators Kennedy, Ervin, and Church joined and concurred with the chairman in the views expressed above.

With that exception, the committee members worked together for three long years of arduous labor. There naturally developed some differences of opinion among our members. It is, however, both remarkable and commendable that so little friction did arise, and that a vast amount of the committee's work proceeded smoothly. That it did so is attested by the record produced, upon which the Congress might depend for drafting the legislation needed to correct the terrible abuses that were exposed.

The roll of the committee should be called once more, since there were changes in the original membership of the Select Committee, which began its duties with Senators Kennedy, Ervin, McNamara, and McClellan on the Democratic side, and Senators Ives, Mundt, McCarthy, and Goldwater forming the Republican contingent, with Robert F. Kennedy as Chief Counsel. Senator McCarthy died in office, and he was replaced by Senator Carl T. Curtis of Nebraska. Senator McNamara resigned from the committee, and he was replaced by Senator Frank Church of Idaho. The late Senator Ives, who was vice chairman, left the Senate at the expiration of his term in January, 1959, and his place was taken by Senator Homer E. Capehart of Indiana. Mr. Kennedy resigned as chief counsel in September, 1959, after splendid service and a brilliant record, and his place was taken by his capable assistant, Jerome S. Adlerman.

The staff of the committee, loyal and persevering and devoted, deserves the nation's gratitude. Each staff member has always had the thanks, deep appreciation, and respect of the chairman.

CHAPTER 14

"I Decline to Answer..."

Persons who have been shocked by the testimony, and at times by the lack of testimony, from witnesses at the hearings often ask why the Congress doesn't do something to curb the willful abuses of the Fifth Amendment Constitutional privilege. About 22 per cent of the witnesses who appeared before the Select Committee took the Fifth Amendment. Many of them would tell only their names and addresses and would then decline to answer any further questions. There were a few witnesses who answered some questions and then took the Fifth Amendment on all others.

Many of these un-co-operative ones were obviously attempting to hinder and obstruct the committee in its efforts to get at the truth, more so than they were seeking to protect themselves against self-incrimination. Thus the frequent and flagrant abuse of the privilege attracted such widespread attention and concerned interest that many citizens viewed the ugly spectacle as a national scandal. The use of this device became the subject of many newspaper editorials and cartoons. Television and night-club performers carefully worked the accepted declaration into their routines: "I decline to answer the question on the grounds that it might tend to incriminate me."

Most of our citizens have little to do with Congressional hearings and with courts and judicial proceedings, and therefore they do not always have a clear understanding of the Fifth Amendment, nor do they know its wording, its history, and the broad concept of freedom and justice that it projects.

The amendment was submitted to the people with nine other amendments at the first session of the first Congress to convene under the new Constitution. (All of the ten were adopted and came into effect on December 15, 1791.) Its provisions go to the heart of Anglo-Saxon justice as it developed in Britain during centuries of struggle by brave men against their oppressive rulers —rulers who grossly misused the great powers of nobility and government which they possessed. Its ideals crossed the seas with our ancestors who settled this land, and the principles it declares and vouchsafes to us are now an integral part of our heritage. Its safeguards are the proud possession of free men—they were designed and developed to protect freedom. This is the Fifth Amendment:

No person shall be held to answer for a capital, or otherwise infamous crime, unless on a presentment or indictment of a Grand Jury, except in cases arising in the land or naval forces, or in the Militia, when in actual service in time of War or public danger; nor shall any person be subject for the same offence to be twice put in jeopardy of life or limb; *nor shall be compelled in any Criminal case to be a witness against himself,* nor be deprived of life, liberty, or property, without due process of law; nor shall private property be taken for public use, without just compensation. [Italics mine.]

The language has a splendid dignity, and its meanings should be as clear and appropriate today as they were in 1791. Our deadly enemy, the international Communist conspiracy, provides no such magnificent foundation upon which to establish either freedom or justice for the victims of its enslavement. This nation stands in glory upon its Constitution. The efficacy and grandeur of that sacred document should be, by resolute purpose and dedication, steadfastly strengthened and preserved, and not be whittled at or hacked away by expedient interpretation or by reckless tinkering and irreverence.

Misunderstanding and controversy do not apply to the entire Fifth Amendment, but only to that clause of it which guarantees that "no person . . . shall be compelled in any Criminal case to be a witness against himself." Perhaps other portions of the Fifth Amendment are more important, but none of them have been or are now the subject of controversy in the same degree as the privilege against self-incrimination, nor have any of them been the subject of so much confusion.

A few personal views cannot put an end to all argument about the Fifth Amendment, but there are some things that seem clear, and if they are plainly said, they may be helpful toward an understanding of the issue.

The privilege against self-incrimination lies in the broad area covered by the term "constitutional rights." All too often, we think of our constitutional rights as "something for nothing." We act as though, having done nothing to get them, we need do nothing to keep them. We seem to consider that they cost nothing, and that they entail no obligations on our part.

I do not take the position that it is possible to speak too often or say too much about constitutional rights; the point is rather that not enough has been said about the duties of citizens under the Constitution. Blackstone's *Commentaries on the Laws of England,* written in 1793, makes these points on the rights and duties of citizens:

The rights of persons that are to be commanded to be observed by the municipal law are of two sorts: first, such as are due *from* every citizen, which are usually called *civil* duties; and, secondly, such as belong *to* him, which is the more popular acceptation of *rights* or *jura.* Both may indeed be comprised in this latter division; for, as all social duties are of a relative nature, at the same time they are due *from* one man, or set of men, they must also be due *to* another. But I apprehend it will be more clear and easy, to consider many of them as duties required from, rather than rights belonging to, particular persons. Thus, for instance, allegiance is usually, and therefore most easily, considered as the duty of the people, and protection as the duty of the magistrate;

and yet they are, reciprocally, the rights as well as the duties of each other. Allegiance is the right of the magistrate, and protection the right of the people.

As a related general proposition, the United States has the right to the testimony of every citizen. And every accused person has the right to the testimony of witnesses in his defense.

One great writer on the law of evidence, Dean Wigmore, many years ago expressed the opinion that in preserving the Fifth Amendment privilege ". . . we must resolve not to give it more than its due significance."

His further words are directly pertinent to the discussion of the use of the Fifth Amendment before congressional committees, and they should be quoted:

We are to respect it rationally for its merits, not worship it blindly as a fetish. We are not merely to emphasize its benefits, but also to conclude its shortcomings and guard against its abuses. Indirectly and ultimately it works for good,—for the good of the innocent accused and of the community at large. But directly and concretely it works for ill, —for the protection of the guilty and the consequent derangement of civic order. The current judicial habit is to ignore its latter aspect, and to laud it undiscriminatingly with false cant. A stranger from another legal sphere might imagine, in the perusal of our precedents, that the guilty criminal was the fond object of the Court's doting tenderness, guiding him at every step in the path of unrectitude, and lifting up his feet lest he fall into the pits digged for him by justice and by his own offenses. The judicial practice, now too common, of treating with warm and fostering respect every appeal to this privilege, and of amiably feigning each guilty invocator to be an unsullied victim hounded by the persecutions of a tyrant, is a mark of traditional sentimentality. It involves a confusion between the abstract privilege—which is indeed a bulwark of justice—and the individual entitled to it—who may be a monster of crime. There is no reason why judges should lend themselves to confirming the insidious impression that crime in itself is worthy of protection. The privilege cannot be enforced without protecting crime; but that is a necessary evil inseparable from it, and not a reason for its existence. We should regret the evil, not magnify it by approval.

Today there is a school of thought in this country which holds that the Fifth Amendment privilege against self-incrimination should be abolished by constitutional amendment, on the grounds that it somehow clashes with the goals of insuring national security and protecting the public against crime. This is not an acceptable concept. To argue it is to argue that there can be instances in which protection of the public or insurance of the national security demand that an individual be required to incriminate himself. To accept this theory—without, at least, the substitution of some other equally efficacious safeguard, if one can be devised—would be a step back toward the rack and the wheel, the red-hot tongs and the "Iron Maiden."

There is entirely too much temporizing neutrality about the Fifth Amendment. All too many laymen—and also too many lawyers—seem to be afraid to appear either too strongly for or too strongly against the Fifth Amendment. This misses the point that the Fifth Amendment is a part of the Constitution. The privilege against self-incrimination is an absolute privilege. It cannot be overridden. It can be satisfied (as by a valid immunity statute) in such a way as to secure needed testimony while protecting the witness against possible prosecution; but this is a recognition of the privilege, not a defeat of it. A constitutional privilege cannot be defeated or denied. And we must not be "neutral" with respect to a constitutional privilege. We can in conscience only support and defend it. Such support properly may, and should, include opposition to any *misuse* or *abuse* of the privilege. We must always try to be honest in distinguishing between abuse of the privilege and its proper use by some individual or in some connection which we oppose. And we must not blame the privilege for the fact that it is abused or misused.

There have been many occasions when witnesses have refused to answer questions, claiming privilege under the Fifth Amendment, when they were either clearly or probably not legally entitled to do so. These witnesses had no legal right to "take the Fifth" either because they did not honestly believe that a truthful answer might lead to prosecution for crime—perhaps because there was nothing for which they could be prosecuted—or because the facts were such that the question could be answered truthfully without revealing any incriminating information. But the fault in any such case lies, obviously, with the individual who has improperly claimed the privilege, not with the Fifth Amendment clause under which the privilege is claimed.

In my judgment, the problem faced by congressional committees, and indeed by all law enforcement agencies, lies not in the wording of the amendment but rather in the strained and too liberal interpretation that the courts have given to its language. The erroneous construction placed upon it by the judiciary has broadened its meaning and extended its application much beyond its original concept and intent.

The abuse of the privilege of declining to be a witness against oneself, as it is done capriciously and with lack of good faith, could be denied by the nation's courts whenever they judiciously observed that the proper interpretation and application of the letter and spirit and intent of the Constitution had been violated.

In most of the incidents before the Select Committee in which the spirit and intent of the amendment seemed to be clearly controverted, the offending witness was not in danger of being a witness against himself, but rather was obviously declining to answer for the purpose of withholding information from the committee. It was not always easy to make a ruling governed by the concepts of justice and fair treatment when the witness was arrogant and contemptuous of the proceedings.

It was committee policy and staff procedure to interview witnesses privately concerning indictments and other pending criminal processes in which they were involved, but to avoid interrogating witnesses during public hearings on such matters. Indicted witnesses most always followed the advice of their at-

torneys and refused to answer all questions except those concerning their names and addresses.

There was rarely an un-co-operative witness who appeared
without an attorney to advise him. Unfortunately for the job of
exposing crime and corruption, most of the attorneys suggested
to their clients that to give any answer beyond name and address
might very well open avenues of inquiry in which the witness
would, by previous answers, have waived any further right to
hide behind the Fifth Amendment privilege. Thus attorneys
usually advised that the safe thing for the witness to do was
simply to invoke the Fifth and not answer any questions at all—
and that they did. Attorneys believed they were fully justified in
so advising their clients, since court decisions in recent years had
indicated that this was a wise procedure to follow in order to
avoid a Congressional citation for contempt for refusal to answer
pertinent questions. In practice during hearings, this procedure
often sent temperatures toward the boiling point, because all too
frequently the Fifth Amendment was improperly asserted simply
as a subterfuge to avoid giving any testimony.

In December, 1957, the committee heard a Teamster goon
from Tennessee claim the privileges of the Fifth Amendment with
a contemptuous sneer. This man had engaged in arson, beatings,
dynamiting, and throwing rocks through windows. The Chairman
insisted that the man, in order to invoke the privilege and demonstrate good faith, had to say that he honestly and sincerely believed
that if he gave a truthful answer to the question asked, such truthful answer might tend to incriminate him. If his refusal to testify
could not be based upon an honest belief that his answer might
incriminate him, then it was doubtful that the privilege could
properly and legally be invoked. The Chairman continued, "This
country could become a jungle so far as civilization is concerned—
racketeers, gangsters, thieves, thugs, crooks taking over this country. You couldn't do anything about it through law and order.
We would all have to resort to the bullet and to the dynamite and
to the knives that cut tires. We would all be forced to take that

measure of defense for our own lives and for the protection of our property and our loved ones. I would like you to think about it and see if you want to be in that kind of a group." The witness still refused to answer most of the questions.

Another procedure that the committee insisted upon if a witness intended to take the Fifth Amendment was that he do it himself and clearly state his intention. He could not claim the privilege by proxy, in his attorney's voice. This was sometimes difficult to accomplish, as in the case of a Detroit man who was involved in the exploitation of a prize fighter named Embrel Davidson, whose career was promoted with Teamster funds until Hoffa and Brennan discovered that he wasn't a world-beater. The Detroiter, a man who was identified as a leading trafficker in narcotics, claimed his English was too poor to make his meaning clear. His attorney volunteered to translate. This was unsatisfactory, since the committee's staff knew that he had been born in Pennsylvania, had lived in Detroit since 1929, and could speak English quite fluently whenever he wished.

THE CHAIRMAN: The Chair won't hold him to exact language, and if he says, "I refuse to be a witness against myself," that is sufficient in his case ... We can't accept the invoking of the Fifth Amendment by proxy. We are sure he intends to do it, but intending to do it doesn't put it in the record. Doing it makes it a matter of record.

The committee, in a few instances, reported resolutions of contempt to the Senate, citing certain witnesses for frivolous, capricious, and irresponsible use of the Fifth Amendment, and prepared contempt proceedings against them for action by the Senate, in the hope that the nation's courts would clearly define the limitations that could be set upon the use of the privilege. Senator Ervin, after listening to Dave Beck, Jr., refuse to answer whether he knew Dave Beck, Sr., declared that the procedure was becoming a travesty, adding that "if the Fifth Amendment did not have a lot of vitality, it would have been worn out by this procedure."

Severity of language and strong admonitions were not always effective countermeasures for cynical and stubborn refusal to testify. They often brought only sneers and cold contempt to the faces of some witnesses, particularly among the overlords of crime who sat brazenly reading the words their attorneys had written for them. "I decline to answer the question ..."

An interesting and challenging alternative to the use of contempt citations has been suggested as a method of determining whether the letter and spirit and intent of the Constitution has been violated. Both the Senate and the House of Representatives have certain inherent powers that have been rarely used in the modern history of the Congress, but they exist and they could be invoked. To raise the question of the abuse of the Fifth Amendment and to place it squarely before the courts in a proper case, either body of the Congress could call upon its own power to punish contumacy by imprisonment.

Let us use the Senate as an example. A Senate committee could cite a witness for contempt. He might then be called before the Bar of the Senate, where he would be asked the same questions put to him at a committee hearing. If he then still refused to answer, the Senate, by majority vote, could issue orders to the Sergeant at Arms to arrest and imprison him for his contumacy. This procedure would then force the offending witness to be the "moving party" to get his case into the courts by means of a writ of *habeas corpus*. The judiciary would then have before it the direct issue of the abuse of the privilege of the Fifth Amendment, rather than the customary issue, which is the much broader fundamental question of whether the Fifth Amendment privilege was available for the use of the witness.

Every lawyer recognizes that the privilege against self-incrimination, under the Fifth Amendment, is an expanding concept. It has been broadened in numerous ways since the Bill of Rights was adopted as a part of our Constitution, and this expansion has been accelerated by decisions of the Supreme Court in recent years. We may not agree with all that has been done in this process of expansion; but we must accept at least a substantial part of it, because there seems to be, at present, no practical way to reverse the process.

The narrow issue of whether the term "criminal case," as used in the Fifth Amendment, is broad enough to include legislative investigative proceedings has never been placed squarely before federal or state supreme courts for decision. However, the language of majority opinions rendered in the Supreme Court of the United States clearly indicates that should that precise issue be presented for decision, that particular court would rule that the term "criminal case" and "legislative proceeding" would have the same status in the application of the privilege against self-incrimination.

Speaking about an early case in which the privilege against self-incrimination was invoked, Chief Justice John Marshall said: "In such a case the witness must himself judge what his answer will be and if he says on oath that he cannot answer without accusing himself, he cannot be compelled to answer." In an 1892 decision, the Supreme Court extended the definition of the term "criminal case" to allow the privilege to be invoked by a witness at a grand jury investigation. In 1913, the Supreme Court ruled that the privilege was properly used by a witness in a civil proceeding, and again in 1920, the Court extended it to a witness appearing in any official investigation. Three more recent decisions of the Supreme Court, two in 1955 and one in 1957, held that a witness before a legislative committee was clearly entitled to claim the privilege.

In spite of the very substantial expansion which has taken place in the concept of the privilege against self-incrimination, and which has had the sanction of the highest court, we do not have to accept every theory that is advanced which would broaden the privilege.

For example, there is a body of opinion which holds that the

Fifth Amendment somehow is involved with freedom of thought. This is, of course, untrue. The *First* Amendment protects against infringement of freedom of speech or press; and since speaking and writing are the outward manifestations of thought, the First Amendment may be deemed to protect freedom of thought as well as freedom of expression. To claim that the Fifth Amendment *conflicts* with freedom of thought is to say that the Fifth Amendment conflicts with the First. To say that the Fifth Amendment *protects* freedom of thought is to admit the possibility that thought may be a crime—and this concept also conflicts with the First Amendment. The Fifth Amendment, obviously, neither sanctions nor in any other way protects or derogates from freedom of thought. It deals with an entirely different subject—criminal jeopardy and punishment.

Fundamental to an understanding of the Fifth Amendment privilege against self-incrimination is the fact that just as the privilege of the lawyer-client relationship is personal to the client, so the privilege against self-incrimination is personal to the witness.

The privilege against self-incrimination may not be used by a witness to avoid naming associates, no matter how much his testimony may embarrass or even incriminate them, except in one instance. The exception is when the witness himself was in conspiracy with the associates, and to connect himself with them might involve self-incrimination. This exception should be borne in mind when we see the spectacle of a witness claiming the Fifth Amendment privilege and asserting that he does so out of high moral principle, to protect others. Either he is misusing the Fifth Amendment in a way which Chief Justice Marshall declared amounted to perjury, or else he fears that his testimony would incriminate himself as well as the others he might name.

Chief Justice Marshall made the following statement: "If in any such case he say upon his oath that his answer would criminate himself, the court can demand no other testimony of the fact. If the declaration be untrue, it is in conscience and in law as much a perjury as if he had declared any other untruth upon his oath."

But despite what Marshall said, and despite the clearly personal nature of the privilege, witnesses before congressional committees, having learned that they can get away with it, frequently resort to the Fifth Amendment in order to avoid giving testimony which would incriminate others.

The Constitutional privilege of the Fifth Amendment is a privilege that should be treated with the utmost respect. It is my considered opinion it should not be used unless the witness honestly believes his testimony would, in fact, tend to incriminate him. It is for this reason that in each instance where a witness pleads this privilege the Chairman of the Committee insists that it be made a matter of record that the witness is not resorting to the Fifth Amendment frivolously. The witness is required to state under oath that he honestly believes that his testimony would be self-incriminating. All courts and forums where sworn testimony is elicited should insist on this basic requirement.

When the real purpose in declining to testify is only to protect others, or to protect some organization, or simply to frustrate the inquiry, the witness who asserts the claim of privilege probably is guilty of contempt (whether or not he is guilty of perjury, under Marshall's theory).

A point about the Fifth Amendment which is not well enough understood is that the privilege against self-incrimination is not the same thing as a right not to be required to testify. If there is no factor of incrimination, or if the factor of incrimination is removed, there is no possible basis under the Fifth Amendment for refusing to testify. This is the basic principle which has led to the enactment of immunity statutes. Where there is no valid immunity statute, and a witness claims his privilege against self-incrimination, he must be allowed to remain silent unless it is clear that the privilege has been falsely or fraudulently claimed. But this is *not* an absolute right to silence. It is a right which is allowed as the only available way of recognizing the Fifth Amendment privilege.

Where there is a valid immunity statute, the claim of Fifth Amendment privilege can be recognized in either of two ways: (1) by permitting the witness to remain silent on the question; or (2) by requiring him to answer, notwithstanding his claim of privilege, while at the same time removing the factor of incrimination by giving the witness full and complete immunity with respect to the matters and things concerning which he may testify in response to the question. Either course of action—and this is an important thing to remember—amounts to full recognition of the claim of privilege.

The practice of members of an organization—whether a labor union or any other organization—claiming the privilege against self-incrimination as a basis for refusing to answer questions about their officers, or leaders, or other individuals in the organization carries with it the seed of complete collapse for our whole system of law. If a man may validly refuse to answer a question which will only incriminate some other person without incriminating himself, then we shall have no right to testimony in criminal trials unless the witness wants to give it.

We must not lose sight of the fact that the principle involved is the same whether the testimony concerns a crime such as murder, or hit-and-run driving, or conspiracy, or a much lesser offense; and conspiracy is conspiracy, whether it is a conspiracy to rob a bank, to kidnap a child, to assassinate a public figure, to overthrow the Government by force and violence, or merely to swindle some poor widow out of her pension money.

There is a great deal of difference between respect for the Fifth Amendment and respect for one who claims the Fifth Amendment privilege against self-incrimination. Over many years, there has been judicial recognition of the fact that a claim of privilege under the Fifth Amendment carries with it some measure of public opprobrium, or at least the danger of it. The Fifth Amendment will not suffice, if only opprobrium is to be feared, and a

witness under the compulsion of a subpoena must divulge pertinent information even though it embarrasses him or renders him
infamous.

Certainly a plea of the privilege against self-incrimination
should not be considered evidence of guilt, or even an indication
of guilt, in a court of law. But outside the courtroom, there is no
requirement that a citizen must bury his head in the sand like an
ostrich and decline to take notice of the fact that a witness claimed
Fifth Amendment privileges in order to avoid answering questions.

No man's good reputation is guaranteed by the Constitution.
That is something a man has to build and guard for himself.

Anyone who thinks Dave Beck improved his reputation, or
strengthened his position with the Teamsters, or increased his
claim to the respect of the American people, by his repeated use
of the Fifth Amendment, is surely out of touch with the prac-
ticalities of life.

In the law of evidence, it is a general rule that whenever a
civil litigant is peculiarly able to offer testimony on any subject,
his failure to offer such testimony gives rise to the inference that
the testimony, if given, would be unfavorable to the cause of
that litigant. This rule of evidence is not to be suppressed or rendered inapplicable because the refusal to give testimony is under
a claim of the privilege against self-incrimination. It is true that
the inference that testimony withheld would, if given, be unfavorable to the withholder is rebuttable. But for the witness to assert
that the testimony, if given, would tend to incriminate him does
not amount to rebuttal.

Common sense tells us that in most instances where a witness
claims the Fifth Amendment privilege, he has some guilty knowledge he wants to conceal. Use of the Fifth Amendment carries
with it no presumption of innocence. In the United States, a man
is always presumed innocent until he is proven guilty; and for a
witness to invoke the Fifth Amendment is not legal evidence of
guilt. But neither is it legal evidence of innocence, nor does it add

anything to the legal presumption of innocence which is the right of every accused person. A witness who denies connection with a crime may be cross-examined about his answer. A witness who takes the Fifth Amendment in response to the same question escapes such cross-examination; but it certainly cannot be said that the claim of privilege is as strong in the witness' favor as the denial.

There has been a tendency on the part of the public to equate the Fifth Amendment provision against self-incrimination with the testimony of supposed Communists before congressional committees. There is lately, however, a trend upon the part of such witnesses to have recourse to a claim of First Amendment privilege. The theory they rely upon is that there is a right to "freedom of association" under the First Amendment, and that this right protects even such an association as participation in a conspiracy to overthrow the government of the United States by force and violence.

So far, alleged Communists seem to be the principal claimants of this asserted "First Amendment freedom of association." Labor racketeers and various other kinds of malefactors seem to have found the Fifth Amendment more suited to their purposes. It must be admitted that in law there is little difference between "association" in a conspiracy to overthrow the government by force and violence, and "association" in some other kind of illegal conspiracy; and it remains to be seen whether conspirators in fields other than Communism will yet avail themselves of the asserted "First Amendment freedom of association."

Hundreds of witnesses have voiced the privilege of the Fifth Amendment in a variety of statements and in many different tones —sullen, cynical, frightened, supercilious, arrogant, contemptuous, shamed, bellicose. Their attitudes toward the claiming of the privilege do not change the broad scope of the problem that we face, which lies not in the existence of the privilege but in the people who abuse it. The claiming of the Fifth Amendment without proper grounds for doing so, the misuse of it in order to deter, hamper, or block a legislative investigation, is the gross transgression with which we are concerned. Let us again quote Chief Justice Marshall: "If the declaration be untrue, it is in consicence and in law as much a perjury as if he had declared any other untruth upon his oath." Therefore, it is clearly demonstrated that the abuse of the Fifth Amendment privilege in our country today is an outstanding example of "crime without punishment." Under present procedures, it can be committed with absolute impunity.

CHAPTER 15

Heads I Win; Tails You Lose

I F THE reader whose eyes are presently scanning these pages will glance at his watch occasionally as he reads along, he will be able to measure the statistical crime rate in the United States by checking off the crimes as they occur, on the average, while the minute hand of his timepiece moves along. Every fifty-eight minutes during the year there is a willful homicide in this nation; there is a forcible rape every thirty-four minutes, a robbery every six minutes, an aggravated assault every four minutes, and a car theft every two minutes. Each time a single minute ticks by, there is a major larceny in the United States. There is a burglary every thirty-nine seconds.

Those statistics on crime come from the latest available figures provided by the top authority on crime in the nation, J. Edgar Hoover, Director of the Federal Bureau of Investigation.

If those figures do not strike home forcibly, Mr. Hoover has others to offer. He says that the Department of Justice believes that the annual cost of these kinds of crime in America is $22,000,-000,000—which is an average of almost $130 for each man, woman, and child in the nation.

We are proud of our schools and our universities. We fondly point to our national educational expenditures as illustrative of what we are doing for generations to come. Unhappily, as Mr. Hoover has pointed out, every time the American people spend $1.00 on education, they spend $1.11 on crime.

We are a nation whose faith and fortitude is based within our religious organizations. Shockingly, Mr. Hoover declares that for every dollar donated to religious organizations, we spend nine dollars on crime.

The statistics cited above are, however, based upon the figures reported by the fact-gathering resources of the Federal Bureau of Investigation. In other words, Mr. Hoover has properly reported the facts that his splendid organization has gathered. He has not minimized them, nor has he embellished them with projections. They are the figures of which he is certain. There are shadowed areas, however, where crimes are committed that cannot be found in the statute books, where criminals successfully pose as respectable and law-abiding citizens, where venality and corruption proceed apace and are in the main ignored or glossed over. These borderline criminal activities add enormously to Mr. Hoover's volume of statistics. Realistic surveys of American crime in all its phases point to a total national crime cost approaching fifty billion dollars, which is more than the defense budget of the United States for the current fiscal year.

In a magazine interview this year, Mr. Hoover, drawing upon his four decades as head of the FBI, declared that the situation in the 1960's has drastically changed from prohibition days.

"We find that the overlords of crime have moved out of the gang hideouts into the mainstream of American life," Mr. Hoover told the magazine *U. S. News & World Report*. "These criminals have great wealth, taken in from organized gambling, prostitution, the sale of narcotics, the sale of obscene material, and other vices. With that money, they have bought into legitimate businesses or set up on their own."

That is the heart of the matter in these crucial decades of the twentieth century, while this country is engaged in an awesome struggle to prevail and endure over an implacable enemy who will relentlessly press for any advantage, ruthlessly utilize any weakness, and viciously probe into the chinks in our armor.

One of the greatest weaknesses, as revealed in the hearings of

the Senate Select Committee, was generated by the changing façade of the underworld. While remaining lawless and conscienceless, it has adopted the bylaws and concepts of a decent society, in-
sofar as they suit and advance its corrupt objectives. It is fairly
easy to liken the ambitious member of the modern underworld to
the young executive in today's big business enterprises; if he has
talent and does his job well and responsibly, he will secure his
future and that of his family, and he will gain almost all the
benefits that industry today regards as standard rewards for its
employees, plus the prospects of almost unlimited power and
wealth.

With those views in mind, after the wide-ranging activities of
the national criminal syndicate were exposed during the three-
year life of the Senate Select Committee, the Senate was asked to
approve the continuation of the investigation of crime and all
its ramifications by authorizing further studies to be made by
the Permanent Subcommittee on Investigations of the Government Operations Committee. The first target of the subcommittee's probes was the main financial support of all of the crime
syndicate's other operations, the national network of gambling
activities.

The startling scope of the gambling operation is shown by testimony of expert witnesses who testified that the amount of money
spent in legal betting at race tracks was $3,500,000,000 in the single
year 1960. This was for horse racing alone. The witnesses with
vast experience declared that off-the-track (almost always illegal)
betting amounted to at least ten times the volume of the money
wagered at the tracks.

To operate this vast national clandestine industry, bookmakers
all over the country have always had to depend upon receiving
accurate information very swiftly concerning the outcome of horse
races at tracks that may be thousands of miles away or perhaps
right in their own cities or states. One of the great benefits of
speedy information for the bookmaker is that it permits the

winner of a race immediately to bet on another one. A huge business service was built up around this need.

Since almost every race track, as well as the laws of some states, prohibit the transmission of immediate information about the horses that ran first, second, and third in a particular race, the wire services that furnish it developed ingenious methods of smuggling the data beyond the track officials' jurisdiction.

Witnesses testified about the various methods—some of them elaborate systems that required knowledge of modern electronics, others so simple that they were extremely difficult to detect and to prevent. Sometimes the system was operated under the eyes of race-track detectives.

Two of these systems were of particular interest to the members of the committee, and the investigations elicited some strange testimony. The first method was described in baseball terminology —it employed "pitchers" and "catchers."

The witnesses were Miss Lucille Rice and Alexander Estrin, who worked as a team at various race tracks. Both were in the employ of a wire service for bookmakers known as the Delaware Sports Service. Both gave their occupations as "reporters." Estrin qualified that, saying he was a "sports reporter." There was no doubt that he was engaged in reporting sports events—the names of the first, second, and third horses in races at eastern tracks.

Estrin was usually the "catcher," since he was barred from many race tracks. Miss Rice was the "pitcher."

THE CHAIRMAN: As I understand, the pitcher is the one at the track that gets it and throws the information out, and somebody catches it, figuratively speaking?
ESTRIN: Yes, sir; and right now I am benched.
THE CHAIRMAN: That wasn't because you made errors, but just because of the sudden change in the weather?

It was a very simple system and could be used anywhere without fear of attracting the attention of track detectives unless they were already keeping Miss Rice and Estrin under surveillance. As soon as a race was over, Miss Rice took a position where she could be seen by Estrin, who occupied a vantage point outside the track, armed with binoculars and keeping a telephone line open to the Delaware Sports Service. If Horse Number Seven won the race, Miss Rice put one hand on her head; if Horse Number Eight came in second, or "placed," she then put both hands on her head. Another signal followed for the third or "show" horse in the race. There were twelve simple signals in all, in the event that any race had a full field of horses. Miss Rice got twenty-five dollars per day for pitching, and Estrin got the same amount, plus expenses, for catching.

Another catcher named Harold Kelly worked the New York tracks; he could look into Belmont Race Track from a pigeon coop atop his house, using binoculars. He described the same kind of system for the same employer, but he said he received only $125 per week, and after hearing that Miss Rice and Estrin got $150, he declared he would ask for a raise.

The pitcher-catcher teams that worked the tracks for the wire services sometimes had an electronic device to do their work for them. It was a small radio transmitter that could send signals from the track to be picked up at some distance by a "patch" installed on a telephone so that the telephone receiver could get the Morse or other code signals instantly as each race finished. Within seconds these results were flashing across the country to subscribers of the wire service. There were several types of transmitters and miniature receivers, most of them worn on belts.

Another electronic instrument was devised by a self-taught technician from Brooklyn, New York. This also served pitchers and catchers at the tracks for limited distances, but its principal purpose was somewhat more sinister and involved some danger for the operator should he ever be caught using it. This also involved a pair of tiny instruments, transmitter and receiver, and it was used to swindle bookmakers in so-called "horse rooms." One confederate would strap the receiver to his arm or leg so that its electrode would give him a series of tiny shocks in code. His companion would post himself in a phone booth near by—not more than half a city block away. He had a phone line open to the wire service to which the pair subscribed. By telephone he received from the wire service the name of a horse winning a race at a certain track. Within seconds that information was transmitted to the confederate in the bookmaker's establishment, who then immediately placed a bet on that horse and collected his winnings a few minutes later when the bookmaker received word of the race's outcome. This is a practice called "past-post betting" and is dependent upon a swift wire service as well as a certain amount of foolhardiness upon the part of the thieves who practice it. In the underworld, a man doesn't stay healthy long when he tries to rob the syndicate and gets caught at it.

If used with discretion, however, the scheme would almost surely work without difficulty, simply because the confederate who did the betting inside the horse room never moved out of view of the proprietor and obviously had no messages passed to him at any time. It was never the subcommittee's intention to give aid and comfort to criminals, but it seems likely that after the wide newspaper, radio, and television coverage of the hearings at which these devices were explained and demonstrated, many a bookmaker stopped taking bets from patrons who stood around casually between races and then quickly placed a large, winning bet just at what the bookmaker believed to be post time.

There was another use for these sending and receiving sets that was described to the subcommittee. They were employed in high-stake card games, where a person standing in a closet that was fitted with a special "two-way" mirror could see the cards held by one player and sometimes two; he would then use his miniature transmitter to relay the information to a confederate at the table who would then know exactly how to bet on his own hand.

The bookmaker who is operating a horse room hundreds and perhaps thousands of miles from the track has no real protection for his business other than the speed with which he receives up-to-the-minute information about the races. Criminals are inventive and ingenious people, and there are many ways of carrying on past-post betting other than with the miniature radios. Therefore the bookmakers have always depended heavily on the wire services, and the subcommittee's investigations and hearings dwelt extensively on those services.

Wire services in operation deal with groups of bookmakers or with individuals at set fees for daily transmission of information. The flashing of race results is almost always done by telephone, and sometimes a description of the entire race is broadcast directly to the horse rooms. The subcommittee found that the wire services often cloak their activities under the names of publications or news services and that they are ostensibly in the newspaper or magazine publishing business.

The proprietor of one of the services, Albert Tollin, who owned the Delaware Sports Service, for which the baseball battery of Estrin and Rice performed, told the subcommittee that his wire service was available only to professional bettors who make legitimate wagers on horse races. He furnished no service to bookmakers and other illegal operators in the field, according to his testimony, and he would shut off his information service to anyone he knew to be a bookmaker. He admitted, however, that he had never found reason to do so, and he further admitted that some of his clients were known to him only by such names as "Jo Jo" and "Biff" and "Charley Eye."

Tollin collected as much as fifty dollars per day from his clients for the results of five races, flashed immediately, but he was insistent that he served no criminals or illegal establishments. He had an explanation to give the subcommittee on the reasons why people subscribed to his service:

TOLLIN: . . . I believe there are people under such tension and anxiety that they would pay me this sum and the touts, also, would pay me . . . in order to relieve their clients . . . and let them know whether they won or lost.

He held to his story in spite of the fact that his father had once testified before an earlier hearing that the information supplied by Delaware Sports Service had little value to anyone but professional bookmakers. And, in spite of Tollin's claim of being only a reliever of anxiety, the hearings clearly demonstrated that he furnished race results for two specific business functions, and those were to sell information to bettors who were trying to beat the bookmakers by "past-post" betting operations, and to bookmakers who wanted to avoid taking bets on a race after it was already run.

The hearings on wire services ranged the country, and the testimony revealed some bizarre practices and subterfuges.

In Providence, Rhode Island, a wire service operated as the Probate Research Institute, ostensibly offering information about estate claims and missing heirs; its elaborate messages were actually horse race results in code.

A Florida witness declared that he made eight calls to Chicago to discuss the purchase of a plastic spray gun. The calls usually lasted less than a minute, which is plenty of time to relay race results. This witness, Elum Caudell, was considered a key figure in Florida wire service operations, and had a record of nineteen arrests, although he was a former Miami policeman.

Another wire service chief, Thomas F. Kelly, Sr., of Chicago, one of the owners of the Illinois Sports News, resorted to the privilege of the Fifth Amendment. He refused to answer questions regarding the reported intimidation of a subordinate who had attempted suicide rather than appear to testify before the subcommittee.

One of the most sinister figures to appear in the wire services probe was the gang-lord of New Orleans, Carlos Marcello, no stranger to the subcommittee or its staff. He had appeared in connection with the inquiry into the crime syndicate during the 1958 hearings of the Select Committee. Just as he had done previously, Marcello took the Fifth Amendment to all questions about his domination of crime in New Orleans, about his connection with the huge wire service operation there, and his criminal associates. Other witnesses testified that Marcello controlled the principal crime, vice, and gambling operations in the Louisiana city and that he was a principal figure in the national crime network.

Another national crime figure, dating from the days of the great bootlegging mobs of prohibition, was Owen (Owney) Madden, who appeared before the subcommittee, coming from his home in Hot Springs, Arkansas, to take the Fifth Amendment on questions about running a wire service in that city. He answered some questions, however:

THE CHAIRMAN: Mr. Madden, did you give us your occupation?
MADDEN: I am retired, Senator.
THE CHAIRMAN: Since when?
MADDEN: A few years, quite a few years.
THE CHAIRMAN: What did you retire from? What was your business or occupation?
(The witness conferred with his counsel.)
MADDEN: I refuse to answer . . .

Most of the witnesses who were connected with wire service operations invoked the Fifth Amendment. Some witnesses were intimidated; several admitted that they were fearful of retaliation for their testimony. Anonymous phone calls threatened many.

No business service can exist without customers; it was conclusively shown that the wire services exist to aid bookmakers outside the law, who in turn run the nation's multitudes of handbooks and horse rooms, and their customers are the national crime syndicate's best friends—the millions of bettors who pour their money into the gangsters' coffers every year. They furnish the revenues that the racketeers use to organize, finance, and operate the lucrative criminal conspiracies that gnaw constantly at the national morality.

Evidence that the gamblers across the nation have operated in complete scorn of federal laws was given by various experts, including the Commissioner of Internal Revenue, Mortimer H. Caplin, who declared that while it was apparent that illegal gambling amounted to perhaps fifty billion dollars annually in the United States, the government had collected revenue in this field of only seven million dollars. The true revenue should have been more than five billion dollars, a sum almost large enough to balance the national budget. Federal law provides that gamblers should purchase a fifty-dollar tax stamp annually and should pay an annual excise tax of 10 per cent of the total amount of wagers placed. In point of fact, during 1961 there were only 9,178 gambling stamps sold in the entire country. Between the major crime of avoiding the excise tax on gambling and the relatively minor ancillary of failing to purchase gambling stamps, the racketeers of the nation have been cheating all the rest of the citizens of approximately five billion dollars which must be made up from the pockets of every taxpayer.

The mockery which criminals make of the law is apparent in some statistics requested by members of the subcommittee for their various states: Washington state (Senator Henry M. Jackson), 2,944 gambling stamps sold in 1961; Arkansas (Senator John L. McClellan), 119 stamps sold; North Carolina (Senator Sam J. Ervin, Jr.), 45 stamps sold; South Dakota (Senator Karl E. Mundt), 16 stamps sold; Maine (Senator Edmund S. Muskie), 2 stamps sold.

In the city of New York, where twenty-six hundred bookmakers were arrested *two or more times* during the year immediately preceding the hearings in August, 1961, there were only 3 wagering tax stamps sold during the year. There were only 30 sold in the entire state of New York. In the city of Boston, a major "lay-off" center for national gamblers, there were 169 stamps sold. (A "lay-off" city is one where the crime leaders have established headquarters to accommodate bookmakers all across the nation who have taken too many heavy bets on one side of certain sporting events; in the event that the bettors should win, the bookmaker would be badly hurt. They "lay off" the bet with the syndicate to protect themselves.) Other national centers for lay-off betting were Biloxi, Mississippi, where 15 stamps were purchased during 1961, and Covington and Newport in Kentucky, one of the nation's greatest gambling areas at the time of the hearings, where 272 stamps were purchased during 1961. Miami, favorite resort of racketeers at rest, had only 10, and the great city of Los Angeles had only 11.

One expert on organized crime, the then chairman of the New York State Commission on Investigation, Goodman A. Sarachan, gave a very lucid and comprehensive review of how the national gambling network operates, which the subcommittee found helpful in considering later testimony. He said that there are four levels of illegal gambling. On the least important of these levels are the street agents or runners, who "operate out of their hats," while those on the second level, the bookmakers, have a permanent place of business, which is called a "horse room" and is generally fronted by a cigar store or pool hall or some other business establishment. Mr. Sarachan talked about the national crime syndicate in describing the third level, where the "bookmaker's bookmaker" reigns.

MR. SARACHAN: He doesn't bother to operate with the small bettor. Where he gets most of his business, of course, is out of the lay-off ... [The small bookmaker] has to lay off some of his bets, otherwise he might be forced out of business. He hasn't got enough capital to take a big loss. So if he finds he is getting too many bets on one horse and he doesn't want to take the risk of losing, he will call up one of these bookmakers' bookmakers ... sort of a wholesaler in the business. It is usually some racketeer or hoodlum who is well supplied with capital. ...

Finally we get to the top, what we call the combine or the syndicate. This is a group of racketeers with unlimited capital ... and these fellows seem to operate openly without any difficulty, and they will take the bets from the bookmaker's bookmaker. ...

After studying illegal betting on horse races, with its myriad evils and tremendous revenues for criminals, the committee examined the national habit of betting on other sporting events, a type of gambling which is also illegal in almost every state in the nation.

In these other sports, the gamblers have a tool that is as valuable in its own way as the wire service is to horse-race betting, and that instrument is "the line." This is simply the probable margin of victory for one team over another, commonly called "the point spread," and it is particularly used in basketball and football games. It is carefully figured by professional handicappers who distribute it in advance for bettors. It is widely published by newspapers throughout the United States, and is consulted by any person who wishes to make a bet on a particular athletic contest, whether it be college or professional sport. The handicappers arrive at this margin of victory by carefully studying such factors as past performances, physical condition of each team, the weather that is likely for the game (particularly in football, of course), and the volume of early betting on one side or the other. Actually, the ordinary bettor around the country is often deceived on the true prospects, because the handicappers consult with the well-known lay-off gamblers to determine what the odds or "point spread" should be.

Those well-known terms on today's national sports pages—"the line" and "the point spread"—lead unhappily but directly to another term that symbolizes one of the most saddening, disquieting scandals to grab national sports headlines since the "Black Sox" exposé in professional baseball in 1919.

The new phrase, coined by the criminals who benefit from it, is "point-shaving." Many a bright dream of youth and many a promising young career has been destroyed in the past several years, since the athletic fans of the country first learned about point-shaving from the glaring revelations in their newspapers. What is it, and how does it work?

It's just another form of "fixing" a sports result. The shameless gamblers are not satisfied to have the line and the point spread carefully figured for their advantage. They are not even satisfied with the co-operation of the big lay-off men in the combine. They have to be sure. So they carefully and cautiously approach an athlete to see if he'd be receptive to making some extra money. If he responds, as so many tragically have done, then they explain very casually and pleasantly—all he has to do is "shave a few points" from his team's total score. If his team is the favorite, he has only to see that his team doesn't exceed the predicted margin of victory; if his team is the underdog, all he has to do is see that it manages to lose by the margin figured in the point spread. Basketball in the nation's colleges has been the principal victim of the greedy, conscienceless gamblers. Who can tell when the star shot-maker deliberately misses a few shots? His fans say that he just "had a tough night." Who can point at the steady player whose opponent scores heavily against him? He was "off his game," or he wasn't feeling well that night. The thousand dollars or the fifteen hundred dollars is quietly passed between gambler and player, and that's the end of it.

Of course, it never is the end. The word gets around. The player is approached again; the money is easy and nobody will ever know. Eventually, however, somebody talks, and then the explosion comes. In the first national basketball scandal more than a decade ago, there were thirty-three players from eight colleges who were involved in point-shaving. Last year it happened again, this time to thirty-six young men in twenty-one colleges.

During the subcommittee's 1961 hearings on gambling and organized crime we heard some testimony about the "fixing" of sports events. One witness was a young man of good character, a fine athlete from the University of Oregon, named Michael Bruce. Young Mr. Bruce described how his college football squad went to Ann Arbor, Michigan, for an important game with the University of Michigan. Oregon was a six-point underdog to Michigan in the point spread established by the handicappers. Mr. Bruce was approached by a gambler named Frank "Lefty" Rosenthal, who suggested that it would be worth $5,000 to him to see that Oregon lost by eight points instead of six. Mr. Bruce pretended to accept, but then went and reported the offer to his coach immediately. He was asked about the man who attempted to bribe him:

MR. ADLERMAN: Do you recognize anybody in this room as that man?
MR. BRUCE: Yes, sir.
MR. ADLERMAN: Who is that?
MR. BRUCE: The man sitting at my left.

The young man then pointed out Rosenthal, who was steadily and monotonously taking the Fifth Amendment about his activities in fixing sports events, conspiring with other gamblers and criminals, and even about how he got the nickname of "Lefty." Mr. Bruce described the circumstances in detail, and then was asked about the Oregon-Michigan game:

MR. ADLERMAN: Incidentally, was that game won or lost by your team?
MR. BRUCE: We lost the game.
MR. ADLERMAN: How many points did you lose it by?
MR. BRUCE: Twenty-one.
MR. ADLERMAN: So all this went for naught. They would have won anyhow. . . .

Rosenthal did not confine his corrupting influences to college football players. He was indicted early this year by a North Carolina grand jury on a charge of offering to bribe a New York University player to shave points in a basketball game with the University of West Virginia. The game was part of an important national tournament held in Charlotte, North Carolina.

Such men as Rosenthal, when they are exposed, should be dealt with to the limit of the law, since their target is the nation's youth and since their heartlessness almost inevitably results in ruined lives for the young athletes who are subverted into reaching for the "easy money." In a realistic view, unless the fixing of sports events comes to a swift halt, there is reason to ask for legislation that will provide harsher penalties for these corrupters than the short jail terms and nominal fines which they now hazard when they attempt their briberies.

In spite of fines and sentences, these criminals have actually committed crimes that go without punishment—for what penalty severe enough can the courts of the land assess upon a man who has ruined a young man's career, and indeed, his entire life?

The guilt lies not only with the gamblers, nor with the young athletes who succumb to the lure of a fistful of greenbacks. It must be shared by all the rest of us who continue to tolerate illegal gambling on sports and who do not protest when the leading newspapers of the country publish in daily prominence the "line" and the "point spread" and the "early odds." It must also be shared by some educational systems that outrageously subsidize young men who will engage in school sports. Colleges go as far as offering cash monthly payments for athletic participation or supplying their athletic stars with automobiles and luxurious apartments—all this done in clandestine fashion through sources outside the college proper, such as wealthy alumni or prosperous local businessmen. There are far too many unhealthy influences upon the young men, who are urged overtly to play hard in the spirit of good sportsmanship, while at the same time they are surreptitiously paid in professional fashion for supposedly "amateur" performances.

Just as the nation's colleges seek by means of scholarships to enroll gifted young scientists and mathematicians and artists and musicians, so might they also round out their activities properly by seeking to find the best football quarterbacks and basketball forwards. The trouble begins, however, when the emphasis on winning is so overwhelming that the young men are paid well,

given special privileges, and allowed to forget scholastic achievements. Academic circles and the general public both gasped in
horror at the revelations of the basketball scandals, at the pictures
in the newspapers of Michael Bruce pointing his forefinger at
Lefty Rosenthal and saying "That's the man."

Realistically, there should be no horror, no shock. For the truth
of the matter is, if our sports-minded academic institutions are
willing to make clandestine payments to a boy for winning, when
they and he both know they are violating the spirit of amateurism,
then why should anybody be horrified when a gambler pays him
secretly for losing? By the time the gambler reaches him, he is
probably sadly confused about moral values, anyway.

Fortunately for the future of sports in America, the overwhelming majority of our young athletes are honest; there is
reason to believe that only a minute percentage of them would
let a bribe attempt go unreported. Certainly a great many of the
arrests and prosecutions of recent years can be attributed to boys
of splendid character in every threatened sport who have listened
to bribery offers and then have co-operated in the apprehension of
the criminals. But there will be threats as long as there is illegal
gambling, and that evil will continue as long as the nation
tolerates it.

It would be wise, our hearings on gambling and organized crime
disclosed, if the man who ventures to play poker with strangers
takes a good look at his surroundings and at the equipment on
the table before he buys chips in the game. The mirror on the
closet door behind him may look like an ordinary mirror, but it
can possibly be a "two-way" fixture, with a pair of sharp eyes
behind it reading his cards and a pair of nimble fingers in the
darkness operating a small transmitter and tapping out a code
that tells all the cards he holds in his hand. The pleasant fellow
opposite him may have a tiny receiver strapped to his leg, so
that he may count slight electronic shocks which will tell him
that the "mark" is holding two pairs against his three of a kind.

The innocent lover of poker games, as well as other card games played for money, would also do well to view suspiciously any opponent who wears tinted glasses at the poker table. It's possible that the colored glasses can bring out otherwise hidden markings on the backs of the cards.

There's one gimmick that the honest but adventurous card-player cannot guard against—contact lenses that enable the gambler to read the backs of marked cards. The lenses are called "ruby red readers," and they are made of red-colored optical glass according to a doctor's prescription. They cost $160, and at the time of our hearings, anybody could buy them by sending in a prescription. He would receive the lenses—if a man had perfect vision, he could get plain lenses that worked just as well—and a deck of playing cards marked with a fluid invisible to the naked eye, but which the ruby red readers could pick out with no trouble at all. A gambler equipped with such lenses and cards can win at poker or gin rummy or blackjack, as he wishes.

According to testimony at the hearings, there are thousands of sets of these contact lenses now in use in the United States, and at the date of this writing, they are perfectly legal. In point of fact, one distributor has told a committee investigator that his business increased appreciably after his testimony was reported in the nation's press. The lenses are, of course, easily procured— no citizen is prohibited by law from viewing the world through rose-colored glasses. The decks of playing cards that necessarily accompany the lenses are easily marked. All a gambler needs is the ink that is invisible to anyone not wearing the special lenses.

The amateur card-player cannot save himself by carefully scrutinizing his opponents; the lenses tend to change blue eyes to a greenish shade, and their effect on brown eyes is only to make them slightly darker. The most observant card-player could only note that his opponent showed signs of a late and somewhat boisterous previous evening.

The safe procedure for folks who like a "nice friendly card game" when they are among strangers is to be sure of the identity of their fellow players. One witness before the committee, Paul Karnov, of the H. E. Mason Co. in Chicago, testified that his firm did four hundred thousand dollars' worth of business in its average year of operations, most of it in crooked gambling devices like the contact lenses, marked cards, and dice that were loaded to favor the operators of crap games. It was estimated that one crap game in every twenty is crooked. The sales of these kinds of crooked gambling equipment were, according to testimony, out in the open, advertised by catalogs delivered in the United States mails.

The victims of this large-scale illicit enterprise have no recourse, since the men who fleeced them are usually difficult to find once the game is over. Even the well-intentioned advice to amateur gamblers to avoid games they are not sure of will be steadily ignored by some of them. There is considerable truth in the old story of the inveterate gambler who came home with empty pockets and was scathingly interrogated by a friend who asked him: "Didn't you know that was a crooked game?" The gambler's reply was to the point: "Sure, I knew it was crooked, but it was the only game in town."

The subcommittee's hearings during the past year on the influences of organized crime on gambling activities throughout the nation have had good results in legislation designed to curtail the most flagrant abuses.

Since September, 1961, there are new laws that severely restrict the national operators of illegal gambling enterprises. It is a pleasure to observe that the Department of Justice, under the energetic leadership of Attorney General Robert F. Kennedy, has been diligent in investigations and prosecutions under the new statutes. The vigorous enforcement of the laws by the Department of Justice has also resulted in various salutary operations on the state and municipal level throughout the country. So it is correct to say that the big-time gamblers of the United States are under more pressure nowadays than they have experienced in several decades past.

These are the vital changes in the laws that permit swift federal action and encourage strong local law enforcement: It is now a crime to travel in or to use transportation facilities of any kind in interstate commerce for the purposes of illegal gambling, prostitution, illegal liquor or narcotics operations, or other forms of racketeering enterprises. It is now a crime to use interstate transportation or communication of any kind for the transmittal of wagering information. It is now a crime to use interstate transportation for the carrying of wagering paraphernalia, except where such material can be used legally under the laws of the state to which it is consigned, as in the state of Nevada. Other laws make it extremely difficult for criminals to flee with subsequent impunity from prosecution or imprisonment, or to carry weapons of any kind after having been convicted of a felony.

These are good laws, and they seem to be working. It has become apparent, for example, that most of the wire services for the purpose of transmitting racing information which existed at the time of our hearings on organized crime have since gone out of business, or they have so curtailed their activities that they can no longer be considered potent aids to bookmaking operations. Some few are still in business but will probably run into the enforcement provisions of the new laws. More study is needed to draft even stronger legislation. It is gratifying to read in the daily newspapers about state and local operations against the illegal gamblers all across the nation. On the very day that these words were written, New York newspapers carried headlines about gambling raids in populous Westchester County—seventy people were arrested in a record roundup that was participated in by the New York State Commission of Investigation, the New York State Police, and local authorities down to the village level.

The apathy of citizens throughout the nation is still a major factor in stalling the control of racketeering, but vigorous action by enforcement agencies gets the kind of publicity that will awaken the citizen's interest and alert him to the huge costs he is paying to support organized crime. The Department of Justice has directed many gambling raids and crime drives in recent months and is likely to continue its efforts. One effect has been unhappily noted in the neighboring nation to the north. It is reported that Canada has suffered an invasion of United States criminals, who are known to have moved across the border because of the heavy pressure put upon them in this country. They are operating in the gambling fields, in narcotics, in stock frauds, protection rackets, and prostitution, as well as in other venal activities.

Probably the most striking effect, however, of the new federal laws and the Justice Department's drive against organized crime, as well as of the awakening of public interest across the country, is seen in two towns in Kentucky, Newport and Covington. Both of them are located near Cincinnati, Ohio, and both of them were known across the nation at the time of the subcommittee's hearings on organized crime as two of the biggest gambling centers east of Las Vegas.

The new federal statutes hit these two cities hard. They were headquarters for the big-time lay-off bookmakers in the east. They had wide-open gambling in their clubs and centers of night life. They had a shocking number of houses of ill fame in open operation. They were both riddled with vice and corruption.

They are now almost ghost towns, and they have unemployment problems and business difficulties for which they have asked federal consideration. Not only have the national laws disrupted the criminal operations that supported their neon-lit prosperity, but their own voters helped to do the job. They elected a reform administration, with the chief law enforcement officer a former professional football player named George Ratterman. Mr. Ratterman was the victim of an attempted frame-up by the gamblers in Campbell County, Kentucky, and his trial on vice charges was a matter of national headlines—until the frame-up exploded in the gamblers' faces. Mr. Ratterman was completely exonerated and then elected to clean up his county. That he has done so, using the new federal laws to backstop his operations, is evidenced by the closing of the two towns as national centers of illegal gambling.

There is need for other legislation directed against the bread-and-butter, basic activities of the men who operate organized crime. It seems likely that the various proposals of the Department of Justice will receive thorough consideration by the Congress and that legislative action will give us further weapons against the criminals. One that is sorely needed will provide for legal wire-tapping while giving proper protection to the rights of the individual. It is no exaggeration to say that when the Congress enacts such a law, it will be one of the most effective weapons that enforcement agencies will have in the battle against the operations of organized crime.

One other that is obviously needed at the time of this writing, and which is provided for in a bill submitted to the Senate, grows from a deficiency in the wire-service law now existing. The present legislation now prohibits only those wire services which are operated by individuals who are engaged in the business of betting. To close the obvious loophole, the law should be amended to prohibit all operations of wire services for the purpose of disseminating information to places where off-the-track betting is not authorized by state law—at present, all off-the-track betting is illegal except in Nevada.

There are frequent arguments advanced in favor of solving the whole situation of organized crime's control of illegal gambling simply by making all gambling legal. This course, say its proponents, will easily take care of the criminals by pulling their livelihood right out from under them, and it will take care of the basic human urge to bet on the outcome of contests, whether they be the rolling of dice or the running of horses or the attempt to hit a ball with a bat safely past a man who is attempting to catch it. Moreover, say the legal gambling proponents, the taxpayers of the nation will profit enormously, as they do now from the pari-mutuel machines at the race tracks. Finally, the legal gambling people say, it is impossible to legislate the nation's moral code. The Volstead Act couldn't do it, and no greater success can be expected from antigambling legislation.

These seem to be insecure, flimsy reasons for barring new laws designed to curb the criminals in gambling, and they are certainly lacking in strength as reasons for making all gambling legal.

The practice of gambling outside the law is an offense against traditional moral standards in this country, and it would still be an offense even if the public were encouraged by law to participate openly, because the criminals wouldn't move on to some other illegitimate enterprises. They would simply welcome legality with broad smiles, and would continue their control of the business, aided by the law's protection.

There is another good reason why legalized gambling would prove to be a curse instead of a blessing. It lies in the nature of gambling itself, which basically survives because millions upon millions of people believe that they are going to get something for nothing. Only a few thousand of them ever do, and they are the ones who gamble once, win, and then quit forever. If gambling were unrestricted and legal, then it would inevitably lead to a sickening slump in the moral standards of our people. Moreover, the crooks who now operate in the field would soon find ways to corrupt legalized gambling with dishonest operations.

The folks who favor legal gambling (and among them, naturally, are most of the nation's gamblers) also say that it is impossible to enforce properly the federal, state, and local laws against the gamblers because law enforcement agencies at every level are corrupt, and that police officers everywhere are "on the take."

This popular and cynical belief, so widespread in twentieth-century America, is simply not true. This nation would be a jungle if it were so. The racketeers would long since have taken over completely.

Most police officers—indeed, the vast majority of them—are hard-working and honest and dedicated. Given the tools and the training as well as the support of the citizenry, they do a splendid job everywhere in the land.

It is true, however, that there are pockets of corruption scattered all across the nation. Almost every police force of any size probably has a few officers, from patrolmen on the beat to high administrative officials, whose records would not bear close scrutiny by experienced investigators. It must be admitted also that some cities, according to testimony of witnesses at our hearings and according to recent news stories, seem to have more crooked policemen than they have honest ones. In these places the criminals operate with impunity in flagrant violation of the laws.

A witness told the subcommittee that, in 1961, the bookmakers alone might be spending as much as $750,000,000 annually to bribe police officers for permission to operate unmolested. That seems to be an unbelievably large sum of money. If it is based upon fact, it represents payments to a great number of policemen in many cities.

Senator Henry M. Jackson commented on that subject. "You know and I know what the trouble is," Senator Jackson said. "They buy off the judges, they buy off the sheriffs, and they buy off the police." The result of such corruption is always a wave of crime without punishment in the affected areas.

Senator Jackson was correct, and while he was not indicting all policemen throughout the land, as the cynics are likely to do, he was making the point that there is not apt to be any widespread gambling operation in any city of the United States that doesn't exist without the knowledge and connivance of local officials on several levels. An honest and energetic city government can put any gambling racket out of business in no time at all.

It may be almost impossible to control the human instinct to gamble, but it certainly is not impossible to put some force into the effort to control its illegal aspects.

That is the work that must be done. Everyone has a part in it. The citizens should demand that their officials exercise vigilance. Good government at every level will provide the kind of police forces, particularly in the urban areas where the racketeers con-gregate, which will put some force into the laws. Heavier penalties for violations may be one solution, but in the long run the answer lies in the certainty and promptness of punishment for breaking the law. The ultimate decision, of course, rests once again with the citizenry. The quality of the police force in any area, over a length of time, will depend upon exactly the kind of police force the voters and the taxpayers really want to have.

The Federal statutes can do severe damage to the national syn-dicate; they are excellent weapons if they are vigorously used, and the Department of Justice has thus far given ample evidence that it plans to so use them. Legal wire-tapping and an amend-ment to the wire-services law will also help immeasurably. It is possible that substantial correction is under way in this particular category of crime that now goes without punishment, and perhaps the chieftains of organized crime will lose a good part of their most lucrative racket.

CHAPTER 16

Manifold Blessings

The Scripture moveth us, in sundry places to acknowledge and confess our manifold sins and wickedness.

Book of Common Prayer

Aʟʟ of the hearings on organized crime, on corruption in the labor and management fields, never produced the same kind of disheartening effect brought about during the investigating subcommittee's probe into the work stoppages and strikes and improper activities at our nation's missile bases.

After years of hearing about the crimes of gangsters and the corruption of racketeers, all of us should have been somewhat insulated against the effects of shocking testimony, but it was sickening to hear details of how some American workmen callously contributed to the Soviet efforts to obtain and hold supremacy in space, a contribution brought about because some union men put their own greed for money ahead of the country's interests.

The dreadful record at the time of the hearings on work stoppages at missile bases showed these figures: in four and one-half years, there were 327 strikes at twenty-two missile bases. Cape Canaveral alone had 109 strikes; the total loss for all bases was reported at the astounding figure of 162,872 man-days of labor.

If the irresponsibility of the workers and their leaders is a sample of America's dedication to the moral values that founded this nation, then we had better admit that the leader of the international Communist conspiracy was right when he said that the Soviet Union would bury us.

That statement from Khrushchev is the basis of the central fact of our existence in the world today, that the free world faces an aggressive and organized force which has the avowed and announced purpose of world domination. The single great barrier to that purpose is the existence of a vigilant and capable sanctuary of freedom. The United States now provides such a sanctuary. We can hold our national character and our dearly purchased independence only by strength, and in today's world of space technology that strength rests in rapid and successful development and improvement of missiles and space vehicles. These facts are so fundamental and so obvious that the schoolchildren of the nation are generally familiar with them.

The shameless attitude of those missile base workers, however, is not a fair sample of America's moral standards. The testimony given to the subcommittee about the elevation of personal greed above the nation's security, about thousands of men spending their time trying to figure out ways of drawing three or four times as much pay as they were entitled to for the work they did, is certainly not a true profile of the American spirit or of the integrity of millions of honest working people in this country. America's crisis today is one of neglect and apathy and laziness, rather than one of spiritual values smashed and irretrievably lost.

The investigation into the missile base problems started with a customary interrogation and inspection trip by subcommittee personnel acting upon complaints received in Washington. Three men—Jerome S. Adlerman, general counsel, Robert E. Dunne, assistant counsel, and LaVern J. Duffy, investigator, went to Florida to check out the complaints. They arrived one morning between eight and nine o'clock at Cape Canaveral. They were mildly astonished to find the place almost deserted. Mr. Dunne asked a site superintendent where everybody was:

MR. DUNNE: . . . We asked where the workers were and what time they started, but he said they usually started about seven o'clock in the morning, but evidently had gone fishing that day. We didn't know quite what he meant. After further questioning, we determined that this was his expression or the popular Cape expression of one of those days when the workmen didn't show up. . . .

The investigators soon found that the walkout was carefully planned. They saw a truck on the highway leading to the base, bearing a sign, *Ironworkers not working today*. It was just like a picket line. Workers wouldn't cross it. They "went fishing" instead. That stoppage, a kind of wildcat strike against the use of four nonunion ironworkers who installed steel platforms for a Titan missile, started on December 21, 1960 and lasted until December 27. It cost 2,688 man-days as follows: 150 man-days on the man-in-space project, 1,000 man-days on Air Force missile contracts, and 1,538 man-days on Army projects.

It is impossible, of course, to figure out the cost or time impact of this loss of work. For one thing, a work stoppage at Cape Canaveral slows down or brings to a complete halt a countless number of other operations going on in plants and research laboratories all across the country. Cape Canaveral, after all, is one of the terminal spots in the space effort. All of us remember warmly Lieutenant Colonel John Glenn's repeated praise for the efforts of thousands of men and women everywhere who contributed so richly to the orbital flight he made this year. One space expert testified that "if you delay tests on a program down there [at Cape Canaveral], you may be able to measure in days, weeks, or months how long the test program was delayed, but that is no measure of how much it was delayed back in the factory and in engineering because we didn't have the information. A month at Cape Canaveral might be many months in the end result of the program."

During its intensive investigation of excessive overtime and exorbitant wages paid for missile base work, the subcommittee's staff prepared close studies of payrolls in two bases, Vandenberg Air Force Base in California and Cape Canaveral, Florida. Mr. Dunne testified on the pay of plumbers and pipefitters at Vandenberg:

MR. DUNNE: The Bechtel Corporation employed fifty-two plumbers and pipefitters ... the lowest was paid four hundred and two dollars and the highest seven hundred and thirty-three dollars. The average weekly earnings of all of them was four hundred and fifty-one dollars ... There were sixty-eight electricians on the payroll ... the lowest paid of those who worked a full week received four hundred and thirteen dollars for the week, and the highest, six hundred and seventy dollars. ...

The commanding officer at Vandenberg Air Force complex is a major general in the Air Force. His total pay and allowances for twenty-five years' service, including his quarters allowance and his subsistence allowance, amounts to three hundred and sixty-five dollars a week.

Each and every one of the plumbers and pipefitters and electricians made more than the commanding general.

His further testimony showed that a foreman of laborers at Vandenberg earned $434 in one week, which was $1 more than the pay of the Secretary of the Air Force and $30 more than the pay of Dr. Wernher von Braun, the missile expert.

Payrolls at Cape Canaveral had slightly lower wage scales, but individuals collected huge pay checks through overtime. An electrician averaged $538 per week. Another apprentice electrician in one week worked only four hours of straight time, but he put in eighty hours of overtime. He received $748 for the week.

It was clearly evident from the testimony that the wildcat strikes, the work stoppages, and the slowdowns were deliberately planned for the purpose of generating overtime pay at double and even triple rates to make up for the time lost by reason of the stoppages. One supervisor testified about his refusals to authorize overtime when he believed it was unnecessary:

MR. ADLERMAN: Mr. Lasky, when you refused to OK this overtime, would you tell us what happened to you personally? Were
you subjected to any harassment and abuse?

MR. LASKY: Yes, sir. I received some service I never requested,
such as delivery of sod or lumber or cinder block. . . . My house
was put up for sale by two various real estate agents who came
to investigate the value, which I had never called for. . . . I
received annoyance telephone calls at all hours of the day,
wherein abusive language may have been used. . . .

Why was so much overtime pay necessary? It wasn't, according to a union official in the witness chair. Robert Palmer, business manager for an electrical workers local, said that he opposed
it. He had members out of work, and he favored spreading the
work around, rather than giving a few men work on an overtime
basis.

THE CHAIRMAN: There is no reason why there can't be two shifts
or three shifts instead of one with a lot of overtime?

MR. PALMER: None at all.

Of course, some of the edge of Mr. Palmer's objection to overtime was taken away when it was disclosed that the apprentice
electrician who drew $748 in one week on quadruple overtime pay
was his brother-in-law.

There were 90,366 man-days lost at Cape Canaveral alone, in
ninety-two strikes. The most serious of these? It was an organizational strike that lasted four weeks and took a total of 30,856
man-days. Who staged it? Once again, a single guess should
suffice. Our old acquaintances—the International Brotherhood of
Teamsters.

Jurisdictional disputes were common at Canaveral, where union
workers objected to having nonunion men on the job, even
though the State of Florida has a right-to-work law, which provides that employees need not belong to a union in order to work.
One company involved in a project at the Cape agreed to avoid

a work stoppage by not taking its own technical employees into the base. In other words, the company wasn't allowed to install the equipment it had manufactured.

Other disputes arose between unions. A staff member, Irwin Langenbacher, described one of the silliest, most asinine, downright stupid excuses for a work stoppage that could possibly be imagined:

MR. LANGENBACHER: . . . In September, 1957, the cement finishers went on strike because the painters were using trowels to fill up small holes and voids in the walls they were painting. The cement finishers claimed that since trowels were used they should do that work. . . .

Out at Vandenberg in California, an official testified, the supervising work was so frustrating that he resigned his job. He said the work was "grossly overmanned, and the productivity of the personnel, both contractors and any others that I could see on the job, was very low."

This official, Ewell H. Hodge, former Air Force contracting officer, testified to the almost incredible account of "blessing the manifold." This tale should be recounted, for it typified the kind of outrageous nonsense that filled the record during these missile base hearings.

Mr. Hodge described the manifold in question, which is an assembly of pipes and valves used in the hydraulic systems on an ICBM launching pad. When the manifolds arrived from the factory for installation, the union pipefitters claimed that they should have assembled the manifold, since the device contained pipes with diameters less than two inches. The pipefitters insisted on disassembling, cleaning, and then reassembling the manifolds, a completely pointless procedure.

It was later decided that it was unwise to take the manifolds apart. It might harm them. So a ritual that became known as "blessing the manifolds" was initiated. It involved absolutely no work at all. The workers were paid for doing nothing.

MR. HODGE: Well, when a manifold came in like this ... we had an agreement with them [the union] rather than tear it apart, "You will so-call bless it." So they would maybe take out one pipe and inspect it and put it back in there to see if it met with the union's standards.

MR. ADLERMAN: They would sit by and wait and watch their time and say, "Well, we blessed it for three hours or four hours," or whatever the case may be, is that right?

MR. HODGE: That is right, sir.

MR. ADLERMAN: Sometimes they would put a mark or a welding bead on it to show that they did some kind of work or a mark to say, "This one was blessed."

MR. HODGE: That is right, sir.

THE CHAIRMAN: Now let me ask you: during the period of blessing, while you were waiting for the egg to hatch and it was blessed, did they sit there and do nothing or would they work at something else?

MR. HODGE: No, sir; they would sit there and watch the piece.

Sometimes the blessing ran into overtime, and not infrequently it was paid for at double time rates.

There were other facets of the situation into which the subcommittee inquired during 1961 hearings. The full story was shocking, and the committee found that while such unjustified extravagance is indefensible, the worst crime of all was the causing of irrevocable loss of vital time in our missile and space program.

Industry and government supervisors and administrators were not altogether innocent during these scandalous work stoppages. Since the federal government paid all the costs, industry made little or no effort to keep expenses down. With few exceptions, the government officials, both civilian and military, were careless, inefficient, and ineffective in supervising the labor aspects of the program.

Furthermore, in the spring of 1962, the subcommittee held hearings on the pyramiding of profits and costs in the missile procurement program. Both military and civilian officials of the government testified at length, as did executives of corporations engaged in missile work. One of the central issues during this series of hearings serves well to illustrate the pyramiding problem. This issue concerned the profits of the Douglas Aircraft Company, Inc., in the NIKE missile program.

Donald W. Douglas, Jr., president of the firm, testified at length about profits that the company charged against the program, real profits which he attempted to minimize in his statements. The facts, as brought out in the record, showed that Douglas Aircraft was paid $63,810,000 in profits on the NIKE program and of this amount $37,300,000 represented "mark-ups" Douglas took on work performed by its subcontractors. During the hearings, a controversy arose concerning which funds were profits and which were proper expenses.

The company, in its testimony before the committee, attempted to charge expenses of nongovernment endeavors—development of certain of its commercial aircraft—against the actual profit on NIKE missile production, in an effort to confuse the committee as to the true nature and extent of its missile profits. This was patently improper and unjustified and could not be approved by the subcommittee.

It was obvious at the conclusion of these hearings that the system of procurement which permitted the taking of profits in that fashion surely required prompt revision and correction. Quick action would have two salutary results: (1) Improve and speed our missile program, and (2) save the taxpayers of the United States huge sums of money annually.

Following the subcommittee's exposures of the labor practices, there was immediate drastic improvement. As an example, our hearings showed that during the period from July, 1956, through March, 1961, there was 1 man-day lost for every 73.2 man-days worked. After the hearings, when the righteous indignation of

Americans everywhere was heard, the rate of loss dropped tremendously during the period from June, 1961, through December, 1961. In this time, there was only 1 man-day lost for every 1,250 man-days worked. Comparing the later figure with earlier experience, there were seventeen times fewer man-days lost for a comparable period of time.

The Air Force also reported that excessive labor costs in overtime had dropped from 26.8 per cent during a period in 1960 to less than 3 per cent during the last quarter of 1961.

As one result of the hearings, the President established the Missile Sites Labor Commission in an effort to reduce work stoppage. This Commission was directed to do everything possible to reconcile differences between contractors and labor groups and between various labor organizations. A no-strike pledge was given by almost all of the labor groups involved.

It is manifestly correct to say that our first manned orbital flight by Colonel Glenn came more swiftly because the work stoppages had been so drastically reduced. It is also true to say that if the four-and-a-half years of outrageous practices had not been allowed to occur, we would have put a man into orbit much earlier than we did. No man can say what the time losses have cost us, or may yet cost us.

In spite of the initial success in correcting these evils, it has been disturbing to watch the strike record creep upward again in recent months, even though the Missile Sites Labor Commission is working to avoid the stoppages.

For example, during the last half of 1961, the work stoppages at missile bases were at a rate of about one-third of the national industrial average. In the first few months of 1962, however, they jumped upward to exceed the national average.

This condition should never be lightly considered or condoned. The nation has too much at stake. Congress will have to act on the matter unless the stoppages for senseless trivialities are ended. It appears unlikely, according to current information, that the responsible people have learned their lessons, and it is probable that they will not perform any better in the future than they have in the past.

It is time for us to have some laws to deal with the kind of greed that jeopardizes the safety and subverts the destiny of the United States. The workers, the union leaders, the supervisors and the government officials at all the missile bases are, most of them, certainly deeply at fault for this outrageous record, but if many of them lost integrity and patriotism in their dealings in this particular field, they are not alone nor are they unique. The behavior of some of them was part and parcel of the insidious philosophy that threads its way through the long record of the Senate Select Committee and the current record of the Investigating Subcommittee. It is the attitude that has burgeoned so alarmingly during the middle years of this century. "What's in it for me?" "What's the deal?" "I'm looking out for Number One." "I've got to have an angle working for me." This is the philosophy of "the angle," and it is the basis of some of the anecdotes that the investigators tell about their work—they seem to run into vast numbers of people who just cannot believe that dedication and selflessness and old-fashioned morality have any meaning, or any longer exist.

While the tales about the missile bases were shocking and disheartening, it is probably true that the men who were slowing down our space program for their own profit, in the face of Soviet accomplishments and danger, were probably no worse in the long run than the other secret operators in the "What's in it for me?" fraternity—the bribe-taking law officer, the industrialist who cynically conspires with others to fix prices and trade conditions, the income tax cheaters, the labor extortionists, the crooked gamblers. They are all part of the same package, and present largely the same problems.

CHAPTER 17

Crimes Beyond the Statutes

THE American people have witnessed in astonishment, during the investigations and hearings of our committee, the exposure of shocking conditions that have existed throughout the nation on almost every economic level, in business, in unionism, and in organized crime and racketeering. Although they were displayed for all to see, many of these evils have gone uncorrected.

There is growing evidence, of course, that when the laws are properly and vigorously enforced, the racketeers in every area of illegal operations will find themselves caught in increasing difficulties with the law. They will not be so arrogant and contemptuous as they used to be. For example, it is unlikely that the leaders of organized crime will soon blunder into another Apalachin conference.

There are, however, many other improper activities that are unpunished and uncorrected, some of them of great national significance. Ordinarily, when we consider "crime without punishment," we are likely to picture the murderer who has gone his way unapprehended, the traitor who vanished behind the Iron Curtain (although perhaps that kind of exile is punishment enough), the housebreaker who is never seen, the rapist who is only a vicious shadow in the night, the embezzler who disappears with his loot.

Crime, however, travels in countless guises, sometimes wearing the various cloaks of benevolence, humanism, and welfare. Activities of this kind are carried on in the plain light of day, in full view of anyone who cares to observe. By their nature they are frequently beyond the investigative scope of a committee of the Congress, and they are within the law as the statutes have established it. They can be aptly described as violations of the moral and spiritual codes upon which our nation was founded. These transgressions have never been defined by statute, nor proscribed by legislation, nor punished by the processes of justice. Yet they remain with us, sometimes changing outwardly with the times, waxing and waning in importance as public values are altered.

Most of them are not generally regarded as criminal violations, and are difficult to define and categorize simply because the deluded citizenry whom they offend and violate has been conditioned to look upon them equally, without indignation, and often with approval.

A good example of this kind of improper activity is the Teamsters' pact with the International Longshoremen's and Warehousemen's Union. As was said previously, if the Teamsters continue to flirt with that element on the far left wing of labor, they may be in for a rude surprise; they may discover that the satellites are governing the parent body. More importantly, however, a national alliance of that kind poses a threat to the transportation lifelines of the nation. To prevent the threat from becoming reality, we need legislation that would specifically prohibit the use of such a powerful weapon by the transport unions, the kind of legislation that would impose controls upon them comparable to those that have for so long regulated businessmen in their pursuit of profits. Our people must be protected from the flagrant abuse of special interests at either end of the economic pole, management or labor.

There are many similar crimes and improper activities that go unpunished. Most of them fit readily into the framework of a broad category of venality that can be designated as crimes against the nation's well-being and security.

This is so broad an area that some specifics are in order.

There are guidelines for us to follow in seeking to achieve our national purpose, the chief objectives and the supreme goals that we seek as a free people in these troubled decades of the twentieth century. They represent and express truly the highest ideals and aspirations of the American people. They are:

The achievement of a just and lasting peace with honor and understanding among all nations and all peoples.

The preservation of a society dedicated to the freedom and the dignity of man.

The enhancement of our cultural and spiritual growth while we make continuous gains in all fields of knowledge and constructive endeavor.

The further expansion and strengthening of our economy to provide greater opportunities and security for all of our people.

All good Americans will agree upon these basic objectives, adding corollaries perhaps, or emphasizing one above another as interests and background may dictate. But there is no serious controversy about them. They were not argued as a major issue during the latest presidential campaign, nor are they likely to form the basis of disagreement in political issues and debates. There may be, of course, a great deal of dispute at times about the means and methods proposed to achieve these blessings. What to do, when to do it, and how it is to be done—these are the sharp divisions among our people in these difficult days.

In the pursuit of these great objectives, the Congress plays a vital role as the chief lawmaking branch of our government and it bears the responsibility for making the right decisions on legislation that will preserve our heritage and move our country forward. This duty is increasingly clear as the world conflict between the forces of freedom and those of enslavement becomes more bitter and savage year by year.

The willingness and capacity of the Congress to measure up in courage, in wisdom, and in the caliber of statesmanship that the crisis demands will clearly determine whether our national purpose will eventually be attained—whether we survive or perish. It is our duty to weigh and consider proposed bills and legislative programs painstakingly in order to determine whether they will have these effects:

Move us further away from another world war, towards the end of the present cold war, and nearer the goal of the universal hopes of mankind for an honorable and durable peace.

Move us towards greater pre-eminence, influence, and power in world affairs.

Move us towards dependable strength and stability in the fiscal affairs of our government.

Move us towards a stronger economy, more abundant opportunities, and greater security for all of our citizens.

If such legislation tends to do any of these, or if it gives promise of favorable results in any of these directions, then it most likely merits support and should be enacted into law. Those are the true guidelines for enhancing and strengthening the national well-being and security.

That is the gleaming side of the coin. Turn it over, however, and see the side that has not been burnished. The Congress should carefully consider proposed legislation to determine whether, in operation and effect, it will simply mean:

More and bigger government.

Increased spending, higher taxes, and greater federal indebtedness.

Rising prices, higher cost of living, and pernicious inflation.

A weakened economy, fiscal instability, and a depleted national treasury.

Less individual initiative, less self-reliance, and less citizenship responsibility.

More centralized government, more government controls, and ultimately, perhaps, a "welfare state."

Proposed measures and legislative programs that would move us decisively in any of these directions, that might produce any of these undesirable results, should be rejected and defeated irrespective of the party label they bear. The national interest and the future welfare of our citizens clearly should become the paramount consideration and the dominating influence in our deliberations and final decision.

In introducing the subject of crimes and improper activities that attack the national interest, therefore, it seems clear that these criteria are excellent guidelines for determining whether certain activities are to be considered crimes, even though they are not so defined by law. What else can they be, when they strike at the ideals and the fundamental principles upon which our liberties rest and upon which our survival as a great and free nation must depend.

One of the greatest crimes of all, in my opinion, is one that is rarely considered by many Americans to be an offense at all for which retribution would ever be exacted.

The full effects of this crime will not likely fall upon the generation that is committing it, but may call for reckoning far in the future, and, unless the present trend is reversed, each succeeding generation will pay more heavily for it. The offense is being compounded annually, and its long-range effects are cause for serious alarm. This is the crime: the generation that controls the economy of this nation today and those who have important government responsibility are callously and mercilessly burdening the livelihood and earnings of the generations that will follow us with a tremendous oppressive national debt.

We are doing this simply so that we can enjoy a national standard of living that we either cannot afford or that we are unwilling to pay for in our own time. We are saddling our grandchildren and our great-grandchildren with the bills for our luxurious living. We have no moral right to do this. Thus, we are inflicting the fruits and penalties of our sins and derelictions upon innocent, helpless children and generations yet unborn.

Americans, as good citizens, usually have nothing but contempt for the deadbeat—the fellow who overextends his line of credit in a community, lives beyond his means, and then tries to evade the responsibility for his accounts. Is there any difference, from a moral standpoint, when a nation throws fiscal discretion to the winds and heads on a careening course towards insolvency? Does not such governmental fiscal irresponsibility fall within the realm of nonstatutory crimes?

Our present course is, I believe, extremely dangerous. There is a perfectly natural human failing that leads us, in troubled times, to eat, drink, and be merry. Another failing accompanies the first—the tendency in elected officials at every level of government to bow to political expediency and yield to myriad pressures to spend and spend without reckoning the eventual cost, and to disguise it with figures that are contrived to make it palatable.

We are in a continuing process of being insidiously weakened by a national tendency to live above our means, publicly and privately. Our moral attitudes relax in the process, our spiritual power as a free people is attenuated. In short, we take it easy.

President Kennedy has warned the nation that we are not likely to see the end of the world tension in our time, and there is every evidence that he is exactly right. In the long and desperate struggle in which we are now engaged with the international Communist conspiracy, we will need every ounce of strength and power that we can command, and that strength and power will not be found in a populace that is relaxed and oblivious to its responsibility. They will surely not be found in an insolvent government, nor in a bankrupt national treasury. Neither will they be found in the process of scoffing at the danger or by labeling it as a typically "conservative" viewing-with-alarm. This is not a matter of disparate political philosophies. It is a vital and urgent national problem. The inevitable accounting will make no distinction between those who sounded the warning and those who disregarded it.

Furthermore, this crime of burdening the future with our own carelessly acquired indebtedness is among the greatest of all the crimes that are not in the lawbooks, because it serves as a gigantic shadow under which all the lesser crimes of its type sprout like mushrooms in the darkness.

While it is unlikely that the citizen who is not directly concerned with the operation of the government will keep the exact figures of the federal budget and the national debt in his mind as a topic for social conversation, he can easily remember the astronomical heights to which they have climbed since World War II, and should readily envision the not-so-distant soaring peaks for which they are destined.

We are moving rapidly toward an annual budget far in excess of $100 billion and toward annual expenditures in all categories that will top $150 billion. (There is nearly $25 billion in annual spending that does not appear in the appropriated budget.) We have a national debt in excess of $300 billion, and that figure promises to grow to such proportions that it will destroy all confidence in our fiscal integrity and will finally compel a repudiation of the government's outstanding obligations. Just as swiftly, most of the fifty states of the Union are pyramiding their expenditures and indebtedness. For example, the total annual costs of all state, county, and municipal governments in the United States was $55 billion in 1961. That figure represents an increase of 141 per cent since 1950, when the comparable total was $22.8 billion. This ratio is far in excess of the rate of increase in our national economic growth.

As an example of the staggering size of our national indebtedness—exactly how much money we owe—let us go back in history to June 21, 1788, when New Hampshire became the ninth state to ratify the federal Constitution, which then went into effect as the basic document of our government. If we total the hours of every day through all the years from 1788 to the time this book was written, in the summer of 1962, and divide those hours into the national debt of about $300 billion, we would find that we owe approximately $195,700 for each hour since the Constitution was ratified and adopted.

There is no end in sight to deficit spending, nor are there enough men in public affairs these days who devote their time, energy, and influence to fighting against it. This is particularly true of elected officials all across the land, who find that the easy way to public office is promising support of governmental spending programs that, in effect, cover a citizen's life from the day he is born until the day he dies. Too few politicians care to take the course of responsibility and wisdom in fiscal matters; it is so much easier to be popular by promising to back programs that offer something for everybody than it is to talk soberly about the necessity for balancing the budget or paying our debts.

The nation is on a spending spree, and has been ever since the fiscal exigencies of World War II were removed. There is disturbing truth in the prophecy that was supposedly offered in the days of the New Deal: "We shall tax and tax, and spend and spend, and elect and elect." That idea was greeted with outrage and indignation by a large section of the country's citizenry, which had been reared in the simple, old-fashioned tradition of respect for economy and thrift. The remark becomes significant today, three decades later, because we have evidence that a succeeding generation greets the same philosophy, although perhaps it is stated in more sophisticated terms, without much more than a murmur of protest. The people are apparently being rapidly conditioned to consider this extremely dangerous economic principle as a just and proper way of life.

Without taking into account what future Congresses will do, but considering only measures that are pending in the present Congress at the time of this writing, the prospects are that the cost of operating the federal government over the next five years will increase by some $30 billion, and by much more than that if the pressures of national security and defense should exact heavier costs than those now anticipated as being required to keep us militarily strong and ready for any emergency.

There can be no doubt that the twin burdens of budget and debt are now serious threats to the health of our free enterprise system. Deficit spending should be stopped. Responsible government can and should find methods either to hold the line or to meet the increased costs without adding further weight to the massive overload of debt that we have already placed on future generations.

One of the phenomena of this age of reckless spending is the school of economists that seemingly has its sole employment in justifying unsound public fiscal policies. Many of them can write scholarly-sounding treatises that explain why an unbalanced budget is beneficial to the national welfare. They see deficit spending simply as a somewhat complex form of consumer credit. They can also elaborate on why there is really no harm in pyramiding the debt.

In the first place, they say, the debt is no problem. A small tax rise of 1 or 2 per cent would take care of it. That is simply not true. If all government revenues were increased about 1 per cent, the increase would amount to less than one billion dollars. How far would that go toward paying off an indebtedness of $300 billion?

The experts on reckless spending also say that inflation will take care of the debt. Inflation, they point out, has been with mankind ever since the first caveman engaged in trade: five mussel shells may have been the price for a sharp stone to make a new axhead; the next time the caveman needed such an axhead, the price had risen to six shells. Why, ask the experts, should a country with such abundant natural resources—the envy of the entire world—worry about mythical amounts of money, however startling the size of the figures, since we owe the money only to ourselves? How irrational can they get?

Their reasoning is reminiscent of that of the people who should have been concerned with annual rampaging floods that swept the rich lands along the Mississippi River in the middle 1920's. Notwithstanding repeated warnings and many positive danger signals year after year, the safeguards of adequate levees and other protective controls were neglected and not provided in time. The waters rose and the floods came as they did every year, but this time they rose higher than they ever had before.

One levee gave way, and then another, and then a series of them, 145 in all, and presently the rich alluvial soil in seven great states was covered by a brown, turbulent inland sea as the great river raged with terrific force, killing and maiming and destroying. Men who had worked and prospered through a lifetime saw their holdings swept away in a matter of hours, saw their capital equipment vanish in the swirling muddy torrent.

There surely had been sufficient warning that the river would one day create great havoc along its course, and the nation's lack of foresight in that disaster resulted in a terrible toll of lives and property. There are other comparable examples of disasters that resulted from shortsightedness and neglect.

Just as the responsible authorities in the days of the 1927 flood relied upon inadequate safeguards, so today the nation seems to be depending upon comforting words and deluding phrases as protecting levees against the inevitable consequences of fiscal irresponsibility. The modern school of economists would have us believe that the levees of words they have raised around our monetary instability will control the tremendous flood of retribution that threatens to inundate us and our descendants. The levees will not protect us, however, unless they are built up and cemented with some good old-fashioned concepts and principles that are not very popular today among the prophets of deficit spending.

The principles of prudence, thrift, and economy should be applied by the architects of our foreign aid program and by those who give approval of it by legislative action. Through the years since the end of World War II, the Congress has provided almost

$90 billion for the restoration of the economies of the war-shattered nations of the world, as well as for the impoverished and underdeveloped countries and for the new nations of the postwar period.

Such a program has never been undertaken before in the history of the world, and it was impelled in the beginning by our altruistic desire to assist and economically rehabilitate our allies and our defeated foes.

While the concept was altruistic, reflecting the generous spirit of our populace, the allocation and excessive amount of funds and the eventual uses to which they have been put, in many instances, have provoked frequent and voluble criticism. At the beginning, the United States considered its assistance to have two basic purposes.

Those two objectives were: (1) economic improvement and the building of trade channels, and (2) the strengthening of free allies of the United States in the maintenance of world peace. The Marshall Plan of postwar days worked well in these areas, and did a particularly effective job of stalling or sidetracking drives for national control by Communist parties in many countries.

Our aid, however, has not always been given wisely nor administered well. In many cases, it has quite evidently been wasted, squandered, or grossly misused. Billions of dollars that were appropriated to bolster shaky economies have been so foolishly and carelessly expended that they have had exactly the figurative effect, as country folks say, of pounding sand down a rathole.

By midcentury, the emphasis in our aid program should have been to secure the co-operation of the nations of the free world in taking up their own proper and porportionate share of the common burden. There have been some steps in that direction, but many of them have been ineffective and bumbling.

A large part of our aid has simply constituted a gigantic giveaway, during a decade in which the average annual deficit in the United States budget has exceeded the total annual budget of most of the countries receiving assistance.

Not many voices have demanded a realistic answer to the question of whether the economy of the United States of America can stand the constant drain upon its resources that foreign aid imposes. Whenever an attempted answer has been forthcoming to the critics of the foreign spending spree, it has been rolled in the sugary and optimistic reassurances of those economists who evidence little or no concern for sound fiscal policies.

The aid picture has changed, however, in the past decade, and the change is alarming. The pace of the giveaway program has been accelerated, and worst of all, a new development has been the incredible amount of military and economic assistance that our government is giving to nations that are ruthlessly governed by Communist dictatorships.

No individual man of means ever attracted true and loyal friends to stand beside him in whatever vicissitudes life might bring to him by using his money to buy their friendship. Let him lose his affluence and he would soon stand alone, wondering where all those friendly people had gone. Just as truly, no nation can buy allies for its cause in a fierce world struggle in the expectation that they will be loyal and steadfast when the hour of decision comes. Allies, just like individual friends, are worthy and true only when the links that bind them are forged of more durable substance than money. True loyalty is not for sale in any marketplace.

Nonetheless, a large part of our foreign aid program seems to be thoughtlessly and fruitlessly directed toward purchasing allies in the cold war, and it assuredly is not successful. One particularly distasteful aspect of this policy has been increasingly evident in our treatment of the very allies that we courted so assiduously in the postwar years. Their favored places seem to have been taken by the nations of the world who are so curiously called "neutrals," although it is somewhat difficult for anyone to ascertain if any of them are truly neutral; i.e., not engaged in assistance or sympathy with either competing side.

The Communist countries like Poland and Yugoslavia have philosophies of government and of society entirely alien to our own, but nevertheless receive U. S. funds to bolster their strength and their economies.

Take the matter of supplying jet fighters to Yugoslavia, and of training the young men who will fly them. Does anyone seriously believe that those jets would ever be launched in combat to fight an aggressor against us or against the free world? Does anyone have the idea that the jet pilots we are training for them will ever fly in defense of American principles and ideals?

Unhappily for the nation, the Congress has never properly equipped itself with facilities and a technical staff to do the kind of job necessary to prevent and eliminate some of the practices that have led to crimes against the national interest and objectives as they are discussed in this chapter. There have been billions of dollars of waste, extravagance, and unnecessary spending in areas which show no gains or benefits to the nation.

One way to gain a material advantage toward achieving the twin objectives of reducing expenditures to an amount below our income and avoiding the criminal pyramiding of our obligations upon those who succeed us is for the Congress to establish a Joint Committee on the Budget. Four times in recent years the Senate has passed such a bill, and four times the House of Representatives has failed to take action.

The proposed Joint Committee and its professional staff would be continually studying the President's budget and the many appropriations bills that come before the Congress, with a view to eliminating waste and duplication and other improper expenditures. Such a committee would institute sound fiscal procedure by recommending steps that might save the taxpayers many billions of dollars over the years.

While the United States is, economically and politically, the greatest nation on earth, our firmest foundations are being progressively undermined by the excessively high cost of maintaining our government and by the national complacency in accepting unbalanced budgets and deficit spending as a necessary concomitant to that greatness. We are in real danger of losing the battle for survival as a free and independent people unless we cast aside this insidious philosophy of living beyond our means. We must follow and stay within the worthy guidelines of our national objectives. The fundamental principles and concepts upon which our nation was founded certainly cannot now be abandoned with impunity.

CHAPTER 18

The Crimes That Go Unpunished

I N the modern criminal underworld," said the President of the United States when he was the junior senator from Massachusetts and a member of the Senate Select Committee, "we face a nationwide, highly organized, and highly effective internal enemy." He then recommended the formation of a separate federal agency, or the expansion of an existing one, to deal with the problem as an intelligence-gathering agency on organized criminal activities. In other words, Senator Kennedy, in March, 1960, advocated the formation of a National Crime Commission. His views were supported by several of his colleagues on the Select Committee: Senators Ervin, Church, and McClellan.

In stating his agreement with Senator Kennedy, the chairman added his own views on the operating procedures of such a federal agency:

"To carry out effectively its objectives, the Commission should be clothed with the power of subpena and charged with the duty of holding hearings and reporting its findings and recommendations to the Department of Justice and to the Congress. It should also be authorized to report at intervals in its discretion to the Department of Justice specific information it may obtain, and which in its judgment would be helpful to the Department of Justice in the enforcement of the criminal statutes of the United States.

"Such Commission should have a permanent status. Its authority

THE CRIMES THAT GO UNPUNISHED 283

and duties should be such as will not in any way usurp or inter-
fere with the functions of the Department of Justice and the FBI,
but only supplement and implement same."

The need for such an agency has not lessened during the years
intervening, even though the Congress has provided some of the
necessary legislation to curb racketeering and even though the
Department of Justice is undertaking the enforcement of the
criminal laws with considerable vigor.

The value of the work of area crime commissions was demonstrated several times during the Select Committee's hearings, as
well as those of the Investigating Subcommittee, during the past
five years. Our investigators made full use of the files of several
such groups, and the experts on crime who work with these commissions proved to be informative witnesses at many hearings
which involved racketeers and gangsters. Among those who offered support and information were the Crime Commissions of
Miami, New Orleans, Chicago, St. Louis, Wichita, and New York
State. Observation of their work strengthens the belief that a
federal agency of similar nature would be a tremendous aid in
the job of fighting organized crime.

The need for the agency has not lessened, for the task is getting bigger every day, as the country grows in population and
as its economy becomes more complex and diversified.

If the Department of Justice succeeds in driving the crime syndicate leaders out of the gambling business—or at least out of interstate operations—let no one suppose that they will be out of business entirely. Their greedy fingers reach out in new directions all
the time, and it is almost impossible for existing law enforcement
organizations to keep up with them. Probably the only practicable
solution to the problem of maintaining national intelligence on
the new ventures of organized crime is a watchdog agency designed for that particular purpose.

Moreover, there is every indication that such an agency might
be extremely valuable in a field that is unpleasant to contemplate
but is nonetheless an existing evil in the United States. That is the

infiltration of gangsters and racketeers into state and local governments. The Attorney General, in testimony earlier this year before a Senate committee, indicated that there were at least three cities in the United States—one in the east, one in the south, and one in the west—where the local administrations were on the payrolls of racketeers. A federal intelligence agency on crime, armed with legal wire-tapping, could keep close watch on such situations whenever and wherever they develop.

Further, existing law enforcement agencies at every level of government are going to be increasingly busy in years to come primarily in dealing with the fields of lawlessness that rarely involve the operators of the crime syndicate. Everywhere in the nation, particularly in cities with burgeoning populations, there is an outbreak of criminal activity that is increasingly violent and vicious.

The rapid growth of crime in recent years is shown in the regular reports of the FBI, which indicate that since 1957 crime has increased five times as fast as our expanding population. In 1960, for example, the crime rate (figured on a basis of crimes per one hundred thousand population) was 13 per cent higher than in 1959; it was 66 per cent higher than it had been in 1950; and it was 96 per cent higher than in 1940. The figures for 1961 indicate a further rise of approximately 3.4 per cent over the previous year.

The FBI also reported that, of every hundred police officers in the cities of the United States, eight were assaulted while on duty in 1961.

In the city of New York last year, 2,525 policemen were assaulted in the course of their duties, and 492 of them were injured. A police official said that the attacks had reached the proportions of "a serious disease," because there were 223 cases of attacks upon law officers by groups of people. In one area, 30 persons were arrested after a mass attack, and in another, 16 people were hauled off to jail after assaulting a policeman. It is a sadly common occurrence in the city of New York for a police officer to be the target of missiles thrown from rooftops of dwellings on congested streets.

In Washington, D.C., the incidence of crimes of violence has risen to fearful proportions. In the city that should be the showplace of the nation and the center of activity for visitors from all over the world, it is literally unsafe to walk the dark streets after nightfall. The city's newspapers have daily accounts of robberies, rapes, holdups, purse-snatchings, assaults and beatings, homicides and so many kinds of assorted crimes of violence that it is impossible to catalog them. As these words are written, the populace is aghast at the beating of a bus driver by a group of young men who assaulted him unmercifully while a busload of passengers watched without intervening. A Congresswoman, leaving her offices after dark, had her purse snatched on Capitol Hill. Indeed, ladies who work for the Government and sometimes stay overtime in federal buildings are continually warned about the dangers of walking alone on the streets of Washington during the night hours. As this is written, Washington newspapers are telling the story of the stabbing and robbing of a Congressional secretary in a church on Capitol Hill.

Daylight, however, doesn't necessarily mean that people are safe from attacks by criminals. Earlier this year, two thugs committed rape during the holdup of a shop in daylight hours. One of the victims was the shop proprietor and the other was one of her customers. There are daily letters in Washington papers expressing the outrage of the populace; there are newspaper editorials appearing every week, along with television and radio commentaries, all deploring the wave of criminal violence.

The city of Washington is supposed to be a symbol for all the nation and for the rest of the world, with its lovely memorials and monuments, its imposing public buildings, its traditions that are rooted in our national heritage. Unhappily, however, it is now rapidly becoming noted for the violence and frequency of the crimes that are committed within its limits.

The police force in Washington, as in other large cities where crimes of violence are commonplace, tries valiantly to do a good job, but the police can never keep pace with the criminals. A distressingly large proportion of the crimes go unsolved, and therefore they go unpunished. Furthermore, in Washington, D.C., the punishments that are meted out seem to be uniformly light. Similar record-breaking statistics of major felonies that pass without prosecution or punishment are being marked in the police ledgers of cities all across the country. Some recent decisions of the U.S. Supreme Court have made law enforcement and punishment for serious crimes more difficult. Let us hope this trend will be quickly reversed.

What is to be done about it? This is no easy problem to solve. In many cases, the need is for increased and intensified vigilance upon the part of local law enforcement officials. There are areas that lack enough policemen to do the job properly; there are others where the officers have neither training nor incentive to develop a top-notch police force. Heavier penalties for insidious crimes are part of the answer. Think of the narcotics "pusher" who entices youngsters into his foul web and then proceeds to ruin their lives and sometimes to cause their deaths by continuing to furnish them with heroin until they are either in prison or dead. Who among us could, in good conscience, object to the most rigorous penalties meted out to such depraved criminals? Probably the most effective answer is for each community to unite in action to eliminate the varied causes for the incidence of crime waves, and to combine all of the corrective actions necessary in order to bring about the certainty of punishment for the perpetrator of every type of crime, from auto theft all along the line of felonies to murder. The man who knows that he will be punished is not so likely to commit a crime.

There were many crimes, of course, that were discovered by the investigators for the Select Committee and the Investigating Subcommittee, crimes that were exposed in the hearings. Many of these actions have drawn no indictments, many have gone unpunished. Knowing that a crime has been committed is one thing; a successful prosecution of the perpetrator is often difficult because of lack of corroborating evidence, the fear of witnesses to testify, the lapse of time covered by the statute of limitations, and many other factors that allow criminals to escape convictions and imprisonment.

While it is unlikely that gangsters and crooks like "Tony Ducks" Corallo and Vincent J. Squillante and Johnny Dioguardi—all of them ousted from the ranks of labor leaders—will ever again be able to grab positions of power in organized labor, let us not blind ourselves to the fact that some of the worst offenders are still riding high.

There is no pleasure, certainly, in turning once again to the International Brotherhood of Teamsters. But it must be done. In the past two years alone, there have been approximately three dozen indictments or convictions of Teamster officials all across the country, including some legal actions against the national officers themselves, headed by James R. Hoffa. He is awaiting trial in Florida under a federal indictment for mail fraud and has been indicted in Nashville, Tennessee, on charges of conspiracy to violate the Taft-Hartley Act.

Prosecution of criminals who appeared at committee hearings has provided some satisfaction to the law-abiding citizens who watched with dismay as the sordid stories were unfolded. A primary result of the committee's investigative work was of course the enactment of new laws, some of which have been cited herein, but also, an important by-product was the exposures made by the investigations that resulted in a good many grand jury indictments at the federal, state, and local levels. Some are still being handed down. Scarcely a week goes by when the daily newspapers do not report indictments or convictions or deportations of men who appeared as witnesses at our hearings. To recount them all would take many pages. Here are some of the more prominent actions, however, almost all of them direct results of the Select

Committee's hearings, combined with vigorous action by law-enforcement agencies:

In Tennessee, Judge Raulston J. Schoolfield was removed from office; later he was disbarred in the state. Teamster funds amounting to twenty thousand dollars were made available to fix a case in his court involving the infamous goon squad that operated in Tennessee. The goons went to jail as a result of later prosecutions and convictions.

In Portland, Oregon, the district attorney, William Langley, was forced out of office.

Dave Beck, master of the Fifth Amendment, was convicted of grand larceny and of filing fraudulent income tax returns for Teamster funds. He is now in prison. His son Dave Beck, Jr., was convicted of grand larceny.

The garbage kings of New York, including Jimmy Squillante, were indicted and convicted in extortion and fraud cases. Squillante's whereabouts are now unknown, and it is possible that he has run afoul of some of his gangland associates.

Barney Baker, Hoffa's strong boy, was convicted of violation of the Taft-Hartley Act in Pittsburgh.

Several indictments and convictions came from the committee's investigations into the fraud and corruption in Teamster Local #107, in Philadelphia.

The union publishers, Maxwell C. Raddock and Bert Raddock, were convicted of extortion practices in Philadelphia.

Mike Singer, who ran the grease business in Los Angeles with a dictator's hand, was indicted and convicted for conspiring to create a monopoly, along with some of his associates.

There were many indictments for contempt of Congress—one of them against Maurice A. Hutcheson, president of the eight-hundred-thousand-member Carpenters Union, whose conviction has been upheld by the Supreme Court; another against William Presser, president of the Ohio Conference of Teamsters; another against Pete Licavoli, supposedly a leader of the old "Purple Gang" in Detroit.

George Stuart, of the Bakers Union, was convicted of embezzlement in Illinois.

Metro Holovachka, who was an assistant prosecutor of Lake County, Indiana, and was involved in real estate ventures with Carpenters Union officials, has been convicted of income tax evasion.

The list of union leaders whose activities were exposed and who are now no longer active in the labor movement is far too long to repeat, but here are some of them: Cross and Stuart of the Bakers, Klenert and Valente of the Textile Workers, William E. Maloney of the Operating Engineers, the Block brothers of the Butchers Union.

The crime syndicate leaders who met at Apalachin suffered heavily for their gregariousness. Indictments against twenty-seven of them for conspiracy to obstruct justice resulted in twenty convictions, although these were later reversed. However, here are some of the current police standings of the Apalachin delegates and their close friends and associates. Russell J. Bufalino has appealed a pending deportation order; Frank Cammarata was deported and went to Cuba, where he was arrested last year by Castro's police for narcotics dealing; Johnny Dio is sojourning in the penitentiary in Atlanta; Carlo Gambino is the subject of a pending deportation order; Vito Genovese is currently doing fifteen years for narcotics violation in Atlanta. Carmine Lombardozzi is on parole for conviction of fraud against the Government. Thomas Lucchese is the subject of a pending deportation order. Anthony Strollo (Tony Bender) has disappeared, and is believed to be a victim of mob violence. John ("Big John") Ormento has been convicted in a narcotics conspiracy and has been sentenced to forty years in prison.

Many others, however, are still holding powerful places in labor, in management, and in the diversified rackets of organized crime, in spite of the exposure they suffered by their appearances at committee hearings. The law, properly laden with safeguards for the rights of free men in a democratic nation, seems everlastingly slow-moving in taking action against them. It does move, however, and every time a Dioguardi or a Squillante or a Barney Baker is convicted, his partners in crime look back over their shoulders. The next blow may fall on them.

Yet it is somewhat disheartening to go over the records of the Senate Select Committee and of the Permanent Investigating Subcommittee, checking out the criminals and checking out the crimes, only to find that the list of crimes that have gone unpunished still heavily overbalances the list for which justice has been administered.

The full list of trials and convictions, impressive though it may be as a step in the right direction, indicates that legal action has not yet cut an appreciable swath through the ranks of gangsters and racketeers who plague the economic health of the United States.

The principal and basic weapon that must be provided is a resurgence of old-fashioned morality in the nation. Apathy must go; it needs to be replaced by the outraged righteousness of a people who rose to greatness in this world through the spiritual values that their forefathers wrote into the Declaration of Independence and the Constitution of the United States. Let us be thoroughly frank about it—there is no better or surer way to stop the advance of crime into every structure of our society.

The entire nation must be roused and morally armed against the criminal army. Every honest man will be required to do his share, no matter how small a contribution his circumstances may permit him to make.

The fight must be strongly waged at the level where fine efforts will pay handsome dividends—among the youth of the nation. Their parents need to instill into them at home the basic fundamentals that differentiate right and wrong; they must give the youngsters a correct appreciation and understanding of the true values of life. Of course, parents cannot do it all. The churches and the schools, the community organizations that specialize in youth work, the children's societies and the probation officers—all of them must double and redouble their efforts with our young citizens, or else the battle may be lost in the approaching decades immediately ahead.

It must not be lost. If the leaders of crime continue their inroads upon our society and their depredations upon our national well-being in the same patterns that have been shown in our hearings over the past five years, then this country will soon be perilously close to clandestine rule by a group of gangsters who will make the current crime chieftains appear to be schoolboys playing simple games.

Delay in giving inspiration to youngsters, in establishing good government, in insisting that laws be enforced, in passing new legislation and strengthening existing statutes—all of these, along with complacency, could combine to bring upon us the disaster that now unmistakably is casting its shadow upon the horizon.

If that shadow sweeps across the land, bringing the darkness of a vast national cartel of crime, wherein present venality would be multiplied many times, what chance would we have in a world where Communism threatens at every point of the compass? No chance at all. We would lie helplessly in the grasp of the criminal leaders, who would be like an all-powerful Mafia, subverting and enmeshing the country.

This book has stressed how serious crimes have gone unpunished at every level of our society and in every sphere of our economic endeavor. This danger will continue and magnify unless we act. If we do nothing, the law of retribution will inevitably exact an accounting. We should remember the fundamental of almost all religions:

> Though the mills of God grind slowly,
>   yet they grind exceeding small;
> Though with patience He stands waiting,
>   with exactness grinds He all.

We cannot, we must not, shirk our responsibility on this grave issue. This challenge can be, and it must be, faced with resolute purpose and effort. The elements of crime and corruption must not prevail. I have a profound and abiding faith that the American people can and will successfully combat this vicious evil and that the forces of law and order will ultimately triumph.

Index

John L. McClellan was born on a farm near Sheridan, Arkansas, in 1896, the son of a farmer and school teacher who later became a lawyer. When he himself was only seventeen, he was licensed to practice law after passing with honors an oral examination before a panel of distinguished attorneys; he had studied in his father's office while still managing the family's farm.

In the early days of the New Deal, he was elected a Congressman, and in 1938 he ran in the primary for the Senate against Mrs. Hattie Caraway. Defeated, he ran again in 1942; this time, without the support of either the national or state Democratic organizations, he won by almost 50,000 votes. He was re-elected in 1948, 1954, and 1960.

Few Senators in our history have carried heavier legislative responsibilities. Senator McClellan serves on three standing committees of the Senate, one joint committee, and fourteen subcommittees; he is chairman of four of these. He was also a member of both Hoover Commissions and is a leader in flood control, navigation, and water-development projects. He is known to millions as "Mr. Chairman," since he still heads the powerful Government Operations Committee of the Senate and its famed subsidiary, the Permanent Subcommittee on Investigations.

DATE DUE

FEB 2 '82			
FEB 16 '82			
FEB 17 1982			
MAY 13 '86			
MAY 18 '86			
MAY 19 '87			
MAY 19 '87			
GAYLORD			PRINTED IN U.S.A.